DEATH OF A CROW

DEATH OF A CROW

Published in 2022 by Seoul Selection U.S.A., Inc.
4199 Campus Drive, Suite 550, Irvine, CA 92612
Phone: 949-509-6584 / Seoul office: 82-2-734-9567
Fax: 949-509-6599 / Seoul office: 82-2-734-9562
Email: hankinseoul@gmail.com
Website: www.seoulselection.com

ISBN: 978-1-62412-147-0
Printed in the Republic of Korea
The Work is published under the support of Literature Translation
Institute of Korea (LTI Korea).

DEATH OF A CROW

Kim Sok-pom

Translated by

Christina Yi

Seoul Selection

Contents

Translator's Foreword

When Japan announced its unconditional surrender to the Allied Powers on August 15, 1945, spontaneous celebrations erupted throughout Japan's (soon-to-be-former) colonies. In Korea, however, the promise of liberation very quickly revealed itself to be a lie, as the intervention of foreign powers led to the creation of the thirty-eighth parallel in August 1945, the occupation of northern Korea by the Soviets and southern Korea by the U.S. from 1945 to 1948, and the establishment of two competing governments on the Korean Peninsula by 1948. Protests against these developments became particularly fierce in Jeju, which in the immediate post-liberation period had benefited from a relatively peaceful transition to local self-governance through the formation of "people's committees" that were guided by the tenets of democratic socialism. Tensions between citizens and the

US military government erupted on April 3, 1948, when hundreds of armed leftist demonstrators conducted raids on police stations across the island. The raids resulted in a yearslong brutal crackdown of any and all suspected communist activity.

In Kim Sok-pom's "Bak-seobang, Jailer" the events leading up to the so-called "4.3 Incident" are described in the following way:

> In April 1948, Jeju became the locus of an armed uprising against the elections that were being conducted only in the South—in other words, in protest against the establishment of the "Republic of Korea" and the partitioning of the peninsula. The people of the island took up handmade weapons and retreated to Mount Halla, the shield volcano that towers over the island. It was there that they prepared for southern Korea's first partisan battle. The astonished Americans and Syngman Rhee swiftly moved to obliterate them. The people of the island were labelled "Reds" and thrown into jail one after another. Every jail was packed to the rafters, so much so

> that it was faster to kill people than to build new cells.

It's estimated that as many as 30,000 people—10 percent of Jeju's civilian population—were killed at the hands of the police and military; many of these individuals, as the stories collected here emphasize, were entirely innocent and had no or only tenuous ties to any "communist" groups. A law passed in September 1948 made it an arrestable offense to even speak of the atrocities of the 4.3 Incident, and the South Korean government refused to publicly acknowledge its complicity in the incident until well into the 1990s.

Born in Osaka in 1925 to parents who were originally from Jeju, Kim Sok-pom had a personal as well as a professional connection to the southern island, having visited it often in his youth. Because Kim was living in mainland Japan at the time of Japan's surrender to the Allied Powers, however, he found himself unable to freely travel back to his homeland after 1945. During the colonial period (1910–1945), Koreans in the Japanese empire had been legally treated as Japanese nationals, albeit with second-class status. But with the signing of the Treaty of San Francisco in 1952, all former colonial subjects were stripped of Japanese citizenship, thus rendering Koreans in Japan stateless, as Japan did not have diplomatic relations with either North Korea or South Korea at the time. The term Zainichi (lit. "residing in Japan"; resident) came to be used to refer to the Korean communities created in Japan by these legal changes in citizenship.

Kim Sok-pom is widely recognized in both Japan and South Korea as one of the most important Zainichi writers of his generation, in part because of the ferocity and political conviction of his fiction. The stories collected here, which were first published in the late 1950s and 1960s, are representative of his oeuvre as a whole. While Kim did not personally witness the events of the 4.3 Incident, as a Korean resident in Japan he was in fact able to write about them at a time when his South Koreans peers could not, bound as they were by South Korea's draconian censorship policies and laws. In an essay published in 1974, Kim writes that the only way he could do justice to the unutterable traumas and horrors of the 4.3 Incident was to use the "crucible of fiction" ("fiction" here meaning falsehoods or fabrications) to "dismantle reality, and then reconstitute it into a different kind of space and order."[1] He then concludes the essay on the following note:

> I write about "Jeju Island" (although it is not the only thing I've written about) because I think it might, eventually, lead to my liberation and self-salvation. I still haven't been liberated . . . To begin with, the fact that I, a Korean, am cursed to write in Japanese is itself a kind of falsehood or fiction. So the fact that I'm trying to use Japanese to achieve self-freedom is completely ridiculous, I know. But I cannot tear myself away from it. I don't know when I'll be able to liberate myself, but it may well be that I can only do it through the written word. If that's the case, then I have no choice but to keep writing—self-contradictions and all.[2]

Acknowledging the painful burden of speaking in the tongue of one's colonizers, Kim points to a path through which the bonds of the Japanese language may be turned into a tool for revealing truth in falsehood, clarity in contradiction, and a certain kind of freedom in constraint. That Kim identifies literature—the ultimate true falsehood—as the key to unraveling all the different competing narratives of nation, home, and belonging is a conclusion borne out by the stories collected here.

In the original Japanese-language texts, Kim will frequently insert Korean words and phrases into his prose, often (though not always) followed by a Japanese gloss or translation in parentheses. One can see this tendency in his prose fiction as Kim's attempts to deliberately defamiliarize and deterritorialize the Japanese language itself—a language inextricably linked to the specific history of Japanese imperialism, as "Feces and Freedom" and "A Tale of a False Dream" both make clear. At the same time, Kim also takes a critical stance against the hypocrisies of the U.S.-backed South Korean government, which perpetuated the very neo-colonial conditions it purported to denounce. In this translation, I have tried to preserve the dual nature of Kim's fiction by retaining the Korean words and glosses as they originally appeared; whatever translations that appear in parentheses are also part of the original text. These moments of linguistic interruption remind us to be mindful of the contested borders of nations and their literatures. Only by understanding the history and fictionality of those borders, *Death of a Crow* warns us, may we find our way to freedom.

This translation is based on the 1971 collection published by Kōdansha. I would like to gratefully acknowledge the invaluable assistance of Haruki Sekiguchi, Minoru Takano, and Olivia Yoo in the preparation of this translation.

1. Kim, "Waga kyokō o sasaeru mono: naze 'Chejudō' o kaku ka'" (That Which Holds My Fictions Together: Why Write About 'Jeju Island'?) in *Kim Sok-pom hyōronshū* 1 eds. Lee Yeounsuk and Kang Sinja (Kyō Nobuko) (Tokyo: Akashi Shoten, 2019), 157. Initially published in the December 1974 issue of *Gekkan Ekonomisuto* (The Monthly Economist).

2. Kim, "Waga kyokō," 173.

Bak-seobang,* Jailer

1.

Pressing his forehead against the wire mesh of the packed prison cell, the stoop-shouldered jailer laughed lewdly and jangled his key ring behind his back. The fetid body odor of the huddled, sleeping female prisoners hung thick in the air. The floor was slick with their drool.

Myeongsun rolled over to her side; Widow Jo's feet were digging into her rear. Normally she slept with her back to the wire mesh, but now she found herself facing the jailer despite herself. That first night, the jailer had stroked Myeongsun's lips with the pad of his finger as she

* Seobang = In the past, a form of address attached to the family name of someone who was not in the civil service. Also a derogatory term for a husband.

slept beside the wire mesh. She had leapt to her feet when she realized what the lout was doing.

"*Aigo*, you're disgusting!"

The jailer had felt a thrill of pleasure almost akin to fear at the snap of her voice. He gave a peculiar, high-pitched laugh—*eeheeheehee*—and said, "You're a real beauty . . . I love looking at you Jeju women and your big asses—and as for your personalities, well, I hear you're only all too willing . . . Eeheehee."

Was it possible that he and this woman shared a special bond? The mere thought made the jailer giddy. The plumpness of her lips reminded him of the barmaid in Mokpo. The waitress had mostly ignored him, though the jailer didn't think of it that way. Women just weren't capable of appreciating a man's worth, he told himself—he was a jailer worthy of great respect, was he not? And in any case, they weren't supposed to confess their feelings so soon. *I—well, I just thought she was pretty, that's all . . .*

But wait. A bond? A bond with that female criminal? The jailer reconsidered. *Careful, she's from Jeju Island—my ancestors would yell at me from their graves if I took up with a Jeju woman.* (Though his ancestors may very well have been from Jeju themselves, as he didn't know who his parents were.) For some reason the thought of losing his bond with Myeongsun made him feel lonely, and then irritated. *C'mon, it's nothing as serious as a bond. She's more like my plaything.* Having reached this conclusion, the jailer began to get drowsy. He licked his finger with a mouth that reeked of alcohol.

Widow Jo had her back against the wall, seemingly asleep, her trousered legs splayed out before her. There was something comforting about the concrete wall with its rough bumps like gooseflesh.

"Myeongsun—" Widow Jo's voice was barbed.

"Now, now . . . What's Myeongsun done?"

"Her thighs are completely exposed from all the rips in her clothing. She looks like something the cat's dragged in . . ."

"Shut up in there!" Unsettled by her words, the jailer shook his key ring again. "That's no business of yours."

For some reason, the jailer couldn't really get into his work without the musical accompaniment of his keys. It was pitiful, almost embarrassing. Still, the dull metallic noise of his keys jangling together immediately roused his spirits.

"Eeheeheehee. Hey, #11, your ass is perfect. From

behind it's got a great shape—looks just like the slopes of Sarabong Hill, eeheehee . . . "

But there was no response inside the cell. *It would be prudent to depart*, the jailer thought with some pomposity. He made his exit, the sound of his odd laugh and his keys trailing behind him. It was what he usually did when he got no reaction.

"That pervert, once it's dark he'll come crawling out of his cave again."

As usual, too, raucous comments followed the jailer as he made his way to his office. He was satisfied with the timeliness of his actions and the fact that they hadn't insulted him to his face. *Pervert? "Great men have great fondness for the sensual pleasures," as the saying goes. I wonder if that means I have some kind of bond with those great men . . . ? The world is disordered, like fibers of hemp . . . There's no reason why I can't be a great man, too.* His mind seized upon the idea, and he fell into ecstasy, imagining the future. But almost immediately he encountered a hurdle: his own self, an old *chonggak* (bachelor) without a woman to call his own. The female prisoner's face flickered in front of his eyes. He tried to shake off his wicked thoughts. *It seems I was originally fated to be a monk, but these troubled times lured me onto the path of a jailer and changed my destiny.*

"Ahh, it's so hot. Myeongsun, aren't you hot? It's days like these that make me wish I had a fresh new handkerchief to wipe away my sweat. This one just won't do—it's no different from a cleaning rag."

Myeongsun's face contorted. Tucked away in her clothes was a fresh new handkerchief. The women in the cell watched Myeongsun and Widow Jo closely. They couldn't stand how Myeongsun had hidden her handkerchief away without even using it once. Widow Jo wiped the sweat from her neck and changed the subject, looking at everyone's faces as she did so. "That pockmarked bastard is nothing but bad news. Ah, look how awful the world's become. Independence? It's the independence of cowards! What good is that? It was better under the *waenom* (Japs). Ah, Japan . . . a place where the streets are paved with gold. You can make money just by walking around! Doesn't matter if it's a piece of wastepaper or an empty bottle, everything's worth money. The country's full of rich people, and even their trash is valuable. It's all there for the taking, and the police . . . well, who cares about them! It's not stealing, after all."

"I've also heard that Japan's a good place to live . . . My son told me—"

"Yes, yes, we know," Widow Jo interrupted. Then she abruptly began to heap abuse on "that senile old bastard" President Syngman Rhee. Apparently there had been a radio broadcast urging people to slaughter the residents of Jeju because they were all *ppalgaengi* (Reds). Widow Jo angrily declared that she'd sink her teeth into any outsider who dared set a toe on the island. "Does he think the people of Jeju are his grandchildren or his servants, to treat us this way? Crazy mainlanders!"

"Auntie Jo," Myeongsun said, "I hear the keys!"

"Have you gone mad, too?" screeched Widow Jo, but there was the jailer once again, smiling smugly and swinging his key ring from his fingers. His tiny eyes gleamed in his dark, cratered face.

"*Aigo*, you pockmarked bastard!" yelled Widow Jo. "What are you so hungry for? Gotten tired of your wife's crotch already?"

Hearing Widow Jo say "wife's crotch" made the jailer a little sad. You couldn't call yourself a real man if you didn't have a wife. *Even if that were true, I'd still be offended. To call me pockmarked!* The jeers of the Mokpo *jigekkun* (laborers who carry things with A-frames on their backs) echoed in his head. "The barmaid is head over heels for your pockmarks. Wahahaha!" Red-faced with fury, the jailer had tried to grab one of them to show off his strength, but instead it was he who had been overpowered. When he retorted that not just anyone could get pockmarks, the *jigekkun* holding him had leaned in close and said, "Sure—only you," then knocked his head against the ground. He thought he saw the barmaid watching from the door, her mouth opens as if in laughter. *There's no doubt about it. Women are cunning creatures.* His tactics changed after that. He decided he would stop picking at his pimples. There was nothing he could do about the pimples themselves; that was his fate . . . But now he was a jailer of great renown. How dare this gaggle of women call him a pockmarked bastard? Even as he thought this, however, his own pockmarks seemed to spread out before his eyes. Startled, he changed his mind about addressing the insult.

"Stop your howling . . . Eeheehee, how about your crotch, then? How does it taste?"

"Try anything and I'll tear you apart."

"Eeheehee, isn't that my line? I'm with the police, remember. You'll be begging me to kill you quickly, but don't worry, it'll be your turn soon enough."

Widow Jo threw herself at the wire mesh. "Go to hell, you *nassumikan*!"

The jailer was taken aback by the unfamiliar word. He had been crouching in front of the wire mesh, but now he sprang back like an agitated monkey.

"Don't forget, I'm your jailer!"

Low moans could be heard from the back of the cell, and weak coughs echoed hollowly inside the night-shrouded jail. The jailer turned his back on it all. He went to his office but did not sit down. It was no fun fighting with that mongrel Widow Jo, and not only had Myeongsun ignored him, he hadn't been able to get a good peek at her ass. He felt disgusted just thinking about it, and he blamed Widow Jo for everything. *Women are just like children, aren't they? Still, it won't do to be ridiculed by a bunch of women. Hmph.* The jailer straightened his shoulders and made his way back to the wire mesh, his keys jangling. There was no logic behind his actions. He was like a dog, driven by an instinctive desire to sniff the female prisoners. Widow Jo looked like she was getting ready to shout something at him again. He spat out a gobbet of saliva, aiming for her mouth, but instead the saliva clung ineffectually to the mesh. Some of it even ended up on his nose.

"Shut up in there!" He should have contented himself with yelling at them. Everyone was laughing. It would be childish to do it again. *I can't retreat now.*

"That's the spit of your master and jailer!" He stamped a foot. "Pay your respects to your master's spit, *nassumikan*!"

"You moron, you're the *nassumikan*!" Widow Jo replied, and the prisoners burst into laughter. The jailer once again regretted his actions. Back in his office, he puzzled over Widow Jo's words. *Why is she calling me a* nassumikan*...? There's no word like that in proper Korean, so no doubt it comes from the hick dialect these Jeju idiots speak. Hahahaha, it's stupid to pay any mind to the words of* sangnom *(people of the lowest social rank) . . .*

But the word continued to worry the jailer all night long. After a long period of careful deliberation, he finally hit upon a brilliant plan. Tomorrow, he would visit the pharmacy *yeonggam* (old man). Nassu *sounds like* nasseol . . . *Was it their word for age?* Mikan . . . *could they mean* milkan? He was completely mystified. *Hmph. The* yeonggam *is educated, and he's lived here a long time. And he's not—not one of those Jeju bastards. Perfect.* He had to clear his head and gather more intel. *I'm a jailer worthy of great respect. That's right, I'll throw cold water on this* nassumikan *business by talking to the old man at the pharmacy.*

2.

The jailer hurried into town immediately following the shift change the next morning, determined to visit Jin Pharmacy in the Chilseongno shopping district. On the way there, he ran into a former acquaintance, a short *jigekkun* nicknamed Little Baek. It seemed that business was booming: Baek's back was bent nearly double under the weight of his packages. The jailer wanted to shout out a snappy greeting to impress the young women who were sashaying past them, but he was beaten to the punch by Baek: "Morning, Bak-seobang."

Well, this was an unforeseen setback! *What's he*

thinking, calling me "seobang"? *I deserve a higher title than that.* The jailer glared daggers at Little Baek. There was little hope of escape now. Baek had clearly been speaking to him. He saw the women turn and glance behind them. The jailer tried to walk on, feigning ignorance.

"Hey, Bak-seobang—you deaf now?"

The jailer's cheeks flamed red. To be addressed so disrespectfully in front of women . . . It was an insult to his police uniform. *The bastard hasn't noticed my uniform.* He tugged his shirt smooth and drew himself up. *Where are my keys? Hmph, who cares if I don't have 'em.* He pulled his police cap low over his eyes and then, springing forward like a jack-in-the-box, gave Baek a sharp slap across the face.

"Idiot! Can't you see what's right in front of you? I'm the great jailer Master Bak, you blind fool!"

Baek staggered, and his packages tumbled off his back. Hearing the sound of a woman's laugh, the Master Jailer felt victorious. Little Baek writhed on the ground and cursed Bak as nothing but a pockmarked candy peddler. Bystanders gradually began to gather around them. Jeju crowds were particularly vicious; their eyes were like daggers. The Master Jailer retreated with a snort.

It had been only about a month since Bak-seobang's "investiture," but his past life as a *jigekkun* and candy peddler had already been completely wiped from his memory. There was no way a Master Jailer could have such a humble history, after all. That past belonged to the Bak-seobang who was from a neighboring village in Hwanghae Province. *I've always been Master Bak. I can't believe Little Baek called me a candy peddler. Hmph, what a day—and it's still only morning. So much for the value of old friends. That scum . . .* He spat and cast a genial look at the crowd, but the women and their swinging hips were already disappearing into the distance.

The sun was shining down on Jin Pharmacy by the time he arrived. White Korean rose petals were strewn on the street, perhaps through some child's mischief. The proprietor's wife was inside, crushing dried pollack heads with a hammer. She was startled to see a policeman at the door, but when she realized who it was, she mumbled out something that was neither "Bak-seobang" nor "Master Bak" and disappeared into the back of the store.

Jin-yeonggam (Elder Jin) sat with his legs crossed as the jailer told his story, combing his fingers through his long, grizzled beard with one hand and tapping his tobacco pipe with the other as he listened. "I see, I see," he said repeatedly. Then: "Please accept my heartfelt congratulations on your promotion, Bak-seo . . . er, Master Bak." A man who put up no resistance to these troubled times, Jin was quite unlike Little Baek. He had an enormous blind spot when it came to Bak and had sometimes hired him back when Bak was still working as a *jigekkun*. Presenting the jailer with some shredded pollack and a glass of cheap unfiltered sake, Jin apologized for not visiting Bak upon his promotion. Bak-seobang stared long and hard at Jin's face, his mouth half open. Jin was the man who had kept Bak busy carrying medicinal powders and other goods for him every time the ships came in. Feeling flustered, Bak almost let the word "Master" slip from his lips as he talked. But he managed to replace it instead with the rather odd title of "Pharmacy Jin." He reminded himself that his policeman's uniform was real. In doing so, he was able to completely forget about Little Baek.

Bak-seobang was pleased by this promising start. But then the old man cut him off, right as he was preparing to announce how "Pharmacy Jin" resembled a *nassumikan*. "So, what's the problem? Diarrhea?" Jin said bluntly, giving him a once-over. Bak-seobang picked at his nose, acutely conscious of the reek of the traditional Chinese medicine in the shop, and replied that he was here for something more urgent than a prescription. The old man tapped his pipe again. Upon being told that the matter had to do with the pharmacy, he tottered to his feet and called for his wife.

"Lately . . . a terrible rumor has been going around," said Bak-seobang.

"Is that so?" said Jin's wife, leaning forward with obvious interest. "Must be something quite serious . . . "

Jin snorted. "No need to hold back. A *seonbi* (classical scholar) should always speak frankly."

Bak, who could be called a scholar only in the broadest, most generous sense of the word, blinked his eyes and explained that there was a rumor that Pharmacy Jin was a *nassumikan*, or rather that he resembled one, and so he had come to visit Jin out of a sense of both professional courtesy and personal friendship in order to get to the bottom of this business.

"*Nassumikan*?" Pharmacy Jin tilted his head. "Hm, I see—a *nassumikan* . . . I suppose you could say that I do resemble one."

"*Nassumikan*?" repeated his wife, staring off into space.

"O-oh, yes—but . . . is that a Korean word?" Bak-seobang was disappointed. It was clear that it was not a legitimate Korean term, so it must be some rural vulgarism. The jailer added that he had unfortunately been unable to do any research on the subject, due to his very demanding schedule. His eyes never left Jin as he spoke. Jin's eyes, on the other hand, shifted restlessly. He stared into space like his wife in an affected manner. The three sat in contemplation.

"*Nassumikan*, you say?" Old Jin sighed deeply. "Am I . . . ?" His wife gave a shorter sigh. The old man stuck his pipe into his mouth by habit and looked over the Chinese medicine display cases. His eyes took in the dried mandarin peels that were hanging from the rafters, but they did not really register. Bak-seobang stared hard at the "Pharmacy" with narrowed eyes. His expression was both reproachful and grave. Even more than the so-called rumors, Old Jin was troubled by the unpleasant possibility of having his learning called into question by his former porter, who now called him "Pharmacy" with such casual familiarity. It didn't help that he had addressed our Bak-seobang as "Master Bak" a moment ago. “Er . . . if we consult the *m* entries in Mun Seyeong’s *Korean Dictionary,*” he mumbled, grasping for an answer in his head. “Or the *n* entries . . . ” But it was a large volume, and there were just too many words.

“They’re false rumors, is what they are!” the old pharmacist finally cried wildly. Just then, a clerk named Gang emerged from the opposite alley with his briefcase in hand, accompanied by four or five other people. “Well, if it isn’t Clerk Gang! Official business, I see.”

Clerk Gang glanced at Bak-seobang and casually clapped him on the shoulder. “Hello there, Bak-seobang!” Bak-seobang lifted his shoulder but did not otherwise respond. *Jeju asshole.* He had not yet had a chance to “research” whether or not being a county clerk was more prestigious than being a jailer.

“So, er, Gang . . . It seems that the word *nassumikan* is being tossed around town.” For the old pharmacist, the fortuitous arrival of Gang, a man who had graduated from a Japanese university, truly proved that “a blind person will find the front gate,” as the Korean saying went—in other words, that everybody had their purpose.

“*Nassumikan*?” The clerk rubbed his chin. “*Nassumikan,*” he murmured again, half to himself.

"Are you referring to the Japanese word? The correct pronunciation is *natsumikan*."

"What?" the old man shouted, both dismayed and exultant in equal measure. "I see—That's right, it's *Ilbonmal* (Japanese)! That's what I thought it was . . . "

Bak-seobang extended and retracted his neck like a turtle with each development in the conversation.

According to Clerk Gang, *natsumikan* was a type of citrus. Pointing to the dried mandarin peels hanging from the rafters, he explained that they were a similar variety of fruit particularly common in Japan. He then made a mocking comment about how comparing Jin-yeonggam to a *natsumikan* was more absurd than the myth of Samseonghyeol (the legendary ruins where it's said the three founding fathers of Jeju Island emerged from three different holes)—though, funnily enough, Bak-seobang's face fit that description exactly.

Bak-seobang found himself faced with utter defeat. It had been a reference to his pockmarks all along! And how dare Pharmacy Jin ally himself with the Jeju bastards? Later, at the bar in the market, Bak drank himself into a stupor. He drank and sang and drank until he passed out, right there in the bar.

3.

Bak-seobang stood on the craggy summit of Mount Yudal, scanning the far-off horizon. (This is before he arrived in Jeju, before he became an exalted jailer.) He shaded his eyes with his hand, feeling like a military general, but saw no limit to the boundless blue. From this height the city of Mokpo looked like a miniature garden, the black streets of the city vivid against a lush green expanse, the islands dotting the sea mere rocks in a pond. All at once, a dark mass of clouds raced across the sky. He felt his heart grow heavy, but he refused to let himself think about the past. He'd been confident that Jeju and its treasure trove of women would reveal themselves to him at any moment, but the island continued to elude him. *Hmph, it's ridiculous how far away it is.* He was disappointed that he couldn't climb higher. And he had been in such a good mood, too! It had taken him some time to come to a decision about his future. It wasn't until he heard someone in town talking about the "three plenties of Jeju" (plentiful wind, plentiful rocks, plentiful women)—a phrase that struck him like an arrow—that he finally resolved to go. He didn't care how wildly the wind blew or how loudly the rocks bashed against each other; nothing beat a beautiful woman. The old *chonggak* chuckled to himself, having already begun to think of the "plentiful women" as his. The salt breeze from the south carried the scent of the unseen women to him, and he raptly imagined a whole island of women waiting for him. *I bet even someone like me could find a wife there . . . a whole harem of them.* Bak-seobang was certain that Jeju was the place where he would finally fulfill his destiny.

If you were to ask him why he remained a bachelor in his late thirties, he would tell you that he just hadn't found a good match yet—which was a dubious claim. Still, you couldn't say that he'd never had any marriage prospects. He'd had exactly one, in fact, though in the end *he* was the one who'd angrily kicked *her* to the curb. It had happened during the "era" when Bak-seobang was a menial servant for the Bak family in Hwanghae Province. He'd been working for them for roughly a decade by that point. It was said that he'd been sold to the Baks by the Yi household in the neighboring village for the paltry sum of fifty-three yen. Whether or not that was actually true is unknown; what's known is that there had indeed been a debt or something of the sort between the families in the amount of fifty-three yen.

One day, while chopping some wood, Bak-seobang heard his master bellowing for him in the usual way: "Baekseon!" At the Yis, he had gone by Gombo (Pockmark), but out of pity (and, even more than that, distaste at following a precedent set by the Yis), Master Bak had bestowed upon him a new name. Baekseon did not know his family name. All he remembered from his childhood was that he had moved around from place to place from an early age.

Master Bak began by complaining—as he always did—that no one paid him the attention he was due in this degenerate world. As Baekseon nodded along—as he always did—tears unaccountably sprang to Master Bak's eyes. "You're almost forty now, and it would be a good thing for you to go to Jeong-saengweon (during the feudal era, a saengweon was a person who passed the lower civil service examination for selecting civil and military officers; it became a honorific title attached the end of an elder's surname)." Seeing Baekseon's sullen expression, he added, "His daughter seems to be quite taken with you." Baekseon was taken aback. The woman in question was built like an ox and pockmarked to boot. *That pockmarked sow?* (It's impossible to fathom how he, of all people, could hate pockmarks so much.) His fury erupted into words.

"She's a pockmarked bitch who only cares about soybean fields! I *hate* soybean fields!" Checked by the sternness in his master's eyes, he hunched his shoulders. "Sorry, master—but she's just not a good match."

As twilight approached, however, he began to get angry all over again, and he downed several glasses of cheap sake before returning home. "Home" was a shed on the Bak property, and as he barreled inside, he kicked at everything he saw, his chest painfully tight. "That pockmarked bitch! She and the master can go to hell!" His toes stung from all the kicking, but his heart felt lighter. After that evening, he and the master stopped being a good match, too. "Can't believe the master's got a worse eye than me." He laughed at his master. It was the first time he was able to laugh so freely. Yes, he and the master were no longer a good match. He cadged some money for travel expenses and abruptly left for Keijo (the Japanese colonial name for Seoul). Everything had come together exactly at the right time.

Baekseon entered the city through Namdaemun.

After he passed through the famous gate, he deliberately bent over and looked at the gate through his legs. "Heh, I suppose it's as big as they say, but it still fits right between my thighs!"

He was very satisfied so far with his first-ever visit to Keijo. He downed a few drinks and then checked into a cheap lodging house. When he awoke the next morning, his bath towel was gone. He was mildly confused at first, but his puzzlement soon turned to complete astonishment when he realized he was the victim of theft. He unleashed his fury on the reception desk, demanding retribution for this crime against him, Bak Baekseon, illustrious scion of the Baks of Gyeongju. Instead, he was thrown out of the premises by two or three burly young men wearing tinted glasses.

Bak Baekseon's next lodgings were inside Keijo Station. Beggars and vagrants crowded against the walls and pillars and thronged the aisles. Before long, Bak Baekseon also found himself holding out his hand and calling out "Master!" to those who passed by. He refused to hold out both hands, steadfast in his belief that he would make it big soon. However, the "masters" would take one look at his pockmarked face and close-cropped hair and slap away his hand with a rolled-up newspaper. *Cheap bastards . . . Even if I got down on all fours, they wouldn't give me a thing. I'll show them, though.* Thinking this, he'd wipe his hand on his *baji* (Korean pants similar to Japanese workpants) and spit.

When independence came, Keijo erupted in celebration. Out of boredom, Bak also shouted *Dongnip manse!* (Hurrah for Korean independence!) and followed a long line of people through the city. He became intoxicated by all the young women waving at the crowd from their windows. The crowd streamed into what looked like a large playing field, chanting and cheering. But then some people got up on the stage and shouted something in Japanese—*Kaisan!*—with their left hands raised high, and the crowd screamed and instantly scattered. Bak was left behind. He was sick with hunger. In the twilight, a deep sadness seemed to have fallen over every inch of the playing field. Well, now . . . Bak-seobang hated sadness. He pushed the feeling aside and gradually made his way back to the station, asking person after person for directions. Back at the station, a fellow vagrant offered him a scrap of bread. "Just you wait," he said, thumping the man on the shoulder. "I'm gonna make it big, and when that happens . . . ”

One day, Bak-seobang made a huge discovery. “What a fool I am for not realizing it until now!” Unlike the countryside, the busy streets of the capital were surely littered with dropped change. He thought hard as he watched countless feet bustling by him. Ambition flared up inside him. He was sure that even now money was fluttering to the ground outside the station. He stood. His discovery must be kept secret. Bringing in accomplices would only reduce his share. It wasn’t as if more money fell when more people looked for it.

“I’m gonna be away for a bit,” Bak-seobang announced in a cheerful voice. He told the other vagrants that he’d located some “really rich” relatives of his in Keijo.

“Amazing! Are you serious?”

“Of course!” He felt like his “secret” might burst out of him at any moment. His homeless peers watched with a mix of envy and awe as Bak Baekseon walked out of the station. *Hmm* . . . A thought had struck him. He strode through Namdaemun, its silhouette now limned with the light of the dawn, and peered at it once more from between his legs. His confidence thus restored, he set off.

Not even half a day went by before his energy flagged,

though. By the afternoon, his eyes were wide as saucers and the blood-red ground was reeling beneath his feet.

He felt like his skull might split in two from the clamor of the traffic. The sunlight was stabbing his eyeballs. He landed hard on his backside in the shade of a building. He had wandered into the busy commercial district of Jongno. The display window behind him shone with goods that would astound even Master Bak. So, this was the great Keijo department store that Master Bak had boasted of with such peculiar possessiveness. He remembered being told that you could find a lot of rich people going in and out of such buildings. Feeling a sliver of hope, he once again directed his attention to the crowds. But no money fell to the ground.

He sat where he was for a long time. He dozed off. All at once he leapt up: someone had crashed into him. "Careful! Watch where you're going, you bastard! Oof, this stuff is *heavy*." A large shirtless man with a *jige* (A-frame) was trying to maneuver his way around Bak. He had so many packages he had to carry some on the *jige* and some in his hands. "Instead of sitting there like a worthless idiot, why don't you help me carry these?" the *jigekkun* (a laborer hired for carrying goods) yelled.

Startled, Bak Baekseon instinctively took the packages from the porter's hands. They were strangely in synch. Bak Baekseon grinned. The two began walking in step together almost as if they had planned it. They arrived at a small shack-like building, whereupon the large man wiped the sweat off his brow and exhaled. He looked hard at Bak Baekseon, a quizzical expression on his face. Baekseon smirked, his face one big rash of pimples. After that encounter, Bak Baekseon never returned to his life at the station. His "honesty" gained him a job as a *jigekkun*. So, his great discovery did lead to something, in the end, and you could certainly say that he acted as if he had made it big. Upon running into a former acquaintance—the vagrant who had given him the bread—at the station one day, he simply tossed out some advice ("You should find some relatives, too. I'm sure they're around somewhere") before sailing on.

A few years passed, but Bak Baekseon never found more success than that. Meanwhile, Keijo transformed into a city of assassins and thieves. One day, a group of people rode into the *jigekkun* stomping grounds on a jeep and began writing up some kind of list. A bareheaded young man with a pistol hanging from his hip announced that they were forming an "association," headed by none other than a member of the nation's opposition party. No one really knew what that meant, but the next day, soldiers arrived and raked up everyone's earnings for the day in the name of "association fees." There were other things Baekseon didn't like, either. The water in Keijo was flat, for example. *This capital is no good . . .* Baekseon came to the realization that in order to really make it big, he'd need an "opening"—a window of opportunity. Keijo had always been crowded with successful people; there wasn't room for any more.

"Jeju Island, Jeju Island..." muttered Bak Baekseon as he stood at the top of Mount Yudal. The wind was chilly. The monochrome expanse of the sea began to blur his vision. Below him, ships raced through the water, leaving white foam in their wake. As he made his way down the mountain, he became increasingly angry at the idiot who had told him you could see Jeju from Mount Yudal. The first time he ever heard the word *Jeju-do* was in Keijo. He had been surprised that such a place even existed in Korea. Even after it was explained that the *do* in *Jeju-do* meant "island" and not "province," he couldn't shake the impression that it existed in some intangible space at the ends of the earth. Apparently Jeju was where "political offenders" had been exiled during the Yi Dynasty. In his imagination it was an island full of desolate cliffs, where the bleached bones of fish that had been snatched from the water by black kites lay in scattered, disheveled piles, disturbed only by the wind. Even as he conjured up the image of a lonely island eroded by the heavy salt wind, however, the "plentiful women" of the "three plenties of Jeju" overtook him, enveloping him in a strange, dreamy fog. This fantasy of an "Isle of Women" kindled Bak Baekseon's passion.

As one might expect, Bak Baekseon was full of excitement when he finally landed on Jeju. The boat ride had frightened him out of his wits. It was his first time on a boat, and the surging waves of Jeju Strait looked nothing less than an immense beast from another world, intent on attacking the small boat with its horrible white fangs. Stormy clouds completely obscured his vision. All of a sudden there was a glimmer of silver from a rift in the cloud cover; the clouds scattered violently, racing across the sky like monstrous birds. The boat continued its mad dance over the water, heading for the valley of darkness ahead. Seasickness robbed Bak of the energy to yell at the captain. The beams creaked with every list and turn, and each nail made a dreadful grinding sound. He worried that the nails might pop out altogether, that the boat would disintegrate under his feet. He glared at the sky and resigned himself to his fate: a tragic, untimely death, like that of a "great man" losing his life at the hands of a terrorist in the capital. His grand scheme was destined to come to naught. But as the beams continued to creak, he soon changed his mind. *I can't die now!* He had remembered that he had no son who could fish his bones from the bottom of the ocean.

However, Bak Baekseon's excitement soon changed to disappointment and dissatisfaction and then—once combined with that peculiar regional bias that is characteristic of all Koreans—to hatred. His hatred was primarily directed against the men of Jeju. For one, why were there so many of them? The very idea of men living on the Isle of Women was enough to make him angry. The fact that they were all so ordinary-looking made it worse. For another, there were too many people who spoke the standard language on Jeju—too many competitors, in other words, narrowing his window of opportunity. He felt as if he'd been abandoned, though by whom he couldn't say. *I was supposed to have my pick of women here!* He was jealous of all the Jeju men. He recalled the barmaid in Mokpo, how she had sometimes filled his cup to the brim. *She wasn't so bad, now that I think about it. I'm sure she was laughing at someone else that day. Yeah, maybe because there was shit on the other guy's pants or something . . .* When he had gone to the storehouse of the Jeju branch, as arranged by the Mokpo shipping company's *jigekkun* boss, he had felt a strange sense of affinity and even satisfaction in learning that the person in charge was a mainlander. It didn't matter, in other words, whether Jeju was a lonely island or a metropolis; it was the unwanted presence of men that so offended Bak Baekseon.

4.

Back in the present, Bak Baekseon left the market bar in a good mood. There had been no complaints about the tab, and he had even received a few compliments on his singing. It was also much more comfortable sleeping there than in the storage shed at the harbor. He made his way to the police station, having completely forgotten about the incident at Jin Pharmacy. Dusk was fast approaching. Bak decided he would ask for an advance on his salary. The room he was currently borrowing from the broker (which he referred to as his "house") was just about the only thing he couldn't put on a tab. Having become a great jailer worthy of respect, he needed to find a place befitting his new status. "Salary, salary . . . " he muttered. While it was true that there was something classy and impressive about receiving a salary, he wasn't used to waiting for his pay. Whether as a candy peddler or a farmhand or a *jigekkun* or a beggar, he'd always been paid in cash. But with this job, he had been given a peaked policeman's cap to set on his head and a smart new uniform to put on his body and a shiny black pistol to hang from his belt . . . It was like a dream come true. He'd been so delighted that he would have gladly paid *them,* but his empty stomach reminded him that you can't survive on pride alone.

He soon found the street that led to the police station. It took less than half an hour to walk from the outskirts of the city to its center. He whistled softly and periodically muttered the word *cash* to himself as he walked.

Someone exited from the partially open main door of

the station just as he was passing through the gate. Bak jumped back in alarm. It was Clerk Gang. Bak Baekseon was seized with a sudden chill. Gang hadn't noticed him yet; he had his back to Bak and seemed to be waiting for someone. An uncomfortable pressure settled over Bak. *I can't run away now. Dammit, if only it were Little Baek* . . . He felt something almost like nostalgia for the runt. *Wait, I should just treat him as if he* were *Little Baek!* Bak Baekseon walked towards the entrance, determined to shout out *Little B*—no, wait, he meant *Gang-seobang.* The door opened wide and three people emerged: a jailer, an inspector of investigations named Bae, and a female prisoner. It was—not Myeongsun. He was puzzled by the relief he felt. Clerk Gang was chuckling.

Inspector Bae noticed Bak. "Well, if it isn't our man Bak! They say that providence always provides, and I see it's true. I know you've just arrived, but I need you and Mr. Gang to escort this one." The inspector gestured to the female prisoner. "What great timing. Jailer Hong, you're dismissed."

"Yessir . . . but where to?" Jailer Bak was suddenly uneasy about going by himself.

The inspector exchanged polite goodbyes with Clerk

Gang, ignoring Jailer Bak. "Give President Yang my regards," he said, and patted the woman's shoulder in farewell.

Bak Baekseon felt miserable as they left the station. "Bak-seobang!" He braced himself—until he realized that it was he who had spoken. His previous resolution to call the clerk "Gang-seobang" had vanished in the wind. *From the way he acted, it's clear the inspector thinks that Clerk Gang is an important man . . . I can't believe he completely ignored me in front of everyone!* He broke out in a cold sweat. *I can put up with being called a* seobang*—just please, please don't call me a* nassumikan. He waited in dread, his chest tight and his heart pounding.

"Heh . . . M-my *na-nassumikan* is something else . . . For one, it's full of craters . . . "

Clerk Gang stared at Bak-seobang in puzzled silence.

"Er . . . These craters of mine are pretty rough to the touch." Bak-seobang stroked his face over and over. "You—that is . . . this morning, you said I look just like a *nassumikan* . . . Well . . . heh heh." He tried to laugh, but his face twisted in a grimace. Having said that, though, his chest felt lighter for some reason.

"What? I have no idea what you're talking about." The

clerk feigned ignorance. "It's quite hot today . . . Jailer Bak, can you come with us to the provincial hospital?"

"Huh?"

"We need you to take us to the provincial hospital on Namdaemun Street . . . It sure is hot."

"The provincial hospital? Sure, I can go anywhere. The heat doesn't bother me at all."

Bak-seobang was disappointed. *He called me Jailer Bak . . . well, that's right, but he's still not showing me enough respect.* He was filled with unexpected dissatisfaction.

The two men had to nearly carry the woman as they walked. The woman kept coughing into her handkerchief. Her name was Yi Something-or-other, and she had been arrested about a month ago. For that whole month she had lain prone on the floor in a corner of the cell, right next to the chamber pot. She was now begging Clerk Gang for something in broken gasps. The jailer found it hard to understand her thick Jeju dialect, but he gathered that she was complaining about the lack of towels in the cell.

Whenever she coughed up blood, she was saying, she'd tried to get it into the chamber pot, but when the pot was full, she'd had to cough on her *chima* (traditional Korean skirt) instead. She'd been forced to tear off part of her filthy skirt just to wipe her mouth, feeling all the while the misery of those who cannot even die. Terrible menstrual pain also stabbed her lower abdomen. But then something white and elegant had risen up from the dark, fetid swamp that engulfed her entire body, like an unfettered swan in the water: Myeongsun's handkerchief. She couldn't stop staring at it. "Just—just a tiny little scrap," she choked out. "If only she could have let me . . . touch it, for just one moment. Let me put it to my lips. Or just a fingertip. My soul could have crawled out of that awful swamp . . . " But Myeongsun had kept it wrapped up tight in her skirt, refusing to let even one finger touch it.

The woman repeated the words "white handkerchief" over and over in a strangely overwrought voice. Halfway to the hospital, Jailer Bak had to lift her onto his back. He could see the hospital lights shining at the top of the hill. The heat of the woman's body made it hard for him to breathe. Blood rushed to his face, and his earlobes felt like they were on fire, crackling and shooting off pale sparks into the darkness. Clerk Gang walked alongside him in silence. Jailer Bak was a little unnerved, but gradually he began to feel like the woman was an extension of himself and that there was nothing to be afraid of. *She's so young . . . eeheeheehee.* This was a perk even better than his salary.

Jailer Bak returned to the police station with all the unsteadiness of a man who had just crawled out of the depths of the ocean. Since there was still time left in the workday, he dropped by the accounting department to ask about an advance on his salary, but was told that he would need official approval from his superior. Bae, the inspector of investigations, was also the director of security. Originally from the Northeast (referring to Pyeongan-do, in northern Korea), he had served as a commissioned officer in the "White Skull" 3rd Infantry Division, the security forces that had led the military subjugation of Jeju, before securing his current post. Jailer Bak passed through the main building and onto the athletic field. He wanted to wait until tomorrow, but was certain he would be yelled at if he left it to the morning. Corpses were strewn all over the field. Rigid arms and legs peeped out from the straw bags that carelessly covered the bodies, the limbs dimly white in the darkness. There were no crows, only chirping insects. He suddenly recalled the woman who had been released earlier that evening. *The inspector mentioned President Yang, or something like that*

. . . I bet I could get 300,000 won for her. 300,000 . . . Even if you pegged the average person as worth only 100,000 won, he calculated, releasing all of the prisoners would still amount to several million won.

The jailer crossed the athletic field into the annex, where the inspector's office was housed. He found the inspector alone in his office, drinking from a liquor bottle with some Western lettering on it. The inspector glanced at the jailer as he came in but said nothing.

" . . . I've come back from the provincial hospital."

"The provincial hospital, eh? . . . What of it?"

"Yessir, I went with Clerk Gang—I mean Mr. Gang . . . to the hospital, just now."

"With Clerk Gang? . . . I see, good job."

Bak Baekseon didn't know how to keep the conversation going. The inspector continued to drink. For lack of anything better to do, the jailer sat down. It looked like the inspector liked his solitude. If he sat there long enough, he'd probably get some sort of reaction at least, even if it was an angry one.

After about ten minutes of this, the inspector sharply brought his arm forward and glowered at his wristwatch. He then ordered Bak to bring Female Prisoner #11 from

Cell #7 for questioning at midnight tonight. The jailer was taken aback. He was talking about Myeongsun! Uneasiness and a strange sense of hope mingled in his heart like cogwheels gnashing together. Delight at the opportunity to touch Myeongsun's hands eclipsed his regret at having made more trouble for himself. The jailer looked timidly at the inspector. "Do you still need something?" the inspector asked. The jailer gave him an obsequious smile and said he wanted to talk about money. The inspector had lit a cigarette and was writing something down, but he laughed at that. Smoke wafted in the air around him, obscuring his notepad.

"Care for a drink?" asked the inspector. Then: "I've known you since you were 'Bak-seobang the *jigekkun*,' so I'm well aware that you're the sort of man who knows his place."

"Yessir." The jailer declined the drink he'd been offered. There was no guarantee that it would lead to his year's salary, after all.

"You probably view your current position as the highest honor, don't you?"

"Yessir." *Uh-oh, this isn't good.*

"Do you know who showed those Jeju traitors of yours

what for? Me. Not the South Korean police forces, but me." Glass in hand, he proceeded to exhort loyalty to the president, but while wearing an inexplicable smile on his face. It was a patronizing smile that didn't reach his eyes. The jailer kept trying to find an opening to change the direction of the conversation. The inspector suddenly shouted, "You're not a real man yet!" and the jailer gave up. No, he couldn't give up. *I know you're a rotten smuggler . . . Just you watch. Even I . . .* But it was his annoying habit to become meek and submissive when face-to-face with a superior. Like Pharmacy Jin, Inspector Bae was someone who had hired Bak-seobang during his *jigekkun* days. Every time the ships came in, Bae made him haul suspicious-looking packages to his residence on Dongmun Street. Then, late at night, Bak-seobang would have to secretly carry some packages back to an unidentified cargo ship. The ship was always hidden away in the cliffs about two miles out from the city. The city curfew was from ten o'clock at night to six o'clock the next morning, so after the ship left, Bak-seobang had to spend the night out on the cliffs, constantly on the alert for policemen and surrounded by the sound of the surging waves. No one told him anything, but once he had seen the inspector accept a wad of money just before the ship's departure. The inspector never hired any of the locals, perhaps because he hated Jeju islanders even more than Syngman Rhee did. It wasn't just them; the people of Jeju were shunned and shut out of their own local politics. The policies of the so-called "Republic of Korea" had therefore created the "opening" sought by Bak Baekseon the mainlander.

Jailer Bak went back to the jail. He squeezed his keys in his hand, which made him feel better. *Doesn't seem like I'll get any dough. Can't believe they're all involved in the black market . . .*

The jailer's office was located just beyond the entrance of the jail, past the iron doors. Next to that was the wire mesh holding cell for female prisoners, then a storage closet, then Cell #6 and Cell #5 . . . the men's holding cells. Those were all windowless. The concrete walls opposite the cells had transom windows set into them. He disliked the men's section. He could see into the entire cell by lifting the cover of the observation window with his finger. Dozens of bodies were stuffed inside a cell that was only about a hundred square feet in size. They formed one giant writhing mass of men, their arms and legs tucked tight like fetuses, backs and behinds wedged against hunched shoulders, some people crammed in so tightly that their feet didn't even reach the floor. Fights often broke out for better positions. Several people died a day in each cell. Their corpses were thrown onto the athletic field. A truck always came at twilight to dispose of them somewhere else. The bodies were pursued by the crows. Sometimes they reemerged in fishermen's nets.

Bak-seobang had found it all exciting at first. It was a form of revenge against the men of Jeju. According to the logic of his fantasies, they had no reason for existing. However, he was amazed at how these prisoners who were on the verge of death still harbored an eerie vigor. He had been too cocky in the beginning and had tried ridiculing them from the observation window, but their eyes had stopped him—eyes like ice, countless eyes, eyes that flared up in the gloomy cell like phosphorescence. Eventually they started mocking him. Someone found out that he used to be a *jigekkun*. Bak Baekseon was terrified that the knowledge would spread to the women. His excitement gradually turned into something that resembled a dog's howl.

Still irritated, Bak-seobang approached the wire mesh

of the women's cell. He began to jangle his keys but then stopped, afraid of that word "*nassumikan.*" He peered into the cell; he couldn't help himself. It was oddly quiet. The space swelled with soft mounds of flesh. Female Prisoner #11 seemed to be crying. Her back was to the mesh. The dark red color of her skirt was faded.

"Tears won't do anything against real sadness," a fellow prisoner commented. "The flames of sadness will burn them up."

"Stop with the bitterness," said Widow Jo. She was using her arm as a pillow. "Things could be worse, right? Yeonsu was able to leave here alive. Though from the way she was carrying on, I can almost imagine her transforming into a handkerchief if they'd buried her . . . "

"I suppose we all feel sorry for ourselves."

"Auntie Jo," said Myeongsun. Jo looked at Myeongsun expectantly. "I couldn't . . . It's mine, so . . . "

"No use thinking about that now. Who does it belong to, really? Me? Yeonsu? Granny Sinchon? No . . . it doesn't belong to anyone, here."

"But I . . . You know I didn't mean it like that . . . I know that death is coming for me. When it does . . . But . . . "

But . . . Myeongsun confessed that her older sister had

died of pneumonia. After a long night of suffering, she had sat up the next morning looking for all the world like she'd been cured. She'd combed her hair in front of the mirror and even put on some light makeup, delighting everyone. But just one hour later, she was dead.

"My, that's not like you. Everybody here is going to die—unless you have money, or you get picked by the governor to be his mistress or something . . . Anyway, what in the world do handkerchiefs have to do with any of it?"

The elderly woman from the Sinchon neighborhood that everyone called "Granny Sinchon" coughed weakly as she spoke. "It's okay, don't cry. It's not your fault. It's the handkerchief's fault! We have to try to get along and let ourselves go to the Pure Land when it's time. We can't appeal to Buddha if we're quarreling with each other. I can relate—I remember wanting to own just one thing that was immaculate and beautiful, back when I was young."

"What nonsense is that?" shouted Widow Jo hysterically. "*I'm* not going to die! Any day now, someone's going to use all their money to come get me! But even if I do die, I'll never be like Myeongsun, with only her handkerchief by her side. Are you going to use it to wipe away your tears when you say goodbye? What sentimental rot!"

Granny Sinchon fell silent. Myeongsun buried her face in her knees and covered her eyes with a scrap of cloth she'd torn from the hem of her skirt. Everyone else's handkerchiefs and towels were ragged and worn; she alone hid her handkerchief deep in the folds of her skirt. The other women's comments were alluding to the fact that she refused to take out her pure white handkerchief even when her fellow prisoners were suffering. Granny Sinchon broke her silence with a prayer to Amitabha Buddha. She chanted *Hail Amitabha Buddha* over and over, bathed in the peculiar reddish light of the cobwebby lightbulb above her. It looked like she was prepared to chant all night.

"'Hail Amitabha Buddha' . . . Hmph, how morbid." The jailer walked to his office. Only once he reached the safety of his office did he jangle his keys.

5.

Bak Baekseon could not calm down. *I can't sit still.* The clock in the office struck eleven. Something gnawed at his heart as it thumped painfully in his chest. *There's nothing to worry about. Just you wait and see, Mr. Inspector—Bae-seobang, you bastard!* He cupped his cheeks with his clammy hands. Those hands still remembered how the sick woman's ass had felt. His hands had slipped down over her curves on their way to the hospital. In that instant, Bak Baekseon had felt so giddy he'd almost stumbled. He conjured up the sensation again. He sniffed both hands, but they reeked from the stink of his keys. The image of the woman's ass split into two and expanded before his eyes. Bak Baekseon tasted desire. His desire wiped away his anxiety. "Well, I'll give it a shot. There's nothing to worry about." He pushed himself away from the desk.

Bak Baekseon took off his shoes. He stealthily opened the door to the storage closet and found a round bar about his height. He strained his ears for any sounds from the cell next door. Were they asleep? *It's too quiet . . .* Baekseon peeked into the cell and stuck out his tongue. *They can't all be sleeping with their faces to the ceiling.* Myeongsun was asleep in the middle of the cell. The jailer nervously swallowed his saliva. Her white feet peeped out of the skirt that enveloped her lower body. The jailer's heart creaked and whined deep in his chest. The faces of Inspector Bae and Myeongsun alternated before him like a pendulum. Now was the time to beat the inspector to the punch.

With his back hunched and tense like that of a cat, the jailer nudged the round bar through the wire mesh. He was shaking and breathless. The bar inched forward. The woman next to Myeongsun was murmuring deliriously in her sleep. "Ahh, it's so hot," she said, rolling to her side. He hastily withdrew the bar. Baekseon checked for a reaction from Myeongsun, but there was none. He used the tip of the bar to silently lift up the hem of her skirt. He thought he could smell her. He was overwhelmed by the sight of the white mounds of flesh that peeked out from the tears in her *baji*. Something divine was hidden just beyond those mounds . . . "Dammit!" The word slipped out. He had been too hasty. Myeongsun made a sudden movement. The tip of the bar was wedged tight. He felt the resistance from her body. Myeongsun leapt up with a scream. Baekseon hid himself in the shadow of the storage closet. He heard the sound of his own blood rushing through his ears.

The cell broke out in an uproar.

The jailer kept running his finger against his cheek and licking it. His fingertips felt like they had touched "it," and he couldn't keep still. Although his original intent had been to preempt the inspector, that was now the furthest thing from his mind. Desire surged through his body. "Pah! She was wearing drawers!"

It was nearing midnight. After about five minutes, he heard the sound of footsteps. It was a policeman on night duty. The jail fell into a strained silence as soon as the iron door creaked open.

"Hey, any beauties in there?"

"Dunno." Baekseon was flustered by how the question hit so close to his own intentions.

"Dunno? What kinda jailer are you?"

"Watch yourself. They're all beauties in my cell."

"Oh yeah? Looks like you got a taste of 'em yourself. . . "

He was about to agree, but hastily said instead, "I hear that Widow Jo tastes pretty good."

"Ha! So tonight was her, eh?"

"That's not what I meant. That is, she's no fun."

Baekseon was determined to keep enemies out of his territory.

The police officer unholstered his gun as the jailer unlocked the door. The cell was full of frightened eyes. They were the only things that looked human in the prisoners' clay-like faces. Several people squeezed Myeongsun's hand one by one. The cell door slammed shut.

Jeju police investigations were such that the "criminals"—it's so ridiculous it may be hard to believe, but in Jeju those who were arrested were executed as criminals without even a trial—were often murdered before they were formally booked.

It began after liberation from Japanese colonial rule on August 15 (1945) was replaced, as many know, with the U.S. military occupation of the southern half of Korea. Instead of Japan, it was now the U.S. that carried out colonial policies and inflicted hardships on the people, and any "lowlifes" who didn't comply with orders were thrown into jail. Under the banner of the "Red Menace," the ruling officials conducted a reign of terror befitting a premodern, ultra-authoritarian state. As a result, southern Korea became a place of darkness in every sense of the term. Seeing their country stolen from them yet again, the people rose up in protest over and over again. In October 1946—the year our Bak-seobang was living in Keijo first as a beggar and then as a *jigekkun*—the "Rice or Death!" riots in Daegu spurred general strikes all over the nation and resulted in over 2.3 million individuals rising up in action. A "people's war" broke out throughout Korea, including on the island of Jeju. In April 1948, Jeju became the locus of an armed uprising against the elections that were being conducted only in the South—in other words, in protest against the establishment of the "Republic of Korea" and the partitioning of the peninsula. The people of the island took up handmade weapons and retreated to Mount Halla, the shield volcano that towers over the island. It was there that they prepared for southern Korea's first partisan battle. The astonished Americans and Syngman Rhee swiftly moved to obliterate them. The people of the island were labelled "Reds" and thrown into jail one after another. Every jail was packed to the rafters, so much so that it was faster to kill people than to build new cells.

Myeongsun's high hips and elegant shoulders saved her to some extent from looking like your typical wretched female prisoner. The hemp *jeogori* (upper garment of a traditional Korean outfit) clinging to her skin had turned nearly see-through with sweat. Or no, that's just how it seemed to Bak-seobang. He stood there in a daze, the handcuffs forgotten in his hands. He glanced at the policeman and saw the bastard looking at her hungrily. "Hey!" Bak-seobang shouted, feeling a sudden surge of courage. "Don't you know your gun is pointed sideways? Where the hell are you looking?" Startled, the policeman turned towards him. Bak-seobang was satisfied. But the feeling evaporated when he tried to fasten the handcuffs on Myeongsun. He quailed beneath her unwavering glare, and something exploded in his chest. He could have withstood her loathing—if only she didn't seem to be looking at the pockmarks on his face.

The jailer huffed and turned his back. "Can't hold it in any longer, I gotta sneeze." Averting his face, he quickly stuck his fingers in his nose and yanked out the longest nose hair he could find. A huge sneeze erupted out of him, shaking the room and making him jump. *Eeheeheehee*, laughed the jailer, and with his eyes downcast he clasped the handcuffs on the woman's hands almost worshipfully.

The jailer departed with Myeongsun. They reached the end of the gloomy hallway of the main building in a flash. He could see the athletic field, surrounded on all sides by walls and buildings. It was submerged in a deep silence.

Myeongsun drew a long breath, as if savoring the smell of the earth below her bare feet. Her pace was neither quick nor slow; indeed, the only one who showed any apprehension was the jailer who held the rope that bound her. He felt a strange reluctance to cross the field. He had walked back and forth across it any number of times without thinking anything of it. The jailer regretted his earlier mischief with the bar, even as he denied his role as the instigator. Unusually for him, his face began to turn red. But wait, he thought. No one had found him out yet!

Without even realizing it, his hand had moved to the woman's behind. He gently stroked it. His palm moved smoothly over its warm curves. There was a throbbing in his wrists. Suddenly he felt the woman resist. No, it wasn't that—as she walked, the jailer had unconsciously begun to drag Myeongsun towards the wall. The jailer came to his senses. There was something he couldn't resist about Myeongsun. Just as when he stood before the inspector, he became aware of his cowardice. There was something oddly comforting about it.

"Hey. It's not . . . not like you're in love with the inspector." The jailer was embarrassed by his own words. "Why not slow down?"

Myeongsun had no reason to hurry. She continued to walk. With her hands cuffed, she could not resist his groping. The jailer followed her like a dog who had caught the scent of a woman's menstruation. She, in contrast, was like a horse: she reared and kicked backwards to fend him off.

All of a sudden, the jailer knelt and threw his arms around Myeongsun's legs. He held them tight and didn't move.

"Ahh! No, no, dammit . . . " Myeongsun struggled violently. "Let go! Let go, you *nassumikan*!" He'd thought he would never let go, but his cowardice got the better of him again. It may have been because of the "*nassumikan*." He stood there in a daze. *Hmph . . .* It was the first time he'd been called a *nassumikan* by Myeongsun. He chuckled softly despite himself. *That's strange. I wonder why I'm not angry that she yelled* nassumikan *at me.* No, he wasn't angry—in fact, a thrill went through his whole body. He nearly dropped the rope tied to her handcuffs.

The rope tautened, and Baekseon snapped back to reality. "Eeheehee, what a moaner." He sneaked a look at her. He couldn't tell if what he was feeling was emptiness or satisfaction. Myeongsun walked in silence, doing her best to ignore him. Feeling bereft, Baekseon grasped her hand. Myeongsun shook it off. "Eeheehee. You just don't get it yet, do you? Everything I do is for you . . . " The jailer tried to get her attention by pointing at the mountain of corpses, but it didn't work. Jailer Bak had thought to scare her, but it took more than that to startle a woman of Jeju. She wouldn't acknowledge that reality until the god of death himself blocked her path.

"What's in that head of yours?" The closer they got to the inspector's office, the more miserable the jailer felt. Myeongsun drew nearer to Jailer Bak. In that moment, his body went numb, and this time it was he who took a few steps back. He saw that Myeongsun was biting her lip. She may have been plotting something—perhaps something that involved seducing the jailer—but that's not something our poor Bak-seobang would be able to recognize. It was a moot question in any case, as they'd already reached the inspector's office.

Myeongsun used her shackled hands to comb her

bangs and neaten her clothes. The jailer hastily adjusted his cap.

Inspector Bae was alone. He glared as his wristwatch as they entered. He didn't yell, but his face was set in a scowl. *Aha*, thought the jailer, *that's a signal that it's twelve on the dot.* The inspector yelled if you were even a little early or late to an appointment. He found pleasure in yelling. Seeing someone arrive right on time satisfied his self-conceit, but since he loved to yell at people it also often put him in a bad mood. It was best not to get too close to him at such times. Bak had no idea what might happen now.

The inspector put away his hand mirror, which had revealed to him thin hair oiled flat over a square face. His imperious gaze did not waver as the jailer brought the woman to his desk. The jailer retreated to a bench in the corner of the room. His role was to assist in the torture that would no doubt start any minute now. Some even called this office "the torture room." The desk was littered with papers and a bottle of imported liquor. The inspector raised Myeongsun's chin with his truncheon. "Look straight at me," he told her. "I will now interrogate you in the name of the law. Confessing honestly to your crimes, in accordance with your conscience and respect for the law, is the best way you can protect yourself." Myeongsun kept her eyes on the glass window behind the inspector. The inspector suddenly let out a bellow. "Where do you think you are? It's not so easy to leave once you're here. Even the brats on this damn island know that."

The inspector's tone was nothing new, but there was something in the lewd gleam in his eyes that set the jailer's heart pounding. He had a vague sense that an ominous fate was about to befall him. Myeongsun looked at the inspector's gold wristwatch; with every tick, it seemed to carve away at the very air itself.

"Water!" The inspector rapped the desk with the bottom of his glass. The jailer fetched some tap water. The inspector drank the water and then closed his eyes.

"What year is it?" he suddenly asked, his tone now casual.

"Year 4281 of the Dangun Era (1948)," Myeongsun replied.

"Ah, very good . . . So you know what I'm going to say."

Myeongsun did not. The inspector began to speak of the events of August 15 (1948)—when, on the very evening the Republic of Korea was established, a "puppet army" had attacked the police substation in Myeongsun's village. "The rebels pillaged the village's provisions. But fish need water to live, as they say. They were abetted by traitors from the village itself." The inspector allowed himself a small smile as he turned a document over. "I see that your household gave them quite a lot of grain . . . "

The inspector's eyes were like inky pools. Myeongsun ducked her head, avoiding his gaze, and denied the accusation. She insisted that the mountain guerillas had threatened them with bayonets and stolen almost all of their barley. "Stop your lying," spat the inspector. "We've got proof." He told her that most of the men who had pillaged the village had "submitted" to the police. Myeongsun replied that she had no reason to lie.

"Ha, you're a brazen one, aren't you? Why did you give them the barley, then?"

"They would have killed us. We were scared. The people on the mountain attack you if you hesitate. But if you give in, then the police . . . "

"You fool!" The jailer jumped, as if he were the one being yelled at. *Now it's going to begin!* The jailer's heart rioted with an enigmatic mix of repulsion and envy. He felt a fresh wave of excitement at the prospect of torturing the woman naked. On one side of the room was a jumble of torture instruments. The ropes, batons, and iron bars were all to be expected, but the soldering iron and bellows made him think of a blacksmith. Almost without realizing it, he selected a whip and presented it to the inspector. It was strange that in that moment, there was not a single shred of sympathy in Bak Baekseon's heart towards this woman for whom he would sacrifice his own life in just a few days.

"Where's your older brother? On the mountain, isn't he? What, you say he's gone to find work on the mainland? Nice try, whore." All at once the inspector stabbed at Myeongsun's collarbone with his truncheon. Myeongsun tottered. She adamantly denied his accusations. The inspector had risen from his chair. "You're shameless," he said, and drained his glass. He began to rant. "Everyone knows that your brother came down from the mountains that evening and met with your family!" His eyes honed in on the tattered hem of her skirt. The jailer followed the inspector's gaze and noticed Myeongsun's pale white bare feet. (In reality, they were black with grime and mud.) *Ahh, something's going to begin after all . . .* The inspector looked fixedly at Myeongsun as she continued to protest. The impotent frustration in his eyes morphed again into a lewd gleam. There was absolutely no doubt about what was going to happen.

Inspector Bae jerked his chin at the door. The jailer didn't know what to do with the whip; neither did he know what to do with his heart. He thought about taking the whip with him. He was ashamed to find himself putting the instrument back in its place. The jailer abruptly turned towards Myeongsun. She looked back at him. Baekseon gave his usual laugh—*eeheehee*—but it sounded frightened. He had to laugh in a way that would also appease the inspector, though, so his face took on two different expressions at once. It was strange how, when their eyes met, neither of their gazes contained any ill feeling at all. The jailer suddenly had the sense that Myeongsun's empty eyes were entreating him for something.

"Do you understand?" The inspector laughed triumphantly like a victorious general. He told her that her brother had already "submitted" and that he could arrange a meeting for her at any time.

The inspector's thin lips shut, even as the woman's

mouth fell open. She stumbled back. "That's impossible!" she said flatly. The jailer thought she had revealed something she shouldn't have, in speaking that way. *But wait, "submitting" is just another word for surrendering, so all that means is that she and her brother don't like to surrender. Well, neither do I! Yep, we're definitely a good match . . .*

"Hmph." The inspector maintained his calm. "I could let you meet him as early as tomorrow."

The inspector just told her a barefaced lie. There's no doubt that Myeongsun's right about him never surrendering. Telling her that he'll let them meet—that's clever, all right. The jailer lingered at the door, watching the two of them. But then the inspector shot him another glare. The jailer gave a hasty salute. The inspector ordered him to come back in one hour.

6.

That hour felt like a thousand years to Jailer Bak. The jailer mechanically made his way to the athletic field. It was dark outside. Filled with resentment, he turned to look back at the light that shone from the inspector's office. Courage surged up in him. *Think I'm a cute little kid, do you?* . . . He became angry all over again as the inspector's words came back to him. "We're around the same age," the inspector had told him, "but you're like a little boy. You're sharp, but you look dumb. Don't think I'll treat you any better just because I pity you, though." *Damn him and his clever words!* The jailer retraced his steps. But his courage didn't extend to opening the inspector's door. He crept down the hallway.

The jailer's imagination assaulted him with the force of a hundred thunderclaps. He clung to the wall like a lizard. The wall throbbed against him relentlessly. He put his eye to a crack in the window and then to the keyhole in the door of the room whose stifling atmosphere was even now spreading outward. His eye couldn't make out much, so he placed his ear next to the keyhole. He was frightened out of his wits by what he heard.

"Heh, I . . . You're my favorite out of everyone so far. Understand? I really like you. Ahahaha."

With a twist of his body, the jailer shot up and grasped the doorknob. It rattled in his grip. If he opened the door, Bak Baekseon's fate would be sealed. Just then, the woman cried out, and the sound tore the jailer's chest in two. He was used to hearing people scream in the inspector's room night after night. It was terrible retribution to have to listen now to Myeongsun's cries. She kept gasping and crying out for help. She was calling for someone. There was no possible reason why she should call for Bak Baekseon, but still he clenched his teeth in anticipation, convinced that her cry of "Master Jailer!" would sink its fangs into his neck at any moment. Splitting his concentration between his ears and fingertips, he slowly but steadily turned the knob with the care of someone handling the pin of an explosive device. He attempted to crack the door open. There was a faint clicking sound. He tried twisting the doorknob again, but it wouldn't budge.

The jailer panicked. He couldn't bear the sound of the woman's choked moans. He felt like his head was on fire, his skull blown open. *Call for me! Call my name—Call for Bak Baekseon . . . Call for* Nassumikan, *like you did before!* He was struck by the urge to break down the door, but he couldn't find the strength that a single call for help would give him. One cry of "Master Jailer!" and he would probably have leapt into the flames of hell itself. That he couldn't break down the door was not Myeongsun's fault, of course, but it was not just because of Bak Baekseon's cowardly heart, either. Although he didn't realize it then, his life had been forfeited the moment the agonizing call of "Master Jailer, Master Jailer!" began to ring deep in his ears. A distant part of himself was saying, *It's all over for me. But they can't do anything about my salary or my bar tab, ahahaha*. That voice howled and rioted inside him.

Jailer Bak did not meet his fate that day. He was despondent: in the end, no angel's call came. *So that's how you feel, huh?* Without knowing it, Baekseon had tied himself up in an unbreakable bond with Myeongsun. It grieved him that he couldn't help feeling deep in his heart that she was a stranger utterly unconnected to him, even though that was by no means the case. Myeongsun was drifting away into the distance. *No, she can't!* Baekseon thought, and his heart immediately began to chase after her.

Bak Baekseon was consumed with jealousy towards Inspector Bae. It was almost pitiful. The shell that was the "Inspector of Investigations & Director of Security" broke apart, and out emerged Bae Gweontae the man. In that moment, the jailer also felt Bak Baekseon the man struggling to emerge out of him. He grimaced and grasped the doorknob, but as soon as he did so the inspector's smug face superimposed itself over the door. "Gah!" He stumbled back involuntarily. His heart always faltered in the inspector's presence, like a crab scuttling sideways.

"You'll regret this, you shitfaced inspector—Bae-seobang, you asshole!" *Stop worrying about her. She's just another cow.* His rebellious heart lowed sadly: *I can't believe you're doing it with Bae-seobang!*

The telephone began to ring. The jailer felt startled but also unexpectedly freed. After a while the ringing finally stopped.

"What? Uh-huh, uh-huh, S. Village . . . Uh-huh, K. Village . . . " Something was up—the inspector's voice was shrill with excitement. "Understood. Understood. I'm in the middle of an interrogation . . . Deployment in the morning, of course . . . six o'clock is good . . . Hello? Don't forget to contact the jail—Jailer Bak's office . . . What's the American army planning? Okay, got it, thanks."

Jailer Bak was thrown by this new development. He hastily peeped through the keyhole for a final time and then crawled away on all fours. The police station was suddenly full of life.

In the hallway that led to the cells, he ran into the officer whom Bae had most likely been speaking to. Jailer Bak feigned ignorance about the call. The fellow officer was wearing a helmet that sat askew over his wildly mussed hair.

"What's going on, you ask? I guess you could say we hit the jackpot this evening." The officer abruptly lowered his voice. "Hey, our 'guest' in the torture room is a woman, right?"

"Er, yeah—"

"Thought so, given how long it took Bae to answer the phone . . . Bet she's a beauty." Jailer Bak was disgusted by the officer's self-satisfied air. Our Bak-seobang would normally have jumped at the topic, but today was too—it was just too filthy and awful. Jailer Bak asked if that was all. "What? No, things are just getting started!" said Helmet Head. He explained that they had just gotten a phone call from the S. Village and K. Village substations saying that they'd been attacked by the "puppet army" (partisans). "The enemy's done for, though. They're like scared little kittens."

"So you're leaving to go help our side?"

Helmet Head clicked his tongue. "No way. Gonna

go home to my wife. Whaddaya think would happen if we left now, when it's this pitch-black? The Reds are like monkeys—and we're like those summer bugs that're attracted to open flames. I've been on duty for three straight days and nights now, and I can't stand it anymore. In the morning—yeah, today'll be my fourth straight day. I wanna go home and strip my wife naked . . . "

"I-I see," Jailer Bak mumbled. At the word "wife," an image of Myeongsun writhing in pain in the inspector's office appeared before him. "So th-that's it?"

"Pretty much. We'll leave in the morning, after the enemy's retreated. The inspector'll understand. We think the same." Helmet Head told the jailer that the Americans would probably put up a fuss, but it'd be alright in the end. Before leaving, he relayed the inspector's phone message and added that the morning shift would probably be cancelled. Jailer Bak secretly rejoiced. He didn't want to be parted from Myeongsun.

The inspector handed the woman over to the jailer and then disappeared into the athletic field. There were no stars, no wind, only some cigarette smoke that drifted aimlessly in the night air.

As soon as he was gone, the woman began to cry in spite of herself. But then her tears abruptly dried. She fell to her knees and looked up at the sky in a daze. The cell skylight shone dimly from across the field. She lay face down on the ground, overcome by choked sobs. The jailer thought back on the inspector's words from just a moment ago: "Those who don't listen need to be worked over." He was still something of a novice, but even he had whipped any number of people who were eventually thrown out of the torture room unable to walk, forced to crawl on all fours like a beast on the verge of death. But he didn't have an ounce of that fortitude left. He let out a nervous laugh: *eeheehee*. He meant to reassure her, tell her she had nothing to worry about now that he was here, but the words wouldn't come out. He had come to realize that he had no right to say such a thing to her. He regretted having laughed. How could he gain that right? He had no idea. With a furtive glance around him, he spat out, "Fuck that shitfaced inspector!" Strangely enough, once he did so his heart began to lift, and he finally began to feel like he'd gained the right to protect Myeongsun.

"Let's go."

Myeongsun followed without complaint. She had no

strength or willpower left. No records or statements had been taken in the inspector's office. That her body would end up dumped on the ground like trash was as clear as day . . . Myeongsun moved her bound hands near her thighs and grasped for the white handkerchief she'd hidden in the inner pocket of her skirt.

"My wrists really hurt." Her wrists were indeed chafed raw from the handcuffs. But she shouldn't say such things, thought Bak. The guards would only laugh at her and swing the butts of their rifles down onto her shoulders. And her voice was shaking too much.

"Oh, I'm sorry." But his chest grew warm with pleasure from her plea. "Yeah, that must hurt a lot . . . "

Bak Baekseon's heart ached with pain. He hated Inspector Bae. An agitated sensation welled up inside him. It wasn't jealousy; it was almost something like a sense of justice. He felt great pity for the woman. He gently touched her wrists; his fingertips came away sticky. The jailer tentatively raised her hands to his cheeks. Myeongsun was shivering. "It hurts!" she groaned, perhaps in response to the way the handcuffs tightened from the movement. The jailer jumped back as though he'd touched a live wire. He'd jumped back because his face had felt smooth and pockmark-free under her touch. It was the first time in his life a woman's hands had touched his cheeks. He desperately wanted to remove the handcuffs.

For the first and only time in his life, Bak Baekseon felt truly heartless. Surrounded as they were by the dark of the night, he could see nothing and feel nothing other than a slight numbness in his entire body. The categories of "jailer" and "prisoner" fell away from his heart. Those round shoulders that almost seemed suspended in the darkness—the sight of them filled Baekseon with anguish. The cells were not far off. He wanted to sit down and silently stay where they were forever. *Should I take off the cuffs at least until we get to the main building?* He hesitated, agonized. *I can't, I can't. I can't break the law.* The jailer remembered the oath of loyalty he'd given to "his excellency President Syngman Rhee." But what good was loyalty when it didn't get you a single red cent? The inspector's face once again floated through his mind. *Yeah, that asshole's no good. He might come back for her again.* As soon as he thought that, his heart did its crab-like scuttle again, and the face he'd seen in the office door rose up before him.

"We're going!"

"Ah—don't pull! It hurts!"

The jailer couldn't stand it anymore. He threw himself to the ground like a madman and clutched Myeongsun's legs. "It's no good, it's no good—I love you . . . It's no good, it's no good . . . " The jailer's body was shaking violently. He may have been weeping.

"*Aigu,* Master Jailer, I'm suffering . . . Please, could you take these handcuffs off? Just for a little while?"

The jailer covered his ears with his hands. *I do understand. I was just thinking the same thing* . . . The jailer didn't give any thought to what she might do after he uncuffed her or what she was planning. *But, but* . . . With deadly earnestness, he buried his head in her knees. The sour scent of woman—She was crouching down—His policeman's cap fell off.

Myeongsun appealed to the jailer once more.

"It's no good, it's no good . . . We have to g-go. It's no good. We can take them off completely once we get back to the cell. Okay? It's really close—right over there."

The jailer abruptly stood up. He let out a series of deep breaths. He took a few dazed steps forward and then back. He grabbed Myeongsun's arms and hoisted her up. Myeongsun was limp at first, but then she shied away from him as she stood and staggered forward, teeth clenched.

"I'm sorry! I'm gonna make this up to you, I promise."

Back to her old self, Myeongsun said nothing more. The jailer was relieved, but deep inside his heart a hard cold lump had begun to form.

7.

A troop of armed police rode towards K. Village in three trucks. From downtown they headed east for about thirty minutes. During the ride, the police opened their mouths wide, as if drinking in the sunlight pouring down on their faces, and sang military songs.

Outside the city limits, the road stretched out white and straight before disappearing into the woods beyond. You could hear the roar of the high sea waves in the distance. The glittering waves surged relentlessly along the coast, which was dense with thatched village houses crowded together like sea lice. The sky was a crisp cobalt blue. Mount Halla loomed far off to the right, surrounded by countless humble hills. At its base, the mountain curved gently upwards along the distant horizon, the highland greenery gradually melting into the deep indigo of the mountain slopes, before rising precipitously towards the sky. Amidst all this graceful beauty, a jagged peak soared up sternly into the clouds. On the other side of those shadowy clouds, the mountainside leisurely disappeared into the horizon beyond at a steady angle.

The policemen gazed at the mountain and sea as the trucks raced along the bumpy main road that was a legacy of the Japanese colonial period. But they had become dispirited by the time they reached the main road and no longer sang military songs. The sound of the siren as they left the station had fired them up, but at some point even the truck horns had stopped honking. Although it was daytime, there was still the possibility of a grenade attack. The three trucks rocked with an icy fear and caution. Someone even fired his machine gun at a flock of crows; he'd been startled by the sound of their wings as they took flight.

Incidentally, Bak Baekseon found the ride exhilarating. He'd never actually seen the puppet army in person. There was something fascinating and even exciting about this puppet army and its ability to scare the well-provisioned police forces of the Republic of Korea this much. In reality, the deployment was a rather miserable matter of obligation rather than a serious action against the enemy. He was amused by the "cowards" on the trucks. He rapturously stroked the M1 rifle that had been formally issued to him. It was the first time he was allowed to use such a weapon. "Make sure you chop off some heads today, too," the inspector had told him. Bak Baekseon didn't know whose heads they'd be, but in any case, he was certain he'd be able to chop off at least two or three. "You'll finally become a man after that," the inspector had concluded. *If I cut off some heads then I might finally be able to receive my salary.* Not only that, he'd been guaranteed that his opponents would not be the puppet army itself.

"Oh, how beautiful." Baekseon began to marvel aloud at the sight of Mount Halla lit up by the morning glow, but was checked by the grim stares of the people around him. *That's right, I'm on Jeju!* "Pah, there's nothing beautiful about those goddamn Jeju mountains!"

As he jolted against the "cowards" on the moving truck, he began to suspect that this incredibly strong puppet army was not just an army of Jeju bastards. The thought enraged him. In that moment the face of Kim Ilsung, the so-called premier of the "puppet regime" above the thirty-eighth parallel, flashed before him. Kim's young, rotund face had often been featured on the signs held by demonstrators as they marched down the streets of Keijo. The puppets of Jeju —they were inhumanly strong, like *gwisin* (demons)! Baekseon shaded his eyes with his hand and gazed towards the horizon. What looked vaguely like land in the distance was in fact a mass of clouds. If the puppet army really was that strong, they'd have to get the mainland involved, too, or else they'd be in trouble. With some relief, he finally recalled how the Reds were also said to be on Mount Jiri and Mount Taebaek. He took in a deep breath of the brisk sea breeze. Before long, his hatred for the puppet army was pushed out of his heart. In its place, a hazy link between Jeju and the mainland began to form.

"Goddammit! Why dontcha come out, you puppet army bastards? Show yourselves!" He had begun yelling without realizing it. The other police officers recoiled in surprise.

"Show yourselves, you cowardly fools!" He couldn't

help but feel an increasing delight at the policemen's nervous expressions. He really did want the puppet army to show themselves. It wouldn't be so bad surrendering to them if they really were that strong.

The trucks rode into the village in a cloud of dust. As they arrived, the sky seemed to cloud over for a brief second. Some crows were flying away, casting a heavy shadow over their heads. The police at the substation gave a perfunctory salute to their superior officers but didn't even go through the motions of welcoming the relief party. The battle was already completely over. There was no trace of the substation barricades anymore, and the roof to the building had caved in and filled the space between the walls with debris. The road was choked with corpses and dyed bright red with their blood. The people of the village huddled among the bodies, weeping as one. They frenziedly hurled rocks at the crows that brazenly alit on the bodies. Every evening, the young adults and even middle schoolers were forced to keep watch around the perimeter of the substation with guns awkwardly placed in their hands. The corpses were almost all middle-school-aged children who had been conscripted into what one could call a "government-manufactured militia."

Some villagers were climbing the wide red-clay hill that led to the coast. They made for an uncanny sight. Every one of them grasped a deadly-looking spear in their hands, but as a group they were strangely downcast. One side of the road was already lined with villagers. At dawn, the substation had used the area's household registries to conduct a thorough investigation of the entire village. If a young man or woman listed in a household's registry was not present at home, they were considered to have fled to Mount Halla and the whole family was branded as puppet army co-conspirators—that is, as Reds.

Surrounded by the policemen's bayonets, the villagers spilled into the schoolyard of the nearby elementary school. The group was eventually divided into two groups, the so-called Reds and everyone else. White dust clouds rose up from the parched ground every time the crowd of some several hundred people shuffled their feet. The police officers shouting angry commands sounded the same as slaughterhouse workers. Whenever a baby began to cry, the mother would hastily swaddle the child with the hem of her skirt as if it were a piece of merchandise.

By the time Jailer Bak stepped down from the truck, he'd already gained a certain measure of respect among his peers, even without having exchanged a single blow with the enemy. *Show yourselves, puppet army!* He looked like he could have given even the infamous "White Skull" 3rd Infantry Division a run for their money. He pulled his blue policeman's cap over his eyes and walked about with his gun pointed indiscriminately at the masses. "Hey! Don't just stand there. It'd be an easy thing to chop off a few heads, you know." He deliberately raised his voice as he spoke. Doing so made the other policemen's voices seem exceptionally quiet. Baekseon was pleased.

Inspector Bae climbed to the roof of the truck. He looked at his wristwatch. For a second, his pitch-black sunglasses flashed with a peculiar light as they caught the gold reflection of the watch. "Attention, everyone!" He glared at the sight of Mount Halla rising up behind the school building. "We, the security police of the Republic of Korea, have been deployed here for two purposes. ONE—to mop up the Reds. TWO—to protect law-abiding citizens. These two things are in fact one and the same." He settled his gaze on the group labelled as Reds. Caught in Inspector Bae's sunglasses were those, for example, who had been swept up because the sons or daughters of the family just happened to be away attending the memorial service of a deceased relative. Inspector Bae orated for over an hour on the roof of the truck. It was just like one of those political campaign speeches that repeat the same points over and over again without advance or retreat. In a word, Bae's monologue was on his hatred against the Reds and his demand for loyalty to the Republic of Korea. To borrow his own words, they were apparently one and the same. He also declared that in order to preserve the public peace of this village and its law-abiding citizens, they had to completely eradicate the Reds who disturbed that peace. It was an overture to capital punishment. Finally, he turned to the people whom he'd sentenced to death and shouted, "Fools, all of you!" Then he climbed down from the truck, still fuming.

Inspector Bae had no doubt wanted to descend from the truck in a resolute manner, but he clambered back up when the platoon security chief began to give the execution order. Bae listened to the execution order with satisfaction. With both meticulous care and boldness of intent, he took a breath and leapt from the truck. When he had jumped down previously, his left hand had struck the side-view mirror that stuck out from the truck like a crab's eyestalk. But he seemed to be quite pleased with the pose he was able to strike with this second attempt (this time he had managed to avoid the mirror), at least based on the fact that he didn't climb onto the truck a third time.

The villagers' punishment was savage. A buzz of voices began to tear apart the heavy silence of the crowd. The "law-abiding citizens" were to use their handmade bamboo spears to stab to death the families of those who were deemed to have fled into the mountains. Neighbor would stab neighbor, relative would spear relative. Because it was a small village, everyone knew each other.

Although Bak Baekseon had boasted about cutting off heads, in reality he was relieved. He was no longer confident that he'd be able to laugh when the head rolled off the shoulders. But he soon found that this new development was much, much worse. At the very end of the row he was overseeing stood a young woman of around seventeen or eighteen with a bamboo spear in her hand. Baekseon's chest tightened as he thought of Myeongsun. One could see the traces of tears still on the young woman's face. She had been told to stab the old woman before her. The old woman had fallen to the ground with her back to the young woman and her hands pressed together as if in prayer. She suddenly unclasped her hands and began to speak in broken gasps. "*Aigo!* What kind of misfortunate world is this? When my son died, I should have passed away, too . . . To live to the point where my face has to touch the ground like this . . . It's unbelievable." The old woman sat up suddenly. "Ahh, Sunhui, I can't believe this, that you have to . . . to kill me . . . It's too horrible . . . "

The young woman didn't say anything. She couldn't say anything. Jailer Bak approached her with his gun. She readied the spear and then lurched at the old woman . . .

The young woman looked vacantly at the blood that gurgled out onto the old woman's white clothes. Baekseon was seized with the urge to comfort her.

"This—this is what you wanted, right?" the young woman mumbled, as if to herself. Her voice didn't sound like that of a human. Her face was as pale as a corpse, and her voice shook like a leaf in the wind.

"Y-yes . . . That's fine—" Baekseon could say nothing else. The young woman took a single, faltering step, the sound of the old woman screaming like an animal still echoing in her ears. She staggered forward like a sleepwalker for a few more paces before collapsing to the ground. She began to cry hysterically.

Just then, Baekseon saw a young man break away from one of the back rows of "law-abiding citizens." "You son of a bitch!" shouted Baekseon for no reason, and began running after him. The young man was racing towards the acacia trees. Just as it seemed like the copse of trees might provide him cover, gunfire roared, and the young man staggered. He fell forward to the ground. The platoon chief had shot him. Baekseon seethed with anger and disgust. It was not because he'd been robbed of his prey or anything like that. He'd run after the young man half-heartedly, out of impulse. He didn't have any intention of killing him or capturing him or doing anything particular to him . . .

A terrible emptiness had formed in Baekseon's heart, but now it was being filled with a deep hatred of his superiors. He loathed the very idea of the police and pitied the young man. He wanted to touch the dead body but was distracted by the irritating sight of the cackling platoon chief. *I'm not a coward!* he thought, and stumbled to a stop.

Roughly half of the village—over two hundred

people—were executed by noon. The late summer sunlight exposed every inch of the schoolyard, which had been bare of even a speck of dirt. Now it was crowded with a mountain of corpses and a sea of blood. Among the dead villagers were some "law-abiding citizens." These citizens had been killed at the hands of the police when they'd been unable to use their handmade bamboo spears to stab their relatives or neighbors to death.

A murder of crows looked down upon the schoolyard from their perch on the roof of the school. Two or three of them flew up and traced an arc across the sky. The sun was high. The sunlight shone down like sticky coal tar on the bodies.

While the truck engines growled to life, Baekseon stared at the young man who had fallen while fleeing. An acacia tree cast shade over the corpse. An old man lowered his *jige* A-frame to the ground and approached the body. Baekseon didn't know if he was a relative or not. The tall old man placed a wooden board across the arms of the *jige* and then put the young man onto it. He hoisted the *jige* to his shoulders, as if carting away just another piece of luggage, and staggered forward with the aid of a cane. As he did so, a yellow butterfly settled on the young man. It looked like a flower petal. Baekseon was seized with the desire to catch the butterfly. He thought back to the time he'd spent as a vagabond in his youth. *I, too, should have a son who's like him.* The hands of the old man gripping the ropes on the *jige* were stained with blood. Baekseon's gaze collided with that of the old man. His runny eyes flashed deep within their sockets. Baekseon hastily averted his face.

The sun was hot. There were no clouds over Mount Halla. For some reason, Baekseon thought of Little Baek, from his time as a *jigekkun*.

8.

Some days passed. It was the seventh month according to the lunar calendar, but the dreary weather continued. Black clouds hung low over people's heads. For a long time, the people of the island were unable to see Mount Halla.

Baekseon, too, was uncharacteristically depressed. His head felt heavy, his joints ached, and his shoulders were terribly stiff. His bar visits became even more frequent.

One evening, after a long night of heavy drinking, he returned to the small shed near the docks and went to bed. The sea was rough and choppy. He woke up the next morning with a hangover. After some difficulty, he left for the morning shift. He stopped by the bar on the way and ordered a drink. As soon as he downed it, he felt his head clear. At that moment there was a flash of lightning, soon followed by a roar of thunder and then a torrent of rain. As he watched the rain come down, his expression was that of someone who'd been relieved of some burden.

Baekseon's bravery had caught the attention of his colleagues. No man had ever thrown down the gauntlet like that while standing boldly on a truck surrounded by enemies, not even in jest. It would have been only just and proper for Baekseon to gleefully use this opportunity to establish himself as a "hero" for these troubled times, but it seems that he was doomed by his membership in the Oriental race and its spiritualism. *The police deserve to be looked down upon.* He'd come to believe that what one called a policeman was no better than a dragonfly without a tail—something incomplete and unfinished—and though they ran around like soldiers, brandishing their guns, there was in fact no use for that miserable lot in this country called the Republic of Korea. It appeared that, for whatever reason, he'd become sick of the whole business. He wasn't someone who could keep things to himself, so instead he narrowed his eyes and told people the following: "I'll be leaving for Seoul soon. I've got a relative who's a pretty important politician, someone who's been making waves lately . . . I can't rot away as a police officer in the sticks forever, can I?" He'd finally mastered the art of speaking down to his colleagues.

Baekseon arrived at the cells reeking of alcohol. The night jailer complained under his breath about his lateness. He then said to Baekseon, "I've got a reputation for my intuition, and my intuition's telling me that there's gonna be a lot of people going to the parade ground (execution ground) today."

Baekseon immediately thought of Myeongsun. "Are you talking about the women?"

"Dunno . . . Probably a mix." The other jailer gave Baekseon a meaningful smile.

"Really?" That smile worried him.

"Why're you so interested all of a sudden? . . . Gotten attached to one of 'em, maybe? Or got your eye on one of 'em but haven't had a chance to enjoy yourself yet?"

Baekseon was taken aback. "You . . . Did you do something?"

"Well, I'm definitely not like you—drunk all the time, bumbling, never getting laid."

"You shitface! You did it, didn't you—you put your hands on Myeongsun!" Baekseon sprang forward and closed his hands around the other man's throat. He was rather impressed at his own strength.

"Hey! Wh-what're you doing? You forget we're inside the police station?!"

"Confess! I don't care where the hell we are. You did it!"

"Did you say 'Myeongsun'? . . . There's been a huge misunderstanding." The other jailer wanted to escape from Jailer Bak and his desperate, crazed expression but was constrained by the hands around his throat. If it came to it, though, he wouldn't hesitate to fight back.

"You wanna settle this now?" The two jailers butted their heads against each other.

"Why not?"

"Let's take it outside!"

"Right here's fine with me!"

In the end, they were so preoccupied with arguing about where to fight that they forgot to actually fight.

Baekseon stood in front of the wire mesh cell, jangling his bunch of keys. To his surprise, Myeongsun approached with her eyes lowered and told him she had a favor to ask. Jailer Bak was ecstatic to have been chosen. "A favor? What kind of favor?" Myeongsun crouched before the wire mesh and asked apologetically if she could borrow a brush and some ink.

"Shouldn't be too hard to arrange . . . but wh-what for?" He would have granted her anything. He wanted her to know that he hadn't actually wanted to keep her cuffed back on the athletic field.

" . . . Please, I'm begging you." Myeongsun hung her head.

Baekseon was about to ask if she needed paper, too, but the thought came to him that she might be writing her last will and testament. He was also acutely aware of his own insufficient ability to read. He broke out in a cold sweat. *My hands shake from palsy, so I can't write.* That's what he should tell her. Even so, his feet refused to move. He recalled the fight that morning. Was Myeongsun going to die? His heart began to beat faster, and for a second Myeongsun looked as if she were standing far off in the distance, amidst a blurry vista. Her eyes were like dark pools. Flustered by those eyes, he drew away from the wire mesh.

Baekseon went and got a brush and some ink from his desk. He then folded a few pieces of calligraphy paper in half and stuck them in his pocket. As he returned to the cell, he debated whether or not he should open the door. There was a slot in the lower part of the wire mesh for inserting meal trays, but the inkpot wouldn't fit through. Myeongsun said that he could just hand her the brush. He passed it through a chink in the wire mesh. The ink she had him place on the ground nearby.

Myeongsun turned her back to the jailer and took out something wrapped in paper from the back pocket of her skirt. She spread it out. The paper disintegrated at her touch, as if it had been soaked in water, revealing her pristine white handkerchief. Jailer Bak remembered how the woman he and Clerk Gang had escorted to the hospital had bitterly complained about Myeongsun. She silently placed the handkerchief on a narrow, unoccupied part of the floor. It was spotless. If purity had a scent, it would have smelled like that.

"I'm going today, I know it," Myeongsun said. "Widow Jo . . . I'm so sorry. I caused everyone such trouble." She fiddled with the ends of the white handkerchief. "Ah . . . I wish I could have visited you in your hometown of Yongdam. You mentioned how there's a beautiful, deep blue pond there . . . "

"Come now. Why are you saying such things? You might be mistaken. Anyway, nothing will come out of that attitude. Think about your brother in the mountains, or your mother who was killed . . . You have to stay strong." Myeongsun involuntarily buried her face in her hands, overcome by these warm words from Widow Jo, a woman who was normally as rough and wild as a boar.

For yesterday's dinner, Myeongsun had received a serving of boiled fish. The women were usually served chestnut rice with two slices of daikon radish pickled in the Japanese style, but occasionally a meal would come with meat, as if someone had remembered that condemned prisoners deserve a last meal. She'd left the fish untouched, unable to eat a single bite. The other prisoners were also too unnerved to eat it. But by morning, it had disappeared.

Baekseon peered into the cell as he made a show of doing his rounds. The calligraphy paper in his pocket had gotten wrinkled. Myeongsun stuck the brush through the wire mesh and into the inkpot. She held it there for a moment, letting it absorb a great amount of ink. Then, overwhelmed by emotion, she jerked her shoulders up and pursed her lips together. Her face was pale. It looked like she'd come to some kind of resolution.

The white of the handkerchief had a piercing purity that almost seemed to emit light. People held their breath as the brush moved and spilled ink onto the cloth. Myeongsun was strangely calm, and the brush tip didn't waver.

Myeongsun gave her thanks and returned the brush to the jailer once she was done writing. Baekseon couldn't move away. Gauging the jailer's mood as he stood there like a rock, Myeongsun hid herself among the other prisoners. And then she slid up her skirt hem and bound her white handkerchief to her thigh so tightly it dug into the flesh. On the cloth, she'd written *Song Myeongsun, twenty-two years old*, and the name of her village, Aewol. Everyone now understood. After she was buried in a heap with all the others, it was possible she might be dug up eventually. By that time, the face and body of Song Myeongsun would have rotted away. What if her grandmother wanted to bury her in a small grave? How would she know which of the countless dead individuals was Myeongsun? She'd clearly pinned all her hopes on that white handkerchief, which would allow her grandmother to find her granddaughter's corpse.

"I'm afraid of disappearing from the world, like a bubble on the surface of the water . . . I'm so very afraid. Widow Jo, please forgive me. But I will die nobly, I know it. This white handkerchief is the only evidence that I was born into this world . . . " Myeongsun had regained some of her composure. Widow Jo gently began telling stories about Yongdam—about how camellias bloomed boldly at the edge of the village pond every winter, about the souls of the young men and women who had fallen into the deep water and died trying to pick those flowers for their lovers. The prisoners listened in silence, looking at their own stained handkerchiefs as they did so. Myeongsun looked up at the sky. Rain was constantly blown into the room through the skylight. Myeongsun watched the raindrops glitter and fall from the spiderwebs in the corner of the ceiling.

Baekseon returned to the jailer's room, but he found he couldn't take it anymore. He banged his hands on the walls with all his might. The walls remained stoically unmoved. His chest throbbed, his stomach growled. He wanted to run out and down a few drinks, one after another. "Goddammit! Nothing happens like it should in this world of ours." Why did quiet and beautiful Myeongsun have to die? His heart anguished over her. He cursed whoever it was who had captured her, imprisoned her, violated her, and whoever it was who would kill her.

While Jailer Bak stood there paralyzed, the situation had become urgent. The iron door to the jail creaked open and several policemen entered, led by Inspector Bae. The deputy inspector, a young man in tinted glasses who served as the head jailer, called out prisoner numbers one cellblock at a time, haughtily shouting "Released!" after each number. Among the Jeju police, "Released!" was a synonym for slaughter.

The iron door opened wide, and several dozen people bound together with rope came shuffling out. Their faces were like masks in which only their eyes gleamed like black voids. Outside the jail, the policemen had their guns at the ready. Torrential rain pummeled the athletic field, throwing up white sprays of water and obscuring the sight of a truck parked on the grounds. The truck had arrived just a moment ago, carrying roughly the same number of prisoners as those who had been "released." The new prisoners were being led to the main building in the rain. They were switching places, in other words.

As the two groups crossed paths, a strange, feverish moaning arose: the prisoners recognized each other. Their poor, miserable voices were muffled by the rain. A broken cry suddenly cut through the commotion on the parade grounds: "*Aigu*, Jailer Bak! It's me, it's me! *Aigu!* I'm here!" Blinking his eyes against the downpour, Baekseon finally spotted the bearded face of "Pharmacy Jin." His mouth was moving, but the rain now obscured his words. What was Jin doing among these prisoners? "Jin-yeonggam!" Jailer Bak howled, but the rain had already driven him further away. He was unsettled by the encounter but didn't pursue it. His heart was as stormy as the sea, and it was all because of Myeongsun.

Silence settled over the crowd once more. Those gathered had noticed that men from the inspection office had arrived. The prisoners in Myeongsun's row were exhausted; people kept stumbling and falling as they walked. If even just one person fell, the entire row had to halt. Their cries sounded ragged, torn apart by the wind and the rain and the spectators' jeers.

The truck's engine roared to life and Bak Baekseon's spirit began to shake and waver, as if he were being squeezed in an unexpected embrace between the heavens and the earth. He spotted Myeongsun's face from behind the shoulders of the people who were crammed under the truck's canopy roof. Their eyes met, or so Baekseon thought. In that instant, Baekseon understood everything. Those who violated Myeongsun were violating the entirety of the world. And that meant they were violating Bak Baekseon, too. Something pierced his thoughts like a shooting star, like a dolorous note from a whistle. Hundreds of thousands of images of Myeongsun's face flickered in the dark sky like stardust.

The main gate to the athletic field opened, and several jeeps drove through. The ringing of a bell groaned its way through the sprays of rain. Baekseon's mouth fell open. The woman's face appeared to him in close-up—only to then become a blinking far-off light. "That's strange, no, that can't be . . . " he muttered mechanically. As the truck turned towards the main gate, Baekseon gave out a sudden wail and began to run after the truck like a madman. He chased after the truck, undeterred by the mocking rain. His policeman's cap flew off. His legs got mired in the mud. He fell forward. Got up again. Fell forward. Got up once again. Kept chasing.

"Wait for me! Please wait . . . Myeongsun, Myeongsun, please wait for me . . . " He waved both hands in the air as he yelled. "Wait for me, Myeongsun! It's me, it's the *nassumikan* . . . Please forgive me! Wait for me! Myeongsun!" He continued to run. The truck passed Gwandeokjeong Pavilion and then disappeared into the distance.

Jailer Bak Baekseon was stripped of his position and "unavoidably" executed four days later. He didn't really need his salary anymore, but since he'd never been paid in the first place, when he died he left behind an "unavoidable" debt. When asked by Inspector Bae if he had any last words, Bak-seobang glared at the inspector's gold watch and said the following.

"I guess we're just—just not a good match, me and the Republic of Korea."

After his death, his jailer's key ring was recovered from

his pocket. On it hung around ten different kinds of keys and locks, including a lock for a traditional Korean chest, a regular padlock, and a lock for a Western-style door. A lot of people laughed themselves silly over the sight of it, but two curious opinions also emerged. The first was that Bak-seobang might secretly have been an affluent person of some importance. The second was that, in his loneliness, he had embraced his key ring while he slept instead of embracing a wife.

Death of a Crow

1.

The rain had stopped. The main road was in a miserable state: having been ridden roughshod by trucks and a slew of combat boots, it was now frozen into a furrowed line of countless deep ruts that stretched obstinately east and west through the city. The sea was so rough today that it could be heard all the way downtown. Clouds loomed low and heavy over people's heads. Occasionally, a silver streak of sunlight managed to leak from a tear in the cloud cover. The wind had subsided. It was a bitterly cold day.

"Hey now, hey! Hey now, hey—"

From his position on the stone steps of the police station, Jeong Gijun distantly heard the disagreeable voice of Old Man Boil, the man who acted as a kind of town crier for the police. Gijun had run into him last night while en route to his secret meeting with the partisans. He was unsettled by a sudden jolt of fear.

Gijun had just come from the military government office. He was supposed to meet with the chief of police (who happened to be a distant relative of his), but for some reason the chief had failed to show up. According to the clock, it was past eleven. The wintry air seemed to darken and blur the colors of the wooden buildings and stone walls that surrounded the spacious station grounds.

Gijun gazed for a while at the police gate. A gravel path lined with cherry blossom trees led from the gate to the main building. He then moved his attention to the withered lawn that extended from the row of trees. The saplings that had once been meant to link the colonies to Japan under the banner of "Japanization" were now gnarled and even hoary, their dead branches stabbing at the air. Corpses from the jail were usually thrown with careless abandon under the cherry blossom trees in the mornings, but today it seemed that someone had cleared the lawn; even the straw mats used to cover the bodies were gone. Gijun hated going to the police grounds and being confronted with the sight of all those bodies, hated walking underneath the trees, hated hearing the gravel crunch underneath his feet. *Just a little longer*, he kept telling himself, but he was still unable to look at the beautiful cherry blossom petals that blanketed the earth like snow in the spring. He was well aware of the mawkishness of it. But he couldn't help what he felt; his emotions were like a visceral ache, rising up from the deepest depths of his flesh. Whenever they threatened to spill out, the corners of his eyes would sting, as if he were a boy again. The scars of that dark time when the homeland had been lost were still engraved into every crevice of his consciousness. The cherry blossoms he saw were not actually cherry blossoms, and the pain from the time when bayonets had been his only companions continued to throb within him.

Gijun averted his eyes from the lawn, took a deep breath, and descended the stone stairs.

"Hey now, hey now, hey—"

Gijun heard the voice again as he passed through the gate into the main road. It was coming from Gwandeokjeong Pavilion. He stopped in his tracks. *Who is it today, I wonder?* He was suddenly tempted to find out. He stood casually beside the barricade as the elderly individual everyone called Old Man Boil drew near. Gijun began striding in the same direction as the old man, abruptly changed his mind, then resumed his walk at a more leisurely pace.

"Hey now, hey! Look at this handsome devil. Talk about having a 'price on your head,' heh . . . What about it, ladies? What do you think of this lady-killer? Hehehe . . . Kind sirs and madams, do any of you know this head? Is there no one who recognizes this bastard's head?" The old man's voice quavered from the cold. But that lecherous, hoarse voice grew strangely thick whenever it was directed towards a woman.

A bamboo basket dangled from Old Man Boil's shoulders, and a shabby felt hat sat snugly on his head. One of his legs was lame, and every time he put his foot down his hips jerked and his whole body gave an awkward shake. His bare feet made a comical wriggling motion when he walked. The road, frozen with the slush thrown by myriad car wheels and combat boots, gleamed in the sunlight like the dull edge of a knife. (The road was so uneven it might make a cripple of anyone.) The head in the bamboo basket rolled around with every tilt of the old man's short frame. He suddenly hunched over and plunged his hands inside the basket with a smirk, his white breath rising in the air like steam.

Gijun could tell from the inflection in his impudent voice that the old man was drunk. His quick dancing movements and the rolling of the severed head also gave it away. It was commonly assumed that Old Man Boil was in his sixties, but where he came from was a mystery. His primary occupation, such as it was, had consisted of healing boils, pimples, and other such skin infections. After he got his "government job," he began offering his special treatment for free. No one took him up on the offer, though; instead, he became the laughingstock of the whole city.

The old man's livelihood had depended upon the swellings that erupted on people's skin. He would place his lips squarely on his client's stiff, steamy purple skin and suck out the pus he found there. Sometimes he bit into it. As the pus pooled into his mouth, he would mumble a request for payment. Afterwards he would go to a bar, his whole face suffused with joy. The more people laughed, the more he was emboldened. As soon as he reached the door, he would deliberately plant his lame leg on the floor and loudly clear his throat. In due course the waste in his mouth would be spit to the ground. He would then gargle with some soju and swallow the liquid down.

Gijun lit a cigarette. He began to amble away, to all appearances lost in thought. The streets were quite busy once he got to the post office by the police station. Women carrying baskets on their backs or in their arms were silently swallowed up by the crowd. Gijun remembered that it was market day today. Old Man Boil had apparently also been attracted by the crowd; he was headed in the same direction. Gijun wanted to find a casual way of stopping him. The outdoor market was packed with a writhing mass of people. Out of the great tumult of noise, he could pick out the hoarse voice of the fish vendor as he hocked his wares and, even closer, the thin cries of someone peddling combs and hair oil. Also being sold were surplus goods from the American military such as pants and socks, chocolates and gum that had completely disappeared a few years ago due to a huge boycott of Western candy led by middle-schoolers, sugar drops, and many other things besides. Gijun stared at the market without really taking anything in. He snapped out of his reverie only when a young woman tossed a sealed letter into the postbox right in front of him and then scurried away. When she reached the street corner leading out of the market, she stopped and looked back in his direction. A stream of passersby jostled their way past her. She gripped the ribbon to the braid that hung over her shoulder and cast her gaze behind Gijun.

The old man that was the source of the young woman's fear had arrived. For him, market day provided an unparalleled opportunity for gathering people to him. The police were nearby, too, and there was a man wearing a khaki-colored American military uniform—ah, it was Jeong Gijun, Old Man Boil realized. The old man promptly tilted his basket and leered at a small group of women nearby.

"C'mon now, there's no need to hitch up your skirts and run away like that . . . I'm not a murderer, you know."

The old man glanced at Gijun. Whenever the old man drew near, the crowd drew back—just like a retreating tide. The fixed distance between them and Old Man Boil never broke. There was mockery in that distance. The wet frozen road cut into the old man's bare feet. All of a sudden, a distant expression clouded his face, as if he were puzzled by something. He began to stomp his feet in a frenzied manner. Gijun had been coolly smoking his cigarette, but he laughed involuntarily at the sight. The old man immediately twisted his body in Gijun's direction and ran towards him, his shoulders rolling wildly from the weight on his lame foot. He was just like a sickly dog who had found his master. He stroked his basket with his hands and looked up at Gijun with his beady little eyes.

"Hehehehe. I know you well, sir. *Very* well. Thank you for treating me last night . . . Hehehe, you always wear nice suits and are always the gentleman . . . "

"That's enough."

Nonplussed by the word "last night," Gijun glared at the old man, who hastily took off his hat and twisted it in his hands. He swallowed his breath and his words and shut his mouth. His head looked like a moss-grown stone, and he stank of alcohol and something fetid. The old man turned around, hugging his basket close and mumbling something as he did so. There, too—there, too, under the eaves of the houses, was the cold laughter of the crowd. Their laughter was knife-edged. He looked imploringly at Gijun once more. In that instant, a cold wind roared through the gap between the old man and the even colder young man, and between the old man and the crowd. The crowd transformed from a group of individuals into a single monster with a million eyes meant to rebuff and reject him. Even the uniformed Gijun looked to the old man like he was there to block his way. He nearly screamed.

Gijun knew that Old Man Boil sought his support—and that he was now afraid of him. The old man looked back and forth from the police to Gijun with a sad, helpless expression on his face. Confronted with that khaki uniform, he regretted having left his previous occupation. Gijun, in turn, was filled not with disgust but with pity when he saw the traces of bloody pus on the old man's stained white clothes. He put his hand in his pocket, thinking to give him a cigarette, but was distracted by some seagulls flying low over his head. As his gaze followed their flight through the chilly cloud-covered sky, they reminded him of summer in a painful way. He lit a cigarette for himself. Seeing the greedy, mucus-crusted eyes of the old man fixed on him, he started to walk away. The old man tugged insistently at Gijun's sleeve. Gijun ignored him. The old man produced a single camellia, tentatively closed Gijun's hand around it, and then waited in silence with his back hunched and his eyes trained on Gijun's face.

"—So you're a florist now?" Gijun said, belatedly remembering how he'd laughed at the old man a short while ago.

"N-not at all!" When the old man finally grasped that Gijun was kidding, he felt a burst of renewed energy. He explained that he had a perfectly respectable job; he simply wanted to give the flower to Gijun, him being a kind young man and all—someone who surely belonged in the Pure Land. Cunning and fear warred in his eyes as he spoke.

More and more people began concentrating their attention on Jeong Gijun. Although they may have looked like curious gawkers, they were not. For the past few years, Gijun had been working as an interpreter and translator for the American military government in Jeju, and there were many individuals who had come to look at him with eyes like daggers. Gijun suffered most from the gazes of those who'd known him for a long time (though there were fewer of them now). Their gazes had eventually merged into a singular sweeping gaze directed at anyone deemed to be a puppet of the American military. Just now at the military office, he'd been told he was being transferred to Gwangju, on the mainland—a change that would free him from this constant siege of hostility. Or, to put it another way, it was a chance for him to escape this island and its many terrible and heightened troubles. But at the same time, the transfer also meant having to disregard the wishes of his allies who knew him better than anyone else on this earth. He didn't know why, but his transfer had been decided very suddenly. To think that just yesterday he had met with the partisan Jang Yongseok . . .

"Heh, I see you've been drinking again," Gijun said, directing a laugh at the crowd. The laugh was not really from him but from "Jeong Gijun the interpreter."

"What's the story behind today's heads? Do the flowers mean they're unusually remarkable, or is it the opposite today?" Gijun threw the camellia flower into the basket.

The old man was puzzled, but he tried to cover his confusion by swinging the basket in a wide arc, causing the head inside to roll around. "There's only one today," he said, thrusting a hand into the basket. And then he repeatedly ran his tongue over his thick, cracked lips and protruding snaggletooth. Like a slave offering a gift to his master, he resolutely raised the head towards the sun. Gijun swallowed nervously. In the winter sunlight, the head of the deceased looked like it was underwater. The young man had been decapitated just under his chin, so the head had no neck. Why did it look so peaceful? Its eyes should have been wide open, nose bulging, mouth agape, tongue loose. But its face was empty of the agony of the living, unmarked by the profaneness of putrefied intent. To Gijun, the almost noble visage expressed nothing less than the tensions of life itself. Its cruelties.

"Hm, that face looks familiar . . . " For some reason, Gijun felt like acting against his own will.

The old man let out a strangled noise and sprang backwards in surprise. He grasped a hunk of hair and lifted the head up. "R-really, sir?!" His voice was hushed. Gijun unexpectedly found himself overwhelmed by the sight of the crippled, hunchbacked old man holding the young man's head as if it were a lantern. The old man inched closer with little twitching steps. Gijun felt nauseated, then angry. He nearly yelled. Instead, he gently told the old man that he just had a vague feeling, that was all. Suppressing his anger—suppressing all of his impulses—was a habit he'd had to cultivate in order to endure his assignment. It was his duty to do so. He suddenly felt embarrassed that he'd allowed himself to linger here. He needed to see the chief of police at once. Even if that basket were thrown into the market crowd or laid bare in some lecture hall, it didn't matter—it wasn't related to his mission. His position was one where a mistake of any kind inevitably led to difficulties. What had made him let down his guard?

Gijun was forced to acknowledge that a deeply submerged part of him clearly felt something akin to liberation at the thought of his "transfer." He also acknowledged that the feeling was accompanied by a certain vulgarity of sentiment—one that made him blatantly hate this blameless old man, and blatantly view the people gathered around them as allies. *You're just trying to run away from your position like a coward. You're not loyal to the organization—you're not loyal to your own self, to the possibilities of the self.* It was a sobering thought. Gijun violently shook his head, as if attempting to throw off something abhorrent, and shooed the old man away.

By that point, however, the residents of the city had already formed an impenetrable wall around them. Old Man Boil was revitalized by this unexpected opportunity. He stretched up on his lame leg and surveyed the crowd, stuffing tobacco into his pipe as he did so. A laugh escaped from Gijun despite himself.

"Ladies and gentlemen, do any of you know this head? If you recognize this *ppalgaengi* (Red) please speak out. Ah, you don't have to speak now—please inform the police later." The old man grasped the head by its hair and held it up high. Bedraggled strands fluttered limply in the wind.

"Is there no one who knows this person? . . . The reward is 100,000 won! I repeat: 100,000! It is also your duty to the state!"

There were clearly those among the crowd who were tempted by the desire to inform on their fellow citizens. They squatted on the ground like frogs, smoking cigarettes with their elbows resting on their knees. One person finally spoke up, glancing at his neighbors' faces all the while. "Looks like a guy I know . . . " Some people left, only to be replaced by others. Those with an interest in informing stayed right where they were. It was a horrible moment. The would-be informants were casting an ingratiating look at Gijun.

This practice of proclaiming news of the dead was fundamentally premised on the act of informing. There was no point to it otherwise. It was necessary to ascertain the identity of partisans who had died in action, or who were captured but refused to disclose information even under torture, so that the police could then investigate their background and family members. Disaster would inevitably descend on those family members in the form of mass arrests. Their entire hometown might even be set on fire by the police and reduced to ashes.

As Gijun attempted to maneuver his way past the wall of people, someone began to loudly proclaim the following: "Yeah, I know him. I know him well, hahahaha . . . I don't mind telling you right here and now, in front of everyone. I don't need the money."

Everyone looked around in surprise. A tall, well-built young man was standing not too far from Gijun. He appeared to be drunk, and his face was half hidden behind his neighbors' shoulders. With a start, Gijun realized it was Yi Sanggeun. A chill went through him. In the next moment, he thought of Yangsun. He always thought of Yangsun, Jang Yongseok's younger sister, whenever he was frightened, as if her face were etched into that emotion.

Yi Sanggeun forcibly pushed his way through the human barricade with his sturdy shoulders. Gijun once again came to a stop. Old Man Boil bent his back like a shrimp, still awkwardly holding the head before him. He started to sidle away. He often saw this young man in town. Sanggeun staggered forward, looking directly down at the old man. The old man took step after step backwards, wearing a frightened, unconvincing smile. The crowd pressed forward against him, then retreated. The old man's smile bent like taffy. Suddenly, he grasped his crippled foot in one hand and began to manically dance on his other foot. The crowd roared with laughter as he hopped about like a spring and warbled out his public proclamation, the head still held high. The laughter of the crowd intoxicated the old man. Sanggeun opened his arms wide, as if he were swimming underwater, and spit some phlegm to the ground. He grabbed the old man, snatched the head from his hand, and looked around him with bloodshot eyes, his fingers thrust into the tangled hair of the dead man even as his own disheveled hair half obscured his face. Gijun was shocked. Their eyes met. Sanggeun gazed steadily at Gijun.

"Listen . . . This is my *relative*." He rolled his eyes and twisted his lips in a clownish gesture. "So I know that my family and I are going to be held culpable . . .

But listen now. This dead bastard's head isn't human. Humans are living beings. Hahahaha, just like me. Which do you think is more appetizing, some dead bastard or one of the heaps of sardines you can catch from our Jeju sea? You see, ladies and gentlemen, this is not the head of a human, it's rotting meat. It's not something that we humans should pay any heed to. That's why it's not actually my relative!" Laughter rippled through the crowd as he finished his speech, followed by jeers. *Nice job, young man! That's 100,000 won for you!* Sanggeun didn't return the laughter. Feeling disappointed, he took a deep, pained breath and closed his eyes. One could gather from his pale swollen face and unbuttoned overcoat that he was most certainly drunk. He stood unsteadily but with composure. His bloodshot eyes moved restlessly about before finally settling in Gijun's direction. Gijun tried to hide behind the people in front of him.

Gijun didn't immediately grasp the meaning behind Sanggeun's actions. Whether they were because he had pity for the dead person or whether it was hatred he felt, or even whether they came from some masochistic impulse that included both these things—whatever the reason, they were the immature actions of someone who, intoxicated or not, knew he belonged to a rich family (and therefore a powerful one, at least in this society).

Old Man Boil suddenly gave a cry and threw himself before Sanggeun. The young man kicked at the old man who had so unexpectedly entwined himself around him. The old man clung to his leg with one hand and attempted with the other to snatch the head back from the young man. The young man looked down at the old man with an exasperated laugh. He drew the severed head closer to his own—but then grimaced, looking nauseous. He shoved the old man aside, throwing the head into the basket that had tumbled to the ground, and advanced towards Gijun in a determined manner. Gijun pushed his way past the human barricade. As he strode away, in dread anticipation that Sanggeun might call out his name at any moment, a memory from last night vividly and unexpectedly flashed before him. Once again he saw Yongseok, dressed in his rough farmer's clothes. Jang Yongseok, limned in the faint white light of the moon as he clambered up the cliff, back to the mountain, away from home.

2.

Yesterday—before he'd known about his transfer—Jeong Gijun had sat at his desk at the Department of Justice in the US Army Military Government in Korea's (USAMGIK) local headquarters, completely preoccupied with the state of the weather. He was supposed to be translating some documents related to the indictments of certain "criminals" and their deaths due to illness or accident—categories applied to those who died from torture or private execution—but was too worried about the rain to focus. A fierce wind was blowing. The wind was pounding endless flowing rivulets of water against the window glass. Normally he could see Mount Halla from the window, but today it was completely obscured by the hazy rain. It was hazy inside the room, too, from the smoke that spewed from the male workers' countless cigarettes as well as from the belching stove. Gijun worried that Yongseok wouldn't be able to come down from the mountain if the rain kept coming down like this. It pained him to think of the fickle weather in that snow-capped place.

The rain and wind finally began to abate by the

evening, though there was still no hint of the waning moon. It suited the nature of their secret communications to meet underneath the faint moonlight. It was an extremely dangerous method of communicating, no matter how you viewed it—the very last resort left to them, you could say. If it failed, then Gijun would most likely have no choice but to join the partisans in the mountains. He might get caught and killed before he could flee. Roughly six months ago, rumors had begun to circulate that Yongseok, one of the leaders of the partisan movement, was hiding in town. Up to that point, the two had communicated by sending coded messages in seemingly unrelated correspondences; sometimes they'd even employed the method of tucking notes into the corner of some dusty bookshelf at a set time and set bookstore. Ironically enough, Gijun himself had been told the rumor at a local bar he frequented. One of the customers had whispered to him that the whole city had been infiltrated by Red spies. The rumors about Yongseok weren't true. He only came into the city when he needed to communicate with Gijun, and he always did so boldly, alone, and in disguise. He may have been able to escape notice the first few times, but no matter how ingenious the disguise, it was difficult to fool the people of this small city for long. It didn't help that Yongseok had lived in the city for many years before escaping to Mount Halla.

Gijun changed into his black double-breasted Macao suit and left his boardinghouse shortly after seven. He was supposed to meet Yongseok at eight o'clock on U. Hill, located south of the city and just under a mile from the mountain. He'd already been able to complete the actions they'd agreed upon roughly half a month before, but as fortune would have it, he was now able to add to his report some urgent information that had just come in that afternoon. Apparently, a police platoon stationed at S. Village was to be mobilized tomorrow to K. Village in the east, which would leave S. Village's police substation only lightly guarded. Gijun had been carefully monitoring the area around the mountain since last night, but had discovered no signal or sign from the partisans. He had seen some smoke signals far away towards the east and west, but they weren't the ones the partisans were supposed to use for Gijun and his engagement tonight. When plans were interrupted or changed, the partisans would raise smoke signals from the mountain hillside about a day beforehand in order to alert their allies. Each group had its own set of codes.

Gijun stuffed a small bottle of whiskey into his overcoat pocket and exited his room. A maid from the boardinghouse was standing at the end of the hallway. "Don't stay out too late . . . " she said to him with a smile, though her tone sounded worried.

"I wonder if you'll follow me, since you're so concerned," Gijun replied lightly, returning her smile.

The heavy rain had stopped, but a cold wind continued to blow mercilessly through the alleys that ran between the low, squat buildings. The electric lighting from the buildings on the main road was weak and sparse, and the area was nearly deserted. Gijun could just make out the stout outline of Gwandeokjeong Pavilion, its curved tile roof seeming to float in the darkness. Gijun kept his hands carelessly thrust in his pockets as he walked. In the back of his mind his concentration was, of course, fully focused, but he made sure to refrain from looking behind him or engaging in other such careless behaviors.

The buildings became a little more cheerful as he moved south on the main road and up a gently sloping hill. The wet streets were still deserted, but here and there the red lights of the brothels and bars shone coldly in the night. A woman's flirtatious voice rang out behind the closed doors of a bar whose walls weren't even painted (it was more like a hovel, really). Jazz music was being played from a scratchy old record. The music almost seemed to flow around a huge silhouette of a woman swaying in the window, but there was something terribly plaintive about the incongruous nature of the reflection. There was no sign of any women on the streets. A few drunks staggered by. One man was pounding his chest as his overcoat flapped open around him and crying something in a voice full of tragic heroism. A group of people were walking down the middle of the street. A tall man amongst them wildly shouted, "I want to go to Japan!" and began singing a Japanese song. Two or three of his companions looked fawningly at his face and cheered him on. Gijun flattened himself into the shadows of a nearby alley. He didn't feel like he was in any particular danger, but it might cause some inconveniences if they saw his face. Although he hadn't had a chance to talk to him very much in the past, he recognized the tall man as Yi Sanggeun. He had a feeling Sanggeun would probably try to drag him to some bar, just because he was a familiar face.

Gijun had to admit he had an interest in Sanggeun. Sanggeun's father was an executive at Siksan Bank and owned a huge parcel of land in Jeolla Province; as one might expect, he also had a certain amount of influence in various institutions of power. With such a father, one might expect the adult son to be the same, but it appeared that they didn't get along very well. Having returned to Jeju after abandoning his studies in Seoul, Sanggeun now spent his days in an aimless, reckless, and almost decadent fashion, worrying his father to no end. It was the kind of lifestyle that only the son of a wealthy family could enjoy. His drunken sprees had become the topic of much gossip around town. When it came to drinking power, it could be said that Sanggeun ranked at the top and Old Man Boil at the bottom. Gijun knew Sanggeun's father and recognized the need to insinuate himself more deeply in the family's good graces, but he was also mindful of Sanggeun's reckless behavior, such as the time he'd drunkenly argued with an MP.

In any case, now was not the time to approach him. Gijun turned into the alley and made his escape. When he reached the pharmacy he decided to stop in and buy some medicine—anything would do. As soon as he began to open the door, however, someone flew at him out of the darkness. It was Old Man Boil. He appeared to be quite drunk. The older man crouched on the ground, threw his arms around Gijun, and began begging him to buy him medicine. Sensing the presence of someone behind the glass door, Gijun moved into the shadow of a nearby stone wall.

"Yessir, I'm drunk," Old Man Boil slurred. "Can't deny it . . . But as you can see, I'm completely cogniz—cogni—I'm fine." He gripped Gijun's hand. "Yessir, d'you know I once helped cure people's boils. They respected me for that! They did, once . . . D'you know, sir, when I'm drunk I can see the stars even when it's pitch-black . . . My eyes are the sky and my tears are stardust, heh heh. But I'm fed up—I can't—can't make a living babysitting these heads . . . " He licked his upper lip. "Can't you spare a cigarette, sir? Just one cigarette." He tried to roll up Gijun's sleeves. Mumbling something about how boils were delicious, he began to frenziedly pat down Gijun's arms, legs, and thighs as Gijun stood there dumbfounded. His whole body shuddered violently as the cold, withered twigs that were the old man's fingers crept into his sleeve. He mercilessly wrenched the old man's hand away. The old man refused to let go.

Gijun pushed some bills at the old man. "Oh, I don't need money—I don't need charity . . . " wailed the old man tearfully, though his fist closed over the cash. It was like he almost wanted to bury himself at Gijun's feet. Gijun roughly pushed the old man aside and made his retreat.

Gijun emerged from the alley onto Nammun Street. It was as deserted as the main road. There weren't even any drunkards. If you followed the street, you'd soon find yourself at Samseonghyeol, one of the famous landmarks of Jeju, but about halfway there Gijun turned left, just before the bridge. As he turned, he glanced behind him. His heart was beating quietly. It might have been his imagination, but he couldn't help feeling that someone was following him. The street cut through the darkness like a dried-up river, surrounded on both sides by endless black stone walls. It felt like Gijun was standing at the bottom of a riverbed, blocked by the shore. In the next moment, he thought he saw a human shadow step away from the stone walls, towards him. It was the first time something like this had happened. The shadow seemed to loom over him, and Gijun thought once again about how hard this whole business was. But surely there was nothing to fear . . . *All I'm doing is walking on this road, right? Whether I decide to take a sip from the whiskey in my pocket right now, or go to a bar, or pay my respects to the dead—it's my right to do what I want, isn't it? And I've got special privileges, to boot.* Feeling himself breaking into a cold, cowardly sweat, he deliberately stopped to urinate in the street. He pissed for some time. A small group of people were crossing the bridge from the opposite direction. He heard a woman talking. On the other side of the bridge was a bar he frequented. For some reason relief washed over him, and he walked across the bridge, coughing a few times as he passed the other group.

Gijun found a seat at the bar. "I came all the way here, but I was afraid you'd be closed. Damn, it's chilly today."

"What're you talking about?" The bar owner brought over a heater. "I'll never take a vacation for as long as I live."

Gijun tipped his cup to the owner, a man who liked to talk. He wondered what he should do. There was really no choice but to casually return to the bridge, he decided. If it didn't work out tonight, then he'd just have to try again tomorrow. (If you couldn't make it to the designated place at the designated time, then the meeting was automatically moved to the next day.) A harsh wind was rattling the old wooden door. Something suddenly thumped against the door—something that was not the wind. Gijun sensed the presence of a person—

The bar owner opened the door with an angry shout. Old Man Boil came tumbling in. "Sir, sir!" he cried to Gijun, before the bar owner could speak. He ran to Gijun, then abruptly turned around and announced to the owner that he had business with Mr. Jeong. In a broken voice, the old man explained that he'd followed Gijun because he didn't need any charity, really he didn't. "I wanted to return your money . . . Thank you for thinking of this poor old man. And, er, could you honor me with a glass of soju, maybe?"

Gijun didn't want to encourage the old man, but he couldn't afford to waste any more time with him. Gijun replied that he'd take back his money, fine, but use it to start up a bar tab so that the old man could come here the next time he wanted a drink. He then exited the bar. Once outside, he let out a deep breath. U. Hill was near the dense pine forests of Samseonghyeol. It was already quite steep there, with no signs of human habitation, and in the night the trees looked even more lush and black. The tangled branches of the tall pines swayed in the wind. Their persistent rustling sounded just like a celestial cry. He recognized the shape of the Samseonghyeol Shrine. Even though its contours were blurred in the darkness, it still had a strangely hushed, weighty quality to it. The flickering lights of the city felt insignificant here, and Gijun had the sensation that he'd come a long, long way to a place of no return. No matter how you viewed it, this was a dangerous business. There were the risks that came from being embedded in USAMGIK, yes, but there was also the fact that if he ever ran into a partisan other than Yongseok (though lately the situation had gotten so bad that they no longer came down this far), Gijun would be unable to reveal his true identity due to the nature of his mission. In other words, he had no choice but to kill his own allies if he wanted to avoid dying in vain.

Once he left the pine forest, his field of vision immediately widened, even in the dark, and Gijun was struck with a bleakness that approached anguish. The wind slashed his face like a knife. Swirling clouds raced and dissolved and reformed at will in the boundless sky, blurring the moonlight. He could clearly sense the moon looming over him. All of a sudden, the moon's reflection turned the cloud cover into a hard, shining shade of lapis lazuli blue. It was like a bottomless abyss, drawing his soul in. The bluish-white moonlight soon revealed the rocky surface of the rugged hills that stretched out ahead, and the ruins of the old castle walls that faced those hills at the edge of the forest. Gijun stood still for a moment, letting the savage wind blow past him. He always felt a sense of fullness here, in the solitude.

U. Hill was just one of the many desolate low hills that dotted the area. It had a deep pool surrounded by cliff walls, and a cave situated at the pool's edge. There were some strangely shaped rocks that looked almost comical in the daylight but became eerie at night. When bathed in the pale, liquid light of the moon, they sometimes made him think of the face of a dead person.

The cliff above the cave was covered with dense shrubbery. It looked like a miniature forest. It was the type of place that, in the daylight, could serve as a fitting playground for boys to horse around. Gijun leaned against a tree and looked around him, straining his ears. The wind that blew across the deserted landscape seemed to settle right above him, but then he finally realized that it was the shrubbery that was wildly rioting against the wind. The luminous hand on his watch told him it was almost eight o'clock. After a short time, an owl call cut through the rustling of the shrubs. It was, without a doubt, Yongseok's voice. Gijun leaned forward and responded with three owl hoots. He found it a little funny how people couldn't help but sound like themselves, even in these circumstances. He heard another owl hoot. Gijun's heart lifted, as if he were a teenager again. He grasped a fistful of dirt and ecstatically threw it into the shrubs.

The two men didn't say anything for some time before going down into the cave, simply clasped hands and embraced. Yongseok's beard had grown out to a comfortable length, and Gijun felt sad as it tickled his cold cheeks. Yongseok wore lined farmer's clothes over his sturdy body and a knit cap on his head, but otherwise was much less warmly dressed than Gijun. Their silent embrace conveyed their mutual joy at each other's safety and wordless empathy over each other's hardships. At times they broke into sobs. Strictly speaking, there was no need for him to come all the way to the cave. In an emergency, they could simply exchange information at the base of the cliff. But just as lovers need a designated rendezvous spot, these two childhood friends needed the peace the cave gave them.

The two climbed down into the cave, whispering together about how worried the weather had made them. The cave was quite deep inside. Yongseok switched on his small penlight, and the two sat in a recess in the cliff wall where they didn't have to worry about a little light leaking out.

"Hey Gijun, did you drink before coming here? You reek."

Gijun laughed. "Don't worry, I just had a few. I didn't have much choice."

"Well, take this with you. If you get too cold on the way back, you can put a little of it in your mouth. Just a little, though, for energy. Be careful of how you dispose of the bottle."

Gijun shielded his lighter with his overcoat and lit cigarettes for both of them. They looked steadily at each other's faces across the flickering red light. The two men grinned like children at the exact same time. With his beard Yongseok looked older than his twenty-three years, but Gijun saw the same strong, baby-faced friend he'd always known. It might have been his imagination, but Yongseok looked thinner than last time. Eyes that had been hardened by the coldness of the mountain now shone like beacon fire under thick eyebrows. Avoiding those eyes, Gijun asked, "Aren't you cold?"

"I've decided to stop talking about things like that. I can handle something as simple as the cold. And anyway, I'm not cold at all."

"How's the snow?"

"Deep. It's up to my thighs now. Looking at it too long can make you sick, but it keeps us on our guard. And it is beautiful."

Gijun sincerely admired Yongseok's personality, his tenacious optimism and lack of discontent. You could say that he was a simple soul, and it was true that he tended not to think too deeply about things unless it was necessary, but that too was nice in its own way. Gijun was full of discontent. It was not unwarranted, but he couldn't count the number of times he'd thought about quitting his job and escaping to Mount Halla. He found it hard to bear the sacrifices required of him for his secret partisan work. But it was strange how easily that feeling evaporated in those moments they were able to embrace or when he saw again Yongseok's snow-tanned face.

Right now they were chewing the fat, you could say. In the scant thirty minutes they allowed themselves to catch up, their feelings raced towards the heavens. But it was hard to capture their feelings in words. As the faint ticking of their watches echoed off the rock face, the conversation sometimes lapsed into silence. During such times, Gijun half expected Yongseok to begin talking about his younger sister Yangsun, but he said nothing about her, nor did he attempt to talk about his parents. The two men sat for a while, their thoughts aligned. The silence swiftly grew heavier.

"—I don't have anything to hand over to you today," Yongseok said. "It's just that . . . well, it's imperative that we liberate the prison camp in T. Township, but the situation on the mountain is tense right now, and we haven't been able to finalize our strategy yet. I want us to meet again next week. Could you gather as much information as you can on the T. prison camp by then? If I can't come, I'll signal you from the mountain with three beacon fires. If your own schedule is thrown off, let's try to meet the next day. Otherwise, we'll proceed as planned."

"Understood. I have some last-minute news, too, but you'll have to decide on its strategic value yourselves. Tomorrow, the substation at S. Village will be almost completely abandoned, just for one night. I learned about it only today. It's written in there . . . Who do you think will go? I know you're pretty familiar with S. Village . . . "

"*What?*" Yongseok shouted. He brooded over the information for some time before eventually replying that he would try to be the one to go if possible. He also emphasized how there was great strategic value in attacking the substations of both S. Village and K. Village since they flanked the prison camp in T. Township. Gijun nodded. He'd given up hoping for news of Yongseok's sister.

It was already approaching 8:30 p.m. The two men looked at their watches and then at each other's faces; both let out deep sighs. Gijun didn't expect anything from Yongseok regarding Yangsun, but he couldn't help feeling a lingering uneasiness in the air that was related to her. Gijun gathered their cigarette butts into the empty cigarette pack and stood up. They walked to the edge of the pool. Muddy water lapped at their feet. The wind was wild above the cliff, but the pool itself was calm, reflecting a stormy, faintly lit nightscape that broke apart and scattered with every ripple. Fish often leaped out of the water during the summer nights. Splashing sounds told them that the same fish were most likely jumping tonight, too. Those heroic noises had often made both Gijun and Yongseok wish they could share their secrets with the fish. Gijun snuffed out the cigarette he'd been smoking, put it into the empty pack, then stuck the pack back into his pants pocket. They were careful to never throw the butts into the water.

Yongseok broke the silence. "Take care of yourself," he said quietly. Then: "I hear my sister's doing fine."

Gijun gave a nonchalant response that was the opposite of how he actually felt. For a moment he froze, but then decided that it was probably better to refrain from talking about Yangsun. He inquired after the safety of Yongseok's parents instead.

"We've had a lot of young people from D. Village join us as partisans . . . My family all seem to be doing well." D. Village was the place where both Yongseok and Gijun were from. Yongseok added that he'd heard his sister also wanted to come to the mountain but had to stay at home for their parents' sake.

"It may be strange to say so now, but I wonder if your sister hates me. No, I'm sure she must."

"Don't be stupid; it's not your fault. Even my sister . . . hahaha, I see how it is. No matter how close you two used to be, it's not my place to say what shouldn't be said. I know how hard it's been for you, too. But I have to do what I have to do."

"I know. I'm the same. But I feel sorry for Yangsun."

"It can't be helped. If she's washed her hands of you because she sees you as a traitor, well—you *do* have all the qualifications of a traitor. Consider it a kind of virtue. You've got a *reputation*." Yongseok laughed. His own laughter seemed to hurt him, like it was slashing his chest open. Gijun also laughed, but the sound did nothing to fill the hollowness in his throat.

"Let's soldier on!" The two men raised tight fists in the air. "You still stink of alcohol," Yongseok said to Gijun, smiling at him with a playful expression on his face. "Make sure you take care of yourself." Gijun had no desire to make excuses about his drinking, but he wondered in this particular case if it were better to tell Yongseok what had happened, especially since his comments were both a form of criticism and an expression of friendship. Gijun had always been a heavy drinker. He quickly explained that he'd stopped at a bar on his way to the cave and had run into Old Man Boil at the bar. Gijun finished his story with a smile, but Yongseok didn't smile back. He could not.

"It's good that it was Old Man Boil," Yongseok murmured, and with some effort finally mustered up a smile. "Guess I'll have a drink, too," he abruptly added, removing the cap from the whiskey bottle. He took a swig but immediately began coughing violently before finally spitting the alcohol out. "It's like fire in your mouth!" Gijun laughed and leisurely took two or three mouthfuls of the whiskey. Yongseok took another sip, letting the liquid roll over his tongue before swallowing it. "Gijun, this is surprisingly good."

It was getting late. They decided on their next meeting time and then said their goodbyes, even as the familiar emptiness that was like an eternal farewell filled both their chests.

"Hey—be careful," said Yongseok, turning around.

"Get going already, you idiot. It won't take me even half an hour to get back." The two parted at the water's edge, in front of the cave. Yongseok began climbing up the cliff. Soon both the sight and sound of him vanished in the wind. Gijun stood where he was for a while, then sat down on a nearby rock. There, by the water, in the dark, he got the sensation that he'd become part of the natural landscape. A deep loneliness overtook him. In that moment his only thought was that he still had some time before the eleven o'clock curfew.

3.

It was a clear, fine day. Jeong Gijun ran into Second Lieutenant Hawk in front of the Department of Justice as he was heading to work. The USAMGIK office was located in a building that used to belong to the Japanese colonial authorities and which now housed the Jeju provincial government, though USAMGIK occupied most of the space. That's why the Stars and Stripes could always be seen on the roof of what was supposed to be the seat of the provincial government. Hawk belonged to the Department of Finance. He told Gijun that he'd just returned by air that morning, then immediately followed up with a quip on how Seoul's kimchi tasted better than Jeju's. Gijun asked if he'd used the services of a *gisaeng* (female entertainer) while he was there, causing Hawk to slap Gijun's shoulders and give a knowing chuckle. He took a photo of a woman from his pocket and showed it to Gijun. *Amazing, amazing*! he said, and gave Gijun a bear hug. Then he strode away.

Jeju General Headquarters was composed of the Departments of Finance and Justice, both of which were overseen by a military governor. In addition to his role as an interpreter for the Department of Justice, Gijun was in charge of translating American military legislation, USAMGIK directives issued to the provincial government, and other such things into Korean and of translating into English documents that had been produced by the Koreans, mostly those related to police matters. He planned to visit Yangsun after first organizing all the documents related to the inspection of the public executions that were scheduled for T. Township and T. Village over the course of the next five days. Submitting this inspection report was the most important task left to him before his transfer ten days from now. The news about the "public executions" and his transfer had come only yesterday, a day after his meeting with Jang Yongseok. It would only take a single day for communication to fail, throwing a wrench into the partisans' plans . . .

During his time at the Department of Finance, Gijun had accompanied Second Lieutenant Hawk to Seoul several times by air. Hawk was genuinely surprised to learn of Gijun's transfer. *That's too bad,* he kept repeating, and told him he'd do everything he could to help him remain at his post. Gijun was confident that he could stop this irrational transfer himself if he really wanted to, even without the second lieutenant's help. The chief of police had been away on business yesterday, so he didn't learn until later that there had been some backstage maneuvering behind the decision to shuffle him to the mainland—a move that was generally considered a promotion. It was thought that the situation on Jeju was becoming too urgent for a mere local police chief to manage, so a former general who used to belong to the "Northwest" was being sent in from Busan. (Geographically, "northwest" refers to Pyongan Province in North Korea, but in South Korea the term came to be used as shorthand for the Northwest Youth League.

Following liberation on August 15, a group of former elites who opposed the establishment of the new political system in North Korea fled to the south and formed an anti-communist organization by that name. These elites soon became Syngman Rhee's most trusted men. Against the backdrop of immense political power, they helped bolster the tyrannical government and its feudalistic acts of terror in a quest to indiscriminately fix the label of "Red" on any and all enemies. As a result, the people quickly came to fear the "Northwest.")

Meanwhile, the police chief had been trying to use Gijun, whose abilities he trusted, to achieve his dream of gaining fame through his assignment to this unfamiliar land, which was considered a demotion. Gijun sensed that Yi Sanggeun's father was also pulling strings in the background, too. Gijun replied jokingly to Hawk that he had to obey the will of USAMGIK. Hawk's blue eyes clouded a little, but he responded amiably: *That's not something a civilian would say.*

Gijun drove to the hospital. He might have caught a cold; he had a temperature, and his body felt sluggish. He had gone out drinking once again last night. Every time he met Yongseok he resolved to stop drinking but then inevitably found himself back at it the next night, usually alone.

The sea could be viewed from the low hill on which the white provincial hospital stood. Although the sky was a clear blue, the sea was black and gloomy and tipped with surging white-capped fangs. A crow perched on the withered branches of the zelkova trees that grew on the hospital lawn, its gaze trained on the darkened entrance of the hospital. When Gijun left the building, it bobbed its head as if bowing to him. A flock of seagulls were flying over the low buildings downtown. Far off to the right, the black bluffs of Sarabong dropped precipitously towards the sea while its peak looked down haughtily at the waves. A lighthouse that resembled an old Western turret nestled in a hollow of the cliffs. Its walls and the seagulls were the same shade of white. Below the lighthouse was the tempestuous winter sea. He knew he should go meet Yangsun, but what would happen when he did? Gijun himself didn't know. He looked at the white road that ran brokenly around the base of Sarabong and chided himself for his vacillation. He stepped on the gas petal. The jeep roared forward without hesitation, as if it were a mere toy following its owner's impulses. Even he found it mysterious how he could so suddenly want a woman from his past whom he hadn't seen in over a year.

He had just rounded a bend in the road when he saw Yi Sanggeun. Today, at least, there was little risk that Sanggeun would try to accost him—although he wasn't wearing handcuffs, there was a policeman on either side of him, hemming him in. The police said hello to Gijun, while Sanggeun simply gave him a thin, unpleasant smile that showed no teeth. He had smiled in the same manner yesterday, as well. Gijun had been trying to make his way out of the crowd, the weight of countless eyes upon his back. His impression that someone was following him was proven right soon enough when a finger gently tapped his shoulder. He turned around and saw it was Sanggeun, who flashed Gijun a crooked smile in greeting. His face was pale, he reeked of alcohol, and there was something sullen about him. Sanggeun had bit out an invitation for a drink, which Gijun politely declined by saying he was still on duty. With his bulk, Sanggeun looked like he might trip over his own feet at any moment. His scornful, tight-lipped mouth had looked even more sullen in comparison.

Sanggeun was now giving the policemen a mean-spirited look. With a laugh, he said, "I've become someone important, too. I was attacked in my sleep. Ha, it's because of yesterday's incident—I'm referring to that incident with the senile old fool. Whaddya call it? That's right—interference with a public servant in the execution of his duties." He took out a cigarette for himself, then came over to the driver's side of the car and offered his metal cigarette case to Gijun. Gijun took a cigarette and lit it with his lighter.

"Letting yourself be taken into custody, well, that's a big honor for the police," Gijun said as a joke. The policemen gave him servile, bitter smiles.

"Oh, well, it's an honor for both of us." Sanggeun looked closely at Gijun. " . . . Just a thought, but I wonder what would happen if you were put in jail. The walls might give way to you. Your expression, Mr. Jeong, has such a wonderful quality to it. I mean that as a compliment. It's like a mask—"

What was this guy going on about? For reasons he did not understand, Gijun felt frightened. "Thanks, I guess . . . I'll take that to mean I should feel self-confident about my looks." *There's no other response I can give,* he thought as he finished speaking. Even though he didn't fully comprehend the meaning behind Sanggeun's words, he still felt his heartbeat quicken a little. Sanggeun's arrest was most likely just for show. He would probably be released by the evening, or by the next morning at the latest. Just then, the wind carried to him the sound of Old Man Boil's proclamations. He was at an utter loss for a second. He leaned his body out of the jeep, in the direction of the voice. The old man was loping awkwardly towards them, the basket cradled carefully in his arms. Gijun spit on the ground and looked at Sanggeun with a smile on his lips. "Ah, the noted physician comes again." With the cigarette still dangling from his mouth, he twisted the steering wheel sharply and drove away at full speed.

It was just before 11 a.m. He would probably reach the village after noon. The bridge and river flashed past. Those camellia flowers had clearly been intended as an offering to the young man's head. Gijun imagined the crippled old man, wandering alone along a clear blue pool, searching for a flower to pluck. The old man must have felt that there was a purpose in life to becoming the target of people's laughter—a fleeting conviction that only in doing so could he maintain others' interest in him.

His field of view widened as soon as he reached the mountain pass. Mountain, sea, road—he could see it all. The translucent sky that served as a backdrop called to Gijun as he drove. He passed through S. Village, then the village next to it, then east again through T. Township. From there, he estimated it would take less than one hour to reach D. Village, where Yangsun lived.

The S. substation that faced the main road had been almost completely destroyed from a surprise attack by the partisans last night. Gijun drove slowly, taking it in from his window, but soon came upon a distressing scene. Some villagers had been rounded up by a troop of armed police and were being made to build a barricade out of sand under their direction. Gijun nodded to the substation policemen but didn't stop his car.

He came to the sudden realization that it was vital that his meeting with Yongseok a few days from now go as planned. If only he could find some way of signaling to Yongseok so they could meet tomorrow or even tonight in order to discuss the problem of the prison camp and, even more urgently, the problem of his impending transfer! Although these thoughts had been with him since yesterday, for some reason a part of him was beginning to turn away from Yongseok. Guilt wracked him. Over half a year ago, in the spring of 1948 (April 3rd, to be precise), the people of Jeju Island came together in an armed uprising. Mount Halla, which loomed at a height of roughly 6,400 feet in the center of the island, became their base of resistance. Gijun had been meeting only with Yongseok on U. Hill for the past several months. As the fighting grew more intense, they became less and less able to meet as scheduled. As one of the leaders of the 1st Partisan Infantry Regiment (primarily in charge of the central region to the north) and as his close friend, Yongseok was the sole tie that connected Gijun to Mount Halla. Even if underground organizations existed in town or in the surrounding villages, there was nothing that linked them to Gijun. In a way, Yongseok was like the narrow neck of a bottle. Only by passing through its opening could Gijun come into contact with the wider, freer world outside, and even then only with great difficulty. Otherwise, he was nothing more than a machine inhabiting the vacuum of a stoppered bottle, mission or no.

Gijun could smell the presence of Yongseok and his nimble maneuvers in the traces of the bitter battle that remained. A black stone wall across from the substation stretched out parallel to the main road, surrounded by fields. Its height easily surpassed that of a child. The wall had been constructed by piling together shards of the volcanic rocks that were common on the island. It meandered uninterrupted along the edges of the fields and yards, reaching even the burial mounds. If the rocks hadn't been gathered for walls like this, they would have littered the ground so thickly that there'd be no room to walk. Yongseok had effortlessly leapt over the stone walls. He'd been required to undergo a grueling training routine to prepare for their partisan battles, which were usually waged on uneven terrain. He'd filled the hems of his *baji* (Korean trousers that resembled Japanese workpants) with sand and pebbles and then bound it all up around his ankles. When he stood, the sand would settle around his shins; when he walked, it was like wading in mud. Each step was a struggle. Yongseok began his training by first getting used to walking and then vaulting over the walls with that weight on his legs. He gradually increased the amount of sand as he practiced jumping over low walls. Only once he'd gotten adept at doing so did he remove the sand from his pants. Gijun could still vividly remember Yongseok's words: "My feet have grown wings." *If only I could be free of this mute life. I'd grab a gun and throw myself into battle, just like him.* Gijun looked out the jeep window to the stone walls that disappeared behind him in an unbroken line along the main road. He finally admitted to himself that the reason he felt such guilt towards Yongseok was because of Yangsun. There was no reason he should be meeting her. He was going to tell her that he was leaving Jeju soon, but that was at most a pretext—one that wouldn't hold up if he managed to meet with Yongseok before then. He was sure that Yongseok would categorically oppose his transfer and urge him to stay at his post for the sake of the fatherland and the party. And he would most likely report as such to the other leaders, as well. As he recalled how thin Yongseok's baby face had looked two nights ago, Gijun lost his nerve. He decided he should try to find a way to stay at his current post, as Yongseok would surely advise.

As he drove into T. Village, his attention was caught by the clusters of people that dotted the landscape. They were crowded around large public execution notices that had been hung on the town hall, the police substation, the post office, and even the gates of the elementary school. The notices seem to have been posted earlier that morning. Printed on them was the following message: *Those who are absent without permission from the proceedings will be severely punished.*

The prison camp stood on a hill by the main road that faced Mount Halla and was surrounded by barbed wire. It always received the full brunt of the wind blowing from the sea to the east due to its location. A guard with an automatic rifle manned the watchtower. He was smoking a cigarette with both arms resting on the windowsill, and the sun glinted coldly off his helmet as he looked Gijun's way. That such a building could exist among all the humble straw-thatched houses, and that he would have to witness tomorrow's events from the executioners' side—Gijun felt numb and hollow when confronted with reality in this way, his thoughts enveloped in fog. He could not ignore the edifice that was right in front of his eyes. It was there, and it would not go away. His feverish body responded to every ripple of heat and every shake of the jeep. The jeep raced on as if inebriated.

The small, isolated community of under two hundred households that Gijun had once called home was located near the outskirts of Y. Village, far away from the sea but close to the foothills that unfurled leisurely and extensively to the east of Mount Halla. During warmer months one could admire the lush meadows of Noksan Ranch, its horses and cattle almost looking like black flowers against the radiant green of the grass as they grazed. When viewed through the silky haze of summer, the scene had often spurred a young and mischievous Gijun to daydream about the future, alongside Yongseok and his younger sister Yangsun. For some reason, Yangsun had hated wearing shoes as a child. Back then, the only footwear they had were straw sandals or cheap rubber shoes. Yangsun decided to go barefoot after a girl from one of the village's more prosperous households began sporting canvas sneakers. The unfamiliar texture of the piercingly navy-blue canvas felt like a dazzling dream to the impoverished Yangsun. She'd always had a stubborn streak in her since childhood.

Nothing could come from chasing the shadow of the long-vanished past, but Gijun was aghast nonetheless at what he discovered in his old hometown of D. Village. His anxieties about his former neighbors' attitude towards him and his uneasy conjectures about seeing

Yangsun also came to nothing: the area, it turned out, was completely deserted. After leaving Y. Village, the jeep finally turned away from the sea and climbed up the steep, bumpy, stone-littered slope that led to D. Village. But there was no sign of anyone when he got there. He had thought some children might come dashing out at the unusual sound of a car engine, but not a single person appeared. He wondered if perhaps the parents had spotted the foreign vehicle from the gaps in the stone walls and were exercising caution. And of Yangsun, whom he had been hoping to theatrically encounter by chance on the roadside, there was not a single sign.

It was much too quiet. Gijun, who had spent two hours being jolted around as he drove, got out of the jeep with much relief. He was exhausted and dizzy, and his ears were ringing. For some reason the sharp angles of the trees and stone walls of the nearby houses leapt out at him when he cut the engine.

As he walked along the deserted road, hearing nothing but the sound of his own footsteps, his uneasiness grew. The wooden doors of the houses were all shut, with nothing but a heavy emptiness stagnating inside their walls. The gardens were cold and barren. *Wait, was that—*

He smiled bitterly. He had been startled by the sound of a lone pig strutting around inside one of the houses. It was nuzzling its nose against the wooden door and snorting. It was possible that the entire village had engaged in a mass exodus and that this pig had been accidentally left behind. If so, Gijun hoped, someone might eventually come back to retrieve it.

In any case, this strange phenomenon of encountering not a single person despite it being afternoon was as eerie as if he'd come face to face with death. The buildings were not in ruins. Ruins had a desiccated honesty about them; the atmosphere here pulsed with something insidiously sinister and heavy. Something was lurking here, like a village that had sunk to the bottom of the ocean. Countless houses stood cold and empty and untouched. There was something uncanny in how the lukewarm breath of their owners lingered in the dark caves that were their rooms.

The village was like a human corpse that was still warm. If death had indeed visited this place, it was not too long ago. He learned only later that the villagers had gone into the mountains very early that morning, before sunrise. Everyone, even the children, had known that the authorities would come sooner or later to torch the place to the ground. They had finally been spurred to action the day before yesterday. The very day that Gijun had met with Yongseok, Yongseok's family—that is, his parents and Yangsun—had been arrested. Under the direction of partisans who were originally from the village, the residents had abandoned their homes and hastily fled to the mountains with their livestock. There, a new life of hardship awaited them all, even the children.

Gijun leaned against the black stone walls that surrounded Yangsun's house and smoked a cigarette as if in a trance. Hunger gnawed at him. His family used to live in a house across the alleyway, but when his mother died, he'd sold it. That was some time ago. He was impressed how the old persimmon tree he'd often clambered up as a child was still standing. There was something almost motherly about it. That tree whose branches had supported Gijun and his pranks may have aged, but unlike his mother, it was still alive and well. Gijun didn't remember his father's face; his father had died when Gijun was very young. Not even a photograph remained of him. On her deathbed, his mother had asked to be buried next to his father. Their graves should still be there, on the outskirts of the village.

Hearing something, Gijun turned his head—only to realize what he'd heard was the second hand on his watch, scrupulously ticking on. It was 1 p.m. in this village now inhabited by a single pig. He decided he might as well look inside Yangsun's house, whose wall he was currently leaning against. As he straightened, a sudden chill overtook him. His coatless body had been hit by a blast of cold wind. He turned up the collar of his shirt and took a few steps, but perhaps because of the cigarette, he felt quite lightheaded. He shut his eyes. Fireworks bloomed on the insides of his eyelids. His stomach roiled from something that smelled like a cross between alcohol and gasoline. The sun hung like a small, dry flour dumpling in the cloudy sky. He leaned against the wall once again and put a hand to his face. With his palm over his eyes, the world turned to night. He definitely had a fever. A low ringing in his ears continued to pound his eardrums.

It was then that he heard it. Yes—he definitely heard it: leather-soled shoes, approaching him with the same scrupulous sound as his watch. The light taps indicated that it was a woman's shoe. The noise echoed clearly in the strained cold air. His eyes flew open, and he saw a young woman in white Korean clothes and white high heels emerge out of the shadow of an old plum tree far opposite alley and begin walking towards him. He was sure it was a woman.

"What's going on? For a woman to be alone in this deserted village . . . What a strange person, to wear high heels with those traditional white clothes, here in the countryside . . . " Although the woman should have seen Gijun by now, she remained silent and did not acknowledge him in any way as she came closer. Her heels clacked against the ground. Gijun unconsciously leaned forward as he stared at her. His head felt woozy, but he was sure that a woman was indeed walking deliberately in his direction. Suddenly he began to shout: "Yangsun! Yangsun! It's me, Gijun!" He ran towards her. The white-clothed woman quickly turned left into a nearby alleyway. She silently swept past his vision like a white breeze. He chased after her, his breathing labored. The alley Yangsun had turned into stretched straight ahead before his eyes, but there was no one there. Had she hidden in one of the houses? It was then that he spotted a single battered crow lying dead on the ground, below a roadside tree. He opened one door after another, shouting out Yangsun's name. His voice echoed hollowly in the dark, deep caves that were the houses. Gijun broke into a sweat. "That's strange. Where did she go?"

When he finally realized that what he'd seen was a hallucination, Gijun's body shuddered violently, as if he'd been drenched in water. His skin shrank taut. A cold shivery air washed over him over and over, making him break out in gooseflesh. He felt nauseous. He gnawed on his cigarette and then spit the sodden thing onto the ground. His mouth filled with a bitter poisonous aftertaste. He got in the jeep and pressed down on the gas pedal. Chills continued to run down his spine. As he drove off, he kept his gaze trained on the shining sea before him, feeling the darkness closing in from behind and the full weight of night and day descending all at once upon his shoulders.

4.

Early the next morning, a platoon of armed police departed for the execution grounds of T. Township.

Gijun was slated to ride with the second troop at 11 a.m. He changed into a suit and left for the USAMGIK office without bothering to put on a coat. The suit was the same one he'd worn four days ago when he had met with Yongseok. The inner pocket of the black double-breasted jacket was large enough to hold his pistol. The jacket now felt saggy and loose, perhaps because it was unbuttoned. He fastened the buttons. He had drunk some alcohol last night as a way of distracting himself from his persistent insomnia, but it had only made things worse. It felt like a thick film coated his brain. He had a splitting headache. "What's wrong? Your face is as white as a sheet," one of his fellow interpreters told him with a lewd, suggestive laugh. Gijun attempted a faint smile as he pressed his fist against his forehead.

They exited the building. At last, he thought, he was finally free of that oppressive place—choked with cigarette smoke and the nauseous stink of the stove—but outside was no better: the granular light that seeped from the gloomy, low-hanging clouds bored into Gijun's skull. On the main road, they ran into Old Man Boil coming from the opposite direction. That was an unpleasant surprise. Gijun suddenly felt thirsty. He reflexively groped in his pocket. His fingers found a crumpled cigarette packet—a red Pall Mall box—which he threw away. Gijun loved Pall Mall's king-size cigarettes, for no other reason than that they were longer than their competitors. He was sure there had still been some cigarettes in there—aha, there they were, in his jacket. He began to light one but was hit with a wave of nausea. He tossed the cigarette away and strode off. *My stomach is queasy.* Even so, he got himself a can of beer and drank the contents straight down.

Once Gijun was gone, Old Man Boil eagerly ran to where Gijun had stood. The empty cigarette pack had looked to the old man like a red flower falling to the ground. The old man snatched up the discarded cigarette and packet like a monkey. When he opened the packet out of curiosity, a number of broken cigarette stubs tumbled out. It was only then that he realized what the packet was. He was quite pleased with this morning haul. He carefully placed the half-smoked cigarette in his pocket, making sure it wasn't bent. He then stuffed some old cigarette butts into his pipe and puffed on the pipe with a rapturous expression. He glanced up at the sky, but sadly the sun was still hidden behind a dense wall of clouds.

"Heh heh, the sun's feeling heartless today, too. Even I

enjoy a Western cigarette now and then . . . hehehe."

"Haha! Hello, *yeonggam* (old man)." It was Yi Sanggeun. Old Man Boil jumped to his feet. In a panic, he attempted to conceal his newfound treasure, although there was no reason to. The old man found the young man intimidating. Sanggeun had spent the night at the police station, although you wouldn't know it from looking at him. He spitefully snatched at what Old Man Boil had hidden away, but when he realized it was nothing more than an empty pack of cigarettes, he let out a bitter laugh. He assumed that it was trash that one of the interpreters or GIs had thrown away. The frightened old man began to defend himself, insisting that he wasn't a thief; he'd simply picked it up from the ground just now. That gentleman could confirm it, he added, pointing to Jeong Gijun. Sanggeun was startled. He watched Gijun's receding back with a sudden keen curiosity. Looking again at the packet, he discovered what looked like dirt-encrusted moss or seaweed stuck to the ends of the cigarette butts.

"Jeong Gijun—Jeong Gijun, you say . . . " Sanggeun murmured.

"Yes, that's Mr. Jeong."

“Be quiet.” Sanggeun began to ponder. He didn’t know why, but he was drawn to the cigarette butts, perhaps for the same reason he was drawn to Gijun’s masklike face. He gave the old man some money in exchange for the cigarette pack and told him to keep his mouth shut. The old man bowed repeatedly and then ran off in delight.

Sanggeun headed straight home. He had a sudden suspicion that Gijun was deliberately avoiding him. *He sped off in his jeep when he saw me yesterday. And the day before that, he refused my invitation to go out, even though everyone else in this town’s got an interest in me. Does he think I’m like all those other drunks? He can’t begin to know how my soul has been tortured and torn in half by this barbaric, primitive society of ours.* He lit a cigarette, but Gijun’s indifferent face continued to haunt his vision. He couldn’t help but be intrigued by how Gijun could remain so calm and collected compared to the other interpreters. It also annoyed him in a way. There was something about those eyes that always seemed to be gazing far off into the distance. And so Sanggeun found he couldn’t look down on Gijun as he did the other interpreters. *That man is greater than I am.* His heart beat faster, protesting the thought. But it was also beating faster because of the odd cigarette butts.

The second troop headed out for T. Township in two trucks. Gijun rode with the director of security, a man named Kim. The director used to belong to the Northwest, and during the ride he talked incessantly about the former general who would most likely be appointed as the new chief of police, how they used to be colleagues and how much he was looking forward to welcoming him here. Gijun nodded along. The clouds today covered Mount Halla from top to bottom, obscuring even the hamlets that were clustered at the base of the mountain. It was as if the sky had fallen to the ground. Out of the corner of his eye, he caught glimpses of the motionless sea. Gijun responded mechanically to the director's words and avoided looking at Mount Halla, as doing so would only fill his heart with pain. He also tried not to think about Yangsun, who was probably even now with her older brother on the mountain, amidst the clouds and snow. To Yangsun, Gijun was a traitor. He was also the man who had abandoned her.

The director had shifted the topic of conversation from alcohol to women and was now ribbing Gijun about what he assumed had happened last night, having completely misinterpreted why Gijun still smelled of alcohol. The director's voice buzzed in Gijun's ears like that of a woman. Gijun shook his head again and again, as if that might clear his head of his terrible hangover, and tried to brush away the white light reflected on the windshield. But in that instant, the light transformed into a barefooted woman in a fluttering skirt, standing on the bonnet of the car. Gijun was seized with the urge to shake off both the white light and his own self. In his feverish state, he could barely stop himself from wrenching the steering wheel towards the mountain and speeding off.

The director was still talking. "A woman is the best cure for a hangover," Gijun said perfunctorily. The road continued to unspool under the car in an endless sinuous line.

"Hah, is that so, Mr. Jeong? Personally, I quite like getting tipsy myself."

By the time the group arrived at T. Township, it was snowing. The road was choked with armed policemen. Droves of residents were trudging up the hill to the execution grounds, with children carried by their mothers and the elderly led by hand. A megaphone had been installed on the police substation barricades. It blared pronouncements on the purpose of the executions and exhorted the crowd to keep moving up the hill. The snow that fell and melted onto the residents' white clothes was inhumanly beautiful against the gloomy landscape. Gijun watched the scene from afar. The thought vaguely came to him that if he were part of the crowd, the incongruity of it all would destroy the chilly beauty soon enough.

The jeep passed through a gate from which hung a banner that said "—— Communal Detention Facility." The building used to be an elementary school. In each corner of the athletic field stood a watchtower fitted with a machine gun. Acacia trees lined the field, though the ones around the watchtowers had had their tops hewn off. He later learned by flipping through the documents in the warden's office that the total number of detainees was close to eight hundred, and that about two-thirds of them were women. Given that roughly half of the detainees were to be "disposed of" over the next five days, he calculated that around eighty people would be killed per day. The warden was quite stout and had a face shaped like a chestnut, with eyes that were disturbingly flat. Constantly tugging at his collar with his finger (it might have been a habit), he was trying hard not to appear intimidated by what he saw as the besuited young upstart serving as one of the U.S. military's only mouthpieces. He was one of those people who thought that uniforms should be worn by everyone and had been completely caught off guard by how calm and collected Jeong Gijun looked in his black civilian clothes. It made him want to flaunt the dignity of his uniform even more.

"Hahaha, here're the facts. It's a waste to use live ammunition on this bunch. It'd be best if we could throw them into the ocean or bury them alive, but being as 'civilized' as it is, the U.S. military has ordered us otherwise . . . " The warden glanced at Director Kim. "Kim and I are old friends from our Busan days. He's quite the gentleman. To be honest, he may be too much of a gentleman. Let me be perfectly honest here. Before we execute the Reds, I want to tell them that their merciful deaths are all thanks to USAMGIK, despite them being a waste of gunfire, but . . . well, the situation's such that we're not allowed to make any mention of the Americans."

"Er, I . . . Thank you." Gijun gave him an easy smile. "We in the American military love mechanical efficiency more than anything. The only thing lost through efficiency is laziness. Please feel free to use as many bullets as you wish. If you run out, Seoul will be able to supply you with more—and if they run out, then his excellency President Truman will surely provide." Using the appellation of "excellency" to refer to the American president was his way of imitating President Syngman Rhee.

The warden looked restlessly at his wristwatch and lumbered to his feet. "Shall we go? After all, our first priority is promptness and efficiency . . . " He added emphasis to "promptness," looking extremely pleased with himself for thinking of the word.

They left the room. Beyond the dark hallway was a snowy square. The white-clothed crowd stood there in silence. Gijun deliberately increased his pace and the length of his stride. Two people were chatting behind him: *When did you get your watch? Is it pure gold or only gold plated? Swiss or American? Mine loses less than twenty seconds in a day.* The warden noisily ran up to Gijun and asked if he'd like to take a tour of the detention facility. Gijun was in no mood to do so. He had witnessed police torture before; many of his former friends had in fact been tortured to death. They'd cursed at Gijun and spit at him, calling him a dog, a cat's-paw, a pig. Even more violence had been brought down upon them as a result. Gijun had borne it all with a cold smile on his face. Gijun accepted the warden's offer, suspecting a hidden purpose in the warden's tone.

The men returned the way they'd come, towards the men's prison camp that faced the sea. They crossed the courtyard outside. The wind drove the snow into their faces. The warden brusquely brushed the snow from his collar and grumbled that they'd need even more bullets now because of the damn weather. Snowflakes alit on Gijun's hatless head like a swarm of gnats, only to instantly melt into water droplets. For a brief moment he surrendered himself to the chilly sensation. It didn't alleviate his fever, but it did feel a little invigorating against his heavy head.

A guard opened the door to the men's facility from within with a salute. "Ugh, it stinks. It's always like this," the warden muttered to himself, pitching his voice so that Gijun could hear him. "I've never owned a pig so I don't know for sure, but I'm guessing this is exactly what a pigsty smells like." The babble of voices inside the building suddenly subsided as the creaking of their footsteps echoed down the wood-floored hallway. The warden kept chuckling for some reason. The building had been partitioned into twelve cells, which were separated from the hallway by wire mesh. The other three walls were windowless. It was the first time Gijun had seen the interior of such a detention facility, but it wasn't much different from the jails back in town. Each 140-square-foot cell was crammed with dozens of people who sat crouched beside each other like chess pieces, their arms around their knees. If someone stood up, he'd have a hard time squeezing himself back in, as his space would immediately be filled by someone else.

Director Kim linked his arms behind his back. "This will take some work," he said, sounding like a store owner making notes on warehouse inventory. The warden protested that it wasn't as bad as it looked. He stooped and stuck a finger through the wire mesh to flick the nose of an elderly man whose face was pressed against the mesh as if in supplication.

"How's that . . . Heh, don't wanna die, hm? You wanna live? You're an honest person—I'm sure you'll go to heaven. Hahaha."

Gijun strode past the cells, giving them only a cursory

glance. He didn't know what kinds of jeers might be hurled at him. He hated what he saw, but he hated hearing the jeers even more. The group had reached the end of the hallway and were just about to leave when it happened. A voice cried out: "W-wait! Wait a minute! Is that you, Gijun?"

Gijun was paralyzed where he stood. He'd heard that voice somewhere before—somewhere far, far away.

The old man who had recognized Gijun pushed his way to the front of the cell and attached himself to the wire mesh. There was no doubt: it was Jang Yongseok's father. There was no doubt about it. Although you could say their meeting was a coincidence, it was not a happy one. Gijun's chest tightened twofold at seeing how much his friend's father had aged in the two or three years since their last encounter. It felt just like a dream. Gijun scarcely saw the other people who writhed beside the old man; the only thing that entered his vision was the old man's face, appearing to him in close-up. His legs began to shake and wobble, as if a joint had come loose.

Just then, an entirely new thought struck Gijun with the force of a tremendous thunderclap. *Yangsun is here! Yangsun is somewhere in this prison camp!* The world disappeared in a flash of lightning. A white light danced atop boundless scorching heat. He realized he was reaching for the wire mesh. He forced out an inane laugh and checked himself with some effort. Yongseok's father was unable to speak for some time, overwhelmed with nostalgia and a sudden dazzling hope that filled him with new life. One could well imagine how he might seek salvation in Gijun, this man who wore a Western suit and appeared to be on equal footing with the uniformed authorities.

"*Aigo* . . . Where are you going? You're Jeong Mantae's son, aren't you? Yes, that's right. You are the son of Jeong Mantae. You—you're Gijun! I'm Yongseok's father. Jang Yongseok—I'm his father!"

Yongseok's father pleaded with Gijun, clinging to the wire mesh like a monkey. The mesh shook. The warden bellowed at the old man, then turned to Gijun and asked if he knew the old man. Gijun nodded. He explained in a flat voice that he was an acquaintance from a long time ago, but that you couldn't live in Jeju if you were going to be bothered by something like that—the past was in the past. He was close enough to the cell that he could have easily touched the fingers reaching out to him if he'd wanted to. The warden turned to the director and chimed his agreement. Apparently quite a few of the younger guards also had acquaintances among the prisoners. It seemed to cause them some pain, the warden concluded with a sympathetic smile. The warden was clearly trying to use his age to bolster his authority. Gijun was relieved by the warden's uncharacteristically considerate words. Not because he believed in the warden's sincerity, but because his words were a kind of shell in which he could conceal the turmoil in his heart.

The old man's entreaties changed from dismay to anger. Even so, he continued to press against the wire mesh, like a mouse scurrying to find a place to escape. At last he began to curse Gijun. But the old man's words were only able to reach Gijun's ears via Yangsun. Yangsun stood between them, blocking the way. Because of that, Gijun felt only irritation. He lit a cigarette and took a leisurely drag. The old man finally seemed to realize Gijun's true nature. He snarled at Gijun, then pleaded with him again, and then finally denounced him as a rotten coward. That last curse had a ring of despair to it. The other two men, meanwhile, peered into the cell as if observing animals in a cage. They turned and said something to Gijun, and he made some sort of intelligible reply. He hadn't actually heard anything they'd said. He felt a compulsion to roar with laughter and shout "The old days are gone!" at the old man in the presence of the warden and director. But he kept tripping over his tongue and couldn't get the words out. He tried standing nonchalantly, but the flesh enveloped by his suit was as stiff as green wood. *Why am I just standing here?* White light flashed across his eyes. Snow was blowing against the glass door. Irritation welled up in him for no reason. It was not the old man's fault. But he still found him irritating.

"He's gone crazy," Gijun murmured coolly, standing beside the director. And then he opened the glass door, into the falling snow.

5.

Gijun did not remember walking across the execution grounds. All he could remember was taking long strides through the snow. He also did not know how he came to be in front of Yangsun. They were simply there, together, separated by the cold wire mesh. There was a vague intangibility to it all. Any reunion would necessarily have to be premised upon a self-awareness of his duties. But what he felt instead, in looking at the woman's prison camp from afar—what he felt, with a horror that froze his blood—was Yangsun's living, breathing body inside the building, even before her presence there was verified. The building seemed to recede further into the distance with every step he took towards it.

"Say, you don't look so well . . . Shall we end the tour here?" The warden pointed towards the women's prison camp as he spoke. Gijun was relieved to find that he was still able to smile. He fixed the warden with a curious, piercing stare and told him with a laugh that he wouldn't be able to live on Jeju if that were the case. Despite the unfathomable force that was now beating at his body, Gijun still wanted to go inside the building and stand before Yangsun. The white light was no longer standing amidst the snow.

Fresh from their victory over Japan, the American military first arrived on this island in mid-September of 1945, roughly one week after having landed at Incheon. The younger generation viewed the Americans as liberators at first, though that impression didn't last for long. The people of the island looked with suspicion at the soldiers of this new foreign country that had replaced the Japanese occupiers. Soon after the war, Gijun returned to his fatherland from Japan with all the joy and hope of his liberated people. Because he had some English language proficiency, gained through his middle school education and an advanced level course at a YMCA language school, he was soon able to get a job as a civilian interpreter, which was in much demand at the time. You could say it was a happy time for Gijun, thanks in large part to the fact that Jang Yangsun and her brother had also found jobs in town.

But the times changed, and Gijun eventually came to regret having become an interpreter. It soon became apparent that the interests of the American military and that of the Korean people did not align, a fact that was manifested in the form of confrontations between USAMGIK and the residents of Jeju. The Americans chose to hide in the background, using others as their mouthpieces—such as the police, as well as local terrorist organizations that included the Halla Corps, the Daedong Youth Corps, and the Northwest Youth League (which essentially acted as storm troopers for the right-wing parties). Yongseok and his sister Yangsun followed almost all the other young men and women of the island in joining the communist opposition. Gijun had also wanted to quit his job as an interpreter and follow them, but . . . Spurred by the killing of six civilians at the March 1 celebrations in 1947, the entire island rose up in protest against the American authorities. Despite the love she'd begun to harbor for Gijun and her acknowledgement that he was her brother's best friend, Yangsun could no longer condone Gijun's position. It was not just her. The people around Gijun began to blatantly treat him as the enemy. But by then, Gijun had already been tasked with his top secret mission through Yongseok.

Thus began a life of anguish, formed out of the rupture between Gijun's inner and outer worlds. Gijun became a loyal disciple of the American military and drove away a brokenhearted Yangsun. He attempted to fulfill the wishes of the resistance forces as if they were his own, namely to marry the daughter of a high-ranking official or some other person of influence so he could further strengthen his position. But then why did he turn back to the woman he'd driven away? Did he violate her precisely because he'd rejected her? He felt a constant remorse about that. But it was only through the weight of his remorse that he was able to maintain a link to Yangsun, and therefore to himself.

She had visited Gijun at his boarding house two or three days in a row, for the first time in a while. Every time he saw her earnest face, Gijun's chest ached and he was filled with an urge to confess that warred with his ironic sense of heroism. *There are surely some things that a man can't tell even his wife*, he'd think to himself, clinging to the comfort and satisfaction it gave him in resisting his dangerous impulses. When he went out he almost always drank soju made from the sweet potatoes that were a local specialty, but with her he drank whiskey that had originally been earmarked for the Americans. As he drank, Yangsun told him that she didn't know what to do and even pleaded with him to quit his interpreting job. She was swathed head to toe in white clothing. The early summer dusk fell upon her as she hunched there on the floor with her chin resting on her upraised knee. She was the only bright thing in the dim room. There was a concentrated beauty to her unmoving, inscrutable figure, a beauty that would blossom extravagantly like a flower bud the moment he touched it with a gentle hand.

She sat in a corner of the room and didn't attempt to move closer to him. Gijun had been leaning against the table, drinking by himself, but he now rose abruptly and offered her a glass . . . He was sure that she'd accepted it. But in the next moment, he heard the sound of the glass shattering against the wall. It was Yangsun who had thrown it. On the wall hung a few ostentatious photographs of half-naked women cut out from *Esquire*.

"You're despicable!" Yangsun's voice was as rough as that of a man. She swiftly rose, walked past Gijun, and tore the women from the wall. Her skirt flapped, and the smell of her body wafted towards him. It saddened him. She was a woman to him after all, but to her he was nothing more than a pseudo GI interpreter. Something base and instinctual thrust up out of his simmering sadness. She tore the photos into shreds and threw them away. She then began to walk towards the door. Gijun grasped her arm. She turned towards him with a twisted face. "You're filth!" she cried, and slapped his cheek. For some reason Gijun found himself swinging hard at her in response. He then pulled her back into the room. She was frightened. She tearfully told him she was leaving, but she didn't leave.

Gijun drank his whiskey in silence. It was all too sad. He had left lasting scars on her cold, soft, immaculate skin. A sense of fullness, like a flood overflowing a wasteland, had spread over their two bodies. There was no sun nor moon there, only a dim light caught between night and day, and a vast gray sky that overshadowed even that light, and a muddy flood spilling senselessly over everything . . . That's what Gijun felt. And with every ripple of the water, the emptiness groaned from below. Yangsun wept. Her cries sounded like groans . . .

The women's prison camp faced the men's camp across the wide square. Gijun stepped foot into the building with the sole purpose of seeing Yangsun. Just to see her—that's all he wanted. Should he go or not? He was consumed with a sensation like dark passion just from the choice. But deep within him something crouched ready and waiting, cold as ice . . . He stood before the wire mesh of the cell and calmly but firmly brushed the snow away from his shoulders. He was surprised to see Yangsun's mother there with her. That in itself was not strange. What was strange was that not even a hint of that possibility had crossed his mind.

The older woman was as shocked and ecstatic as her husband had been. Unlike her husband, however, she gave her thanks to the Buddhist bodhisattva of compassion over and over, crying as she did so, unable to grasp the meaning of this unexpected meeting. Yangsun leapt to her feet in astonishment but then quickly tried to cover up her emotions, as if they were something shameful. She stood behind her mother, biting her lip, but he could still make out the wild heaving of her gently sloped shoulders. The room was dark and dirty. Several lamps hung from the ceiling of the long hallway (they didn't have electric bulbs in the village), swaying slightly. The light blurred the contours of the people crammed in the cell and the checked pattern made by the wire mesh. Gijun felt something like vertigo as he stood underneath the swaying lamps. Yangsun's body, clothed in a white top and black skirt, trembled in the shadows.

"She's got some nerve, this woman—sleeping away her time until she dies," the warden said. He explained that this was the wife and daughter of the old man from the men's cells. He then turned to Gijun and said with a laugh, "You really can't live in Jeju." The director murmured something about how the daughter was a real beauty. Yangsun's round black eyes blinked a few times, growing steadily wider and more dazzling with each blink. Gijun wanted to put his arms around her heaving shoulders. The next moment, Yangsun abruptly half rose to her feet. Brushing her tangled bangs away from her face, she looked at Gijun with eyes like ice—without a shred of emotion, as if he were an inanimate object. Gijun didn't know if it was hatred or fury that dwelled in their depths; all he could see was her denunciation of him as a traitor. The reason he flinched in that moment was because in her eyes he was nothing more than an insignificant pebble, something not even human. The feelings that had welled up inside him drained away. Flames suddenly flared in her frozen eyes, sharp and hard as blades. It was the first hint of emotion she'd shown him, and as he folded it into himself, he finally felt released from her cruel indifference.

But he didn't want her silence, he wanted the fire of her invectives; so when her smooth brow furrowed and her face tautened, he found himself approaching the wire mesh. Yes, that was what he wanted, but when he saw the terrible strength of the fire that threatened to rage forth from deep within her flesh, he realized he couldn't stand it. He couldn't stand it. *Yangsun! Yangsun!* He smothered the yearning of his wretched heart. The warden and director watched the scene with an air of wise benevolence, gossiping about Yangsun and noting how purehearted she was. They also used her misfortune to reaffirm the value of enforcing the policies they'd put so much trust in, disguising their self-satisfaction as that virtue called sympathy. For days afterwards, Gijun was unable to forget how they'd talked. He found it strange how clearly he heard them, as if their words had been filtered into his ears.

The older woman roughly shook her daughter's shoulder and apologized to Gijun for her silence. She grasped her daughter's collar and pointed to Gijun. "Look at him!" she cried. She shook her daughter's shoulders once more, as if she were a ragdoll. It had a huge effect on Gijun. Her hands didn't look like a mother's hands—they looked almost like the hands of the director who stood next to him, or the hands of someone urging a woman to sell her body. Not the hands of someone who might arouse the love buried deep in Yangsun. "That's enough!" Gijun said firmly, his own voice ringing in his ears. The warden laughed. For the first time, something that could be called an expression surfaced on Yangsun's face—a hint of contempt and sadness. Illuminated by the lamp that swayed above them, her deep, glittering eyes shone like black pools behind the striped pattern of the wire mesh. A wave of unbearable anguish overtook him. The wave rippled over the taut ties that bound her clothes to her chest. Gijun was unable to look Yangsun in the face. He looked instead down the long hallway. He saw at an angle the wire mesh of the various cells that faced each other across the hall. The fingers that grasped the wire mesh were writhing like a mass of insects. A guard was looking steadily in their direction as he stood at attention, darkening the backlit glass door at the end of the hallway. All of these things began to sway and tilt like a boat on unsteady waters, then steadily flow away from his feet. There was a harsh buzzing in Gijun's ears. He closed his eyes and leaned against the wire mesh. As soon as he did so, Yangsun instantly receded into the infinite distance, just like the white light had done, and stood motionless within that far-off landscape. Then, once again, a white light danced down from above and settled over her. A sound like splattering oil ran incessantly through his head.

That thing that was lodged like an iceberg in his unhappy heart—without it, he might not have been able to endure it until the end. The moment his hands touched the wire mesh, his eyes were struck blind and he was pierced with the desire to let out a wail and prostrate himself right there, in the hallway, and confess everything. In that moment he wanted to give it all up, break apart the wire mesh, and fly to her.

Yangsun was going to die, she was going to disappear forever. He, too, had to die. He would die inside her. He would die like a dog. Above his head he heard the solitary truth break into two with a snap. As it did, the opportunity to reveal his true self died forever. *But she'll transcend me when she dies, leaving her curses behind.* How much better it would be if he were actually a traitor. A traitor who was not a traitor . . . Although it was she who was now facing the end of her life, she would deliver the final blow to him. Gijun felt like he would drown from the remorse that surged relentlessly around him like the tide. Why had he been unable to utter even one word of the truth to her, rules of the organization be damned? There had been so many opportunities. Why wasn't he allowed to do so? Even his remorse was now poisoned.

His remorse couldn't harm him. For the party, for the fatherland! In that moment, those things only made him more miserable, and he found himself unable to cast aside his prejudices and selfish desires. He had killed his own people and broken Yangsun's heart, all for the peace and security of a terrible conscience. Then what was it that had interposed itself between them? The party and fatherland under whose name he'd broken Yangsun's heart were not worthy of even a single drop of her tears. Gijun hated Jang Yongseok, hated the party, hated his fatherland. And he wanted nothing more than to stab to death the two men laughing next to him.

"Well, this has been quite a day . . . Mr. Jeong, you look like you're in some distress. Remember, it's about efficiency first and foremost. Hahaha!" Hearing the warden's voice, Gijun realized that he had, in fact, been able to endure it until the end. It was all over. He was forcefully made aware once again of the thing like ice lodged deep in his dark heart.

"Really, I'm fine," Gijun finally responded. He was no longer able to look directly at the wire mesh. For the first time, he was able to feel the great sorrow surging within him. He wanted to hear Yangsun voice her heartfelt hatred and contempt. He wanted to immolate himself in the flames of her fury. *I'm a foolish man besieged by waves of remorse from which there's no longer any redemption. It is I who am unworthy of even a single drop of her tears. I'm nothing but a coward who overreached himself.*

But Gijun turned back. He took a deep drag from a fresh cigarette, then let it fall to the ground. He looked down as he put out the cigarette with his shoe while absently brushing a hand over his shoulders, even though the snow had already melted. Yangsun's mother was weeping. The clamor of the prison camp started up again. Yangsun stood there unmoving. Separated by the wire mesh, her glittering eyes took in the figure of the miserable man as he walked away. She was a statue: face pushed against the wire mesh, neck twisted, mouth contorted into a warped, frozen smile. For the first time that day, she flashed her teeth at him. Gijun caught it from the corner of his vision. In the end, she didn't say a single word. The hallway groaned underneath Gijun's shoes. It was all over. A voice murmured to him from the far edges of his consciousness.

The executions were finished by the afternoon. The snow was so heavy that it delayed the schedule by an hour. Yongseok's sister and parents disappeared from the snowy execution grounds. Their deaths tore at his heart to the very end.

Not even the ringing echo of the siren announcing that the executions were over could elicit any deep emotion from Gijun. A row of stakes had been driven into the dirt near the stone walls of the execution grounds. The wind blew about the snow that blanketed the square. A few crows dotted the winter landscape with black splotches here and there. In this place, there were no effusive shows of sorrow or roars of wrath, nor did any wild beasts howl for blood. Gijun felt an impotent irritation at the silence of the witnessing crowd. Their silence resembled the deep and mounting snow.

From the guardhouse window, Gijun watched the crowd that watched the executions, even as the snow continued to pile up. From there he also watched the executions of Yangsun and her parents, which occurred around the halfway mark.

He poured some whiskey into the tea that had been offered to him and drank. Yangsun and her mother came stumbling out of the building that was to the left of the guardhouse with their hands bound behind them. The older woman kept tripping. The police officer yelled at her as she desperately struggled to get back to her feet. The father had exited his building first, but they were finally reunited outside and were able to walk across the square together. When the three met, Yangsun turned her head and seemed to be looking for someone. But the wall of police in front of the guardhouse blocked her view, and she was unable to see Gijun. Gijun saw her.

The parents walked together and Yangsun followed behind. There was a policeman to the right and left of Yangsun. She looked up at the dark sky and then toward the mountain, which was currently obscured. With the snow in her hair, she seemed to be wearing a beautiful white veil. As they reached the center of the square, a loud quarrel broke out between the mother and father. They jabbed at each other's necks as they fought. "I don't want to die!" the old woman cried. Her voice wormed its way into every crevice of the square. "It's because of *your* son. I'm going to be killed because of the son your flabby rotten prick made. It's all your fault, you bastard—you and your horrible prick. I don't want to die! I don't, I don't!"

The old man wasn't going to take that lying down.

He struggled against the rope and kicked at his wife, showering abuse on her. "Bitch! What about your flabby rotten slit? He was born from there, wasn't he? It's because of that I'm going to be killed. I don't want to die, either, you old whore!"

The old woman tumbled forward. A young policeman blankly watched the fight unfold with a magnanimous attitude, like an adult supervising a spat between children. Although he didn't laugh, some laughter broke out from a corner of the square where the upper management had congregated. Suddenly, two young policemen hissed at the couple and brought the butts of their guns down on their heads. The old woman's wails echoed underneath the snow-laden sky. Yangsun bit her lip and walked quietly through the snow, her head hung low.

Gijun saw every detail of it. He thought of Yongseok. Why were they fated to die in this way? Just before dozens of carbines roared, spitting out their fire across the snow, he heard it: the broken and broken-hearted voices of Yongseok's parents, crying out for their son. "*Aigo*, our son! Our precious Yongseok!" In that moment, Gijun gave thanks—though to whom or what he couldn't say. He thought he could also hear Yangsun call out her brother's name. Hidden in the shadow of that name was a boundless curse against him. *That will do.*

Gijun watched all of the executions to the very end. The mountain of corpses was thrown into a nearby field, transported there by the same truck that had carried the policemen. The bodies were buried with the snow in a mass grave dug by the villagers. Gijun recalled the warden's words and the expression on his strangely stiff, flat face as he spoke: *Crops grow well in fields that have been fed with human blood. The farmers welcome it.*

It would continue tomorrow, too. He would have to climb higher and higher, dragging his heavy heart along. Gijun found it so hard to endure. *These things happen; there's no helping it*, he murmured to himself. *To make certain actions possible, there are things we must give up . . .*

That day, Gijun hallucinated over and over that he was the one who had killed Yangsun. After she was executed, he searched for Yangsun's ghost, but for some reason she didn't appear before him as she had before. The white light no longer shone anywhere, either, not even in the transparent emptiness of the jeep's windshield that the wipers cleared over and over again.

6.

Instead of dropping by the USAMGIK office, Gijun went straight home. Well, he intended to go home. Instead, he found himself passing through the flimsy curtain that served as a door for the local bar. It wasn't technically a bar but an establishment that presented itself as a Chinese restaurant. It had a straw roof and a dingy interior. Gijun had a sudden dread of returning to his own dark, cold room. A lump lodged deep in his throat moved with every breath he took. He was exhausted.

He sat at a table situated behind a partition at the back of the restaurant. Twilight shadows hung in the air, as if they'd seeped out from the gloomy walls that retained the heavy smell of cooking oil. There were only two or three other customers, all seated near the entrance. Gijun sat in a trance with his elbows on the table and his head in his hands. He took no notice when the surly old woman who worked there approached his table. He finally raised his head at her voice and quietly said, "Soju."

"Anything else?"

"I'll eat anything."

The old woman looked at him suspiciously, but in

the end she brought him only alcohol. Gijun intended to drink just a glass or two and then go back home. He briefly considered going to a brothel, but no matter how he tried he couldn't muster up any desire. The glasses piled up before him as he sat there, hidden behind the partition.

At one point he raised his head, sensing the presence of another person, and was taken aback for some reason to see it was Yi Sanggeun. "Hey there!" Sanggeun said as he took off his overcoat. "S-sorry for interrupting. I was curious to see who was here . . . " He asked Gijun if he could sit with him. Gijun mechanically responded yes. Sanggeun pulled out a chair and sat across from Gijun with a smile. He looked calm, but in fact he'd taken off his overcoat because he was not a little flustered.

The table that shone black with the oil from countless people's hands and the traces from countless people's breaths suddenly seemed to take on the expression of a living being at the appearance of this new person called Yi Sanggeun. Gijun didn't speak.

The atmosphere around the gleaming black table wanted something other than silence, though. Sanggeun started off the conversation by saying that he himself quite liked the dingy gloominess of the restaurant and the aura created by the greasy walls, but was surprised to see Gijun in such a place. He smiled as he spoke. Gijun returned the smile with one of his own. "Is that so?" he replied. "I don't think it's a very gloomy place at all. In fact, the sound of the splattering grease dries me out." He thought it strange how Sanggeun was missing his typical sullen smile.

When the old woman brought over the next round of alcohol, Sanggeun handed his overcoat to her. Gijun saw that Sanggeun's clothes were all black, even his muffler. Like Sanggeun, Gijun also just happened to be wearing black. For some reason, it made him think of his earlier experience at the execution grounds. *I need to go home soon and get some sleep.*

"It's impressive how you spotted me way back here."

"To be honest, it's because I always sit here when I come."

"In that case, I'm the one who's intruding," Gijun said with a laugh, getting up from his seat. He was relieved by Sanggeun's words, but he also couldn't help feeling that today's meeting was not by chance. "I should go. I'm tired, and I've already drunk quite a lot."

Sanggeun put his hand on Gijun's arm as if to stop him. The motion was so sudden and agitated that it caused the table to sway and the legs to creak. Sanggeun didn't want to let Gijun go. It was a complete coincidence, him running into Gijun like this, and it gave him the first opportunity to test out a theory he had about the other man. He was also, quite simply, interested in knowing what it was like to drink with him.

He thought back to his encounter with Gijun earlier that day. He was oddly fixated on the cigarette butts he'd received from Old Man Boil that morning. A pack of Pall Malls contained twenty cigarettes. There were less than ten butts in the empty packet, which meant that Gijun must have discarded about half of them somewhere else. But even supposing that Gijun had used the box as a kind of makeshift ashtray, that didn't explain why the butts in the packet had dirt and moss on them. After returning home, Sanggeun had made the additional discovery of something that looked like dried grass. It was clear that the cigarettes had been smoked outdoors, but the weather had been stormy these past few days. "Haha, I wonder if this was his way of observing what people call 'public morals,' by going to smoke in the middle of some open field . . . " Sanggeun threw himself onto his bed and roared with laughter. With nothing else to do, he took out the broken cigarette butts one by one and laid them out in a neat line on the table. At last he stuffed one of the butts into a short pipe and lit it. He puffed. He half expected something to materialize from the smoke. He tried imagining what Gijun's thin, naked body looked like, as if he were a woman. But the masklike expression of his face jarred with that naked body. He looked at his own reflection in the mirror, but the only thing that appeared through the smoke was Yi Sanggeun himself. It might be that the only realistic answer to the mystery of the cigarette butts was to be found by approaching the mask directly. To meet Gijun by chance, to silently hand him the evidence and sound out his reaction—that was surely the ideal way to turn up a clue.

Meanwhile, Gijun remained unaware of his own blunder. They were the remains of the cigarettes that he had smoked with Yongseok. On the way home that evening, he had run into someone in town. They had gone to a bar together and drunk quite a lot. When he changed his clothes the next morning, he completely forgot about the cigarettes.

The instant that Gijun got up from his seat, Sanggeun felt his plan descend heavily upon his consciousness as if it were some external force. His body tensed. "If that's the case," Sanggeun said, "how about a change of venue? Somewhere a little livelier, perhaps . . . " Gijun told him he needed to return home. The two silently drained their cups and finished smoking their cigarettes. Gijun found Sanggeun more congenial than he'd initially thought. He savored the bitterness of the cigarette clamped between his lips and looked down at Sanggeun's sculpted fingers. Sanggeun could feel the weight of that gaze as if it were a physical sensation but didn't withdraw his hands from the table.

Sanggeun had the cigarettes in question in his pocket. For some reason, he found himself unable to take them out. As he hesitated, he could feel the pressure bearing down upon him from the other man. Despite his mild demeanor, there was something dangerous about Gijun's expression today. It permeated his entire face, creating its own kind of atmosphere. His face always looked as if his expressions had been pasted onto his thin skin. Today, the shadow on his shaven high cheekbones keenly balanced his tapered nose. His eyes were filled with a deep calm light. The subtle movement of those eyes lanced Sanggeun's chest with a pain like poison. Even so, his haggard face also gave off the impression of great fatigue. Sanggeun made some vague comments and decided to put off his inquiries for another time. *There's always tomorrow,* he thought, trying to bolster his faltering courage. He wanted to tell Gijun that his face looked different today, but for some reason the words wouldn't come out. Instead, he found himself blurting out the following: "In the past I thought about becoming a spy."

It wasn't that he thought Gijun was a spy or anything like that. If he had, he probably couldn't have said such a thing so easily; instead, he would no doubt have been able to overcome his faltering heart and silently present the empty packet before Gijun, just as planned. But reality didn't work out like that. When confronted with the living, breathing human being that was Gijun, the thread linking Gijun to Sanggeun's fanciful idea of him snapped and fell away. He had confessed the thoughts in his head without any ulterior motive. Gijun had merely been the catalyst. But as one might expect, his words gave Gijun a terrible shock.

"Huh!" Gijun knew he had to say *something.* "I see.

That's an interesting thought—" Gijun abruptly felt like he was outside of himself, distantly watching a different self sitting there small and shrunken in the chair. The faces of the director, the Americans in the USAMGIK Department of Justice, and even Yongseok flashed before him, one after the other, as if bathed by the light of an electric bulb. Sanggeun sat with his arms spread wide and his chin resting on his hands. He wore a brazen expression, and there was something about his penetrating gaze that made Gijun feel a pressure that resembled fear. Fortunately, their surroundings were only dimly lit. Gijun sought safety in the cigarette he had just lit. He took a drag from the cigarette as naturally as possible, and with heavy deliberation. The cigarette trembled faintly as he moved it away from his mouth, and ash threatened to fall from its tip. Holding back the deep breath he had been about to expel, he decided it would be dangerous to remain silent. "I'm not really familiar with the subject, but I bet there are lots of different types of spies," he said, leaning forward with feigned interest. He had to make sure his smiling face was composed and neutral. "Newspaper companies spy on each other, for example, as do businesses . . . I suppose you're talking about political spies—but in any case, I'm sure that's more relevant to big cities like Seoul, not a place like Jeju."

"That's true." Sanggeun's expression was exceedingly earnest. "But I wasn't talking about any political reality. I simply wanted to consider the ideological aspects. Spies are like a small intestine after an enema. That is, they're like a dissected human whose skin is the only thing keeping it together. To put it crudely."

Gijun was reassured by Sanggeun's tone, if nothing else. It sounded like someone expounding on a random theory. "It's not a subject I'm really familiar with," Gijun repeated, as convincingly as he could.

His words did seem to have an effect. Sanggeun downed his drink and also leaned forward. "In other words—no, I mean—you—" He seemed intoxicated by his own words. "I want to know what you think of my definition of a spy. It's not a question of politics. As a rule I don't trust anyone who's involved in that thing people call politics. Let me give you an example. Right now the Reds and I . . . Haha, you want to know about the Reds? Haha. I don't have any interest or concern about such things, but we're being manipulated everywhere by them. You may be surprised to know that the police have been scouring the streets day and night, looking for them. But it's too late—they're swarming everywhere in this city, no matter where you go. They may look innocent, but they're all Reds—even the elementary school kids. Are you okay, by the way? This is just my opinion—but what I meant to say is that the situation is such that you could easily become a spy for either side, if you really wanted to. What are your thoughts on this tricky human position? That's what I want to know. Given your profession, you must have considered the question before. What does it really mean to trust another human being? I'm someone who can manipulate two organizations—what you might call two different worlds—like puppets on a string."

Gijun knew he should leave. Sanggeun spoke frankly and without any hesitation, but hearing the word "spy" over and over strained Gijun's nerves to their limit. There was also the fact that customers had finally begun to spill over into the partitioned section. Gijun glanced at the old woman who sat in the corner like a statue. He was assailed by an extremely languid tension.

"This conversation has exhausted me. It's a complicated issue, I know, but I'm afraid my interest in it doesn't run that deep." Gijun wondered if standing up now would look unnatural.

"No, please stay. You must have some opinion." Sanggeun took out a handkerchief and wiped his forehead. "I want an inner soul like yours. Sorry, I apologize—I'm not saying that you're a spy. It's just that whenever I look at you, I'm reminded of a mask. I can't help but feel there's something hidden behind it . . . That's what I want."

That afternoon, Sanggeun had in fact peered at his own face in the mirror while thinking of Gijun. You could say it was either an expressionless expression (the true essence of Gijun's masklike face, possibly) or an expression of expressionlessness. In either case, Sanggeun wanted the latter for himself. He had tried wiping all emotions from his face, but in the end all that remained was Sanggeun's same old self. His face, in other words, was that of a man who gnawed on abstract concepts even as he shut himself away from the world of action. It was precisely that face he wished to disavow through some masklike means. Or else it may be that he wanted to find a way out of himself. Yi Sanggeun was like those people who, unable to find a foothold for action within a reality in turmoil, gradually retreated deeper and deeper within themselves. The reality around him was not just in turmoil, it had exploded—and the shock waves were continuing to spread. That reality was constantly demanding an answer from Sanggeun, for example by thrusting before him the figure of a young man who had been murdered. He acknowledged that he had to find some kind of answer. But there was nothing within him he could use as a fulcrum for action.

Gijun now abruptly stood up, interrupting Sanggeun's words. "I admit I'm also drunk, but I wish you weren't so cynical with people." The old woman in the corner stared at them suspiciously. Gijun pulled out a cigarette and lit it. The light flickered like a melancholic will-o'-the-wisp, and in that light Sanggeun's face suddenly looked so small and shrunken it might fit into his palm. The sight bewildered Gijun, to say the least. *Shouldn't it be the opposite?* How strange. "I think the description applies more to you," he said with a laugh and a flash of his teeth. As he laughed, he was acutely aware of the cold sweat gathering along his spine.

But at that moment, a thought struck Sanggeun with the force of a lightning bolt. It was so sudden and wild that it unsettled even himself. It couldn't possibly be true.

It was only a simple whimsical notion: Jeong Gijun, this man standing before him, was a spy. When he had said the word "mask," angering Gijun, Sanggeun's brain had conjured up a clear image of those old cigarette butts. He was overwhelmed by the force of the conjecture even as he tried to reject it. He pressed a hand to his chest as if his heart pained him. His heart was beating so loud and fast he was half afraid the other man might be able to hear it.

Gijun was looking down at Sanggeun. Sanggeun gently grasped Gijun's wrist and said, "I didn't mean it like that. I didn't mean in the least to be cynical with you." *If this man really is a spy, then today's no good. If I want to face off against him, I'll have to show him the evidence like I first planned without any advance warning.*

Gijun silently sat down and took a drink from his glass. He apologized to Sanggeun and told him to go on. He realized he was drunk. Why hadn't he kept his mouth shut and let him finish what he had to say . . . Sanggeun gave a self-conscious laugh and shook his head. Gijun urged him to continue, saying that he was finally starting to feel the effects of the alcohol but that he found the conversation fascinating.

"Really?" Sanggeun took the overcoat that the old

woman was holding out to him and shrugged it on. "Aren't you cold?"

"No, I'm fine."

Sanggeun returned to the topic at hand. "For example, I wonder what people thought when I took that head out of the basket. It may be that they assumed I was the same kind of person as Old Man Boil. But for me, the action was meaningless. Or else it might just have been a whim brought on by alcohol. That's what I thought, anyway, that night I spent at the police station. But the police deemed it 'interference with a public servant in the execution of his duties'—ha, can you believe that *he's* considered a public servant?—and, by extension, treason against our very own Republic of Korea. Everyone else in this city, meanwhile, regards me as a despicable bastard who desecrated their precious revolution—a traitor to the people. On the other hand, I could also be seen as resisting authority . . . "

Sanggeun's voice had gotten heated. "But I'm neither," he concluded. He then downed his water like a parched man. Gijun forced himself to nod as he picked at the fatty pork on his plate. *What an extravagant man.* Gijun reminded himself that people who got drunk off their own words still had some good in them. The sense of danger had receded. His lassitude immediately returned to take its place.

"I'm neither," repeated Sanggeun. "My actions were shunned by both sides, and in that sense I am free. Spies must be something similar. If so, then I might be able to reach the top of the pyramid. Like a tower with no door. The wind may blow all around my body, but I'll just stand there, unmoved. That's where my freedom lies. I want to stretch myself across an empty space with no politics, no stratagems . . . Or else, haha, like I said before, spies may just be dissected humans, barely held together by skin . . . Moreover—"

"—Moreover, the strength of a mask's expression . . ." is what Sanggeun wanted to say, but instead he drained his glass. His gaze fixed on a point beyond Gijun, as if he were trying to see through the door to what lay outside. But even as he avoided Gijun's eyes, another part of him was busy drawing up a new plan. Gijun felt his tension start to ease along with his exhaustion. Sanggeun couldn't possibly know anything about the murky world of the spy. He couldn't possibly know that it was nothing like standing at the top of a pyramid—it was, rather, like being trapped at the bottom of a deep, dark hole, swinging constantly between feeling like a hero and feeling like the devil, and shuddering with fear the whole time. "Well—real spies are not like that." Gijun's throat felt like it was full of treacle. He only barely managed to control his voice.

7.

As soon as he entered his room, Gijun threw himself onto the bed in exhaustion. His whole body felt like it was being swallowed up by the bed. His tears wouldn't stop. Four days from tomorrow—again, again, he would have to climb that steep hill once again. Gijun wondered if Yongseok, with his guileless nature, would be able to understand his anguish. He told himself that he would reveal everything about himself that he found so difficult to bear and once and for all go up into the mountains; that, or he'd go through with the transfer. But the more he set his mind to abandoning his mission, the more he felt that doing so would mean losing everything. He was terrified that everything supporting him would crash to the ground, plunging him into a bottomless hell. He was quite inebriated, and so exhausted his body felt boneless. Still, Gijun found himself unable to fall asleep. "Ahh, why do I always become so sad whenever I get drunk?"

The insistent voice of the boardinghouse maid brought Gijun to his feet. Her presence wasn't necessarily cause for alarm; it was already 7:30 in the morning. He wondered, however, why she was bothering to wake him. He asked her if it was snowing. The girl had been knocking on his door rather hesitantly, but at his question she said in a sudden formal matter that it wasn't snowing now but that it looked like there might be some heavy rain later. She then giggled. For some reason her voice on the other side of the door didn't sound as it normally did. She told him there was a visitor for him. He acknowledged her with some irritation. He was more interested in confirming that the owner of the voice was indeed who he thought it was.

He knew, of course, that it wasn't Yangsun. But he thought of her as he walked down the hallway of the veranda. He suspected that he'd caught a cold; his throat was warm, and he had a headache. The snow in the courtyard had turned slushy, and a fine rain was falling. The pile of snow under the single poplar tree that towered in the corner of the courtyard was punctured with countless black holes from the water droplets that fell from the tree's branches. They reminded him of the hole in his own heart, and again he thought of Yangsun. But even if she were to appear now, it would be as just another ghost in a crowd of ghosts. She'd stand there underneath the poplar tree, surrounded by comrades who had been tortured to death, looking at him but pretending not to recognize him. The ghosts who narrowed their eyes at him were no longer his comrades, nor were any of them Yangsun. Gijun grieved for his own rebellious heart. This life surrounded by allies who constantly rejected him, Yangsun's final, sad smile when she had flashed her teeth at him—Gijun laughed at his own sentimentality. In the end, weren't the icy eyes of the ghosts who hung in the air the same as those of Yangsun? They were the enemy! Gijun let out a deep breath.

The elderly police janitor was waiting under the eaves of the shed next to the front gate. When he saw Gijun approach, he looked down and noisily blew his nose into his hand, then began hurrying towards him across the courtyard. He produced a police envelope from his breast pocket and kept his eyes trained nervously at Gijun's feet. "I am very sorry to bother you at home," he said, bowing his head again and again. Several decades ago, the elderly janitor had been one of the people made to plant cherry blossom seedlings in the police yard under the watchful eyes of the "*waenom* (Jap) police chief" and others in his command. Gijun asked the old man to stay put for a minute and went to fetch a pack of cigarettes for him.

Soon afterwards, Gijun left for the police station. The contents of the letter were simple: *Meeting called. Come at once to station.* That was it. Gijun felt a vague apprehension at the unusual request. He threw on his raincoat and headed straight to the station. As he emerged onto the main road, he happened to glance to his left, towards the Catholic church on Nammun Street. There, he spotted Yi Sanggeun, dressed as always in black. He was suspicious at first, but then remembered that he was in the red-light district. It looked like Sanggeun had stayed out all night. Sanggeun acknowledged Gijun from a distance with an uncharacteristically affable nod. Gijun found it extremely discomforting. Was that the kind of greeting you gave someone after having come out of a disreputable place? Gijun returned the nod but continued to cross the intersection without stopping. He saw that a sentry had been posted at the police station barricade.

He entered the chief of police's office. The chief of police, director of security, and vice commander of security were already seated around the table. Having settled deeply in their armchairs, the three men did not bother getting up to greet Gijun. The chief was silently looking at the portrait of Syngman Rhee that hung on the wall behind him. The director was using a toothpick to get at something in his teeth. Although all three remained silent, there was something theatrical about the young vice commander's attitude. His big, bulky body was splayed uncomfortably over the armchair. He was smoking a cigarette and his eyes were closed at the moment, though later Gijun saw him frequently half open his eyes and squint at the cigarette ash stuck on his nose.

The meeting turned out to be an important briefing session for the police, in advance of a secret meeting scheduled for 10 a.m. at the USAMGIK office with the police and security forces. The briefing began roughly half an hour after Gijun's entrance, with the arrival of the American general. Gijun soon realized the terrible nature of the meeting. When it was announced that President Syngman Rhee and Minister of Defense Shin Sung-mo would soon be arriving on the island, he felt his voice go faint and hoarse. That was all he was allowed to know for the moment, but it was enough. Things would become clear enough in time. Like a prospector panning for gold, he hoarded the information that spewed from the police chief's mouth. An alarm was going off inside Gijun, and he felt like his body was expanding uncontrollably. The room was almost too small to contain his agitation. He now understood why the chief's expression had been so gentle just a moment ago: given this abrupt change in circumstances, the chief's transfer would be delayed, necessarily affecting Gijun's transfer, too. The chief rose and opened the window a crack. The wind stirred the curtains, revealing the view outside. The window faced a stone wall that was now being pounded by the rain. The police chief, who was originally from this island, said he wanted to remain here and watch the islanders massacred with his own eyes. Gijun resolved to do everything he could to prevent his transfer if worst came to worst.

In the early months of 1949, the South Korean president, the minister of defense, and other government leaders held two secret meetings with the head of the American military for the purposes of subjugating Jeju Island. In those meetings, the Americans took a hard line on three points: first, that Jeju was in a strategic geographical position; second, that the complete suppression of opposition on the island was an essential condition for defeating North Korea; and third, that regaining control of Jeju would also help relations with Japan. As a result of these meetings, leaders from South Korea and America landed on the island. Minister of Defense Shin Sung-mo and others led on-site operations under the direct command of Brigadier General W. L. Roberts. Declaring that "failure to surrender will result in the wholesale slaughter of the 300,000 inhabitants of the island," they carried out an unprecedented mission to annihilate the Jeju partisans. Thousands of military reinforcements from the mainland were mobilized, alongside right-wing terrorist organizations, the American navy, and several American military aircraft.

Gijun left the room feeling as if he'd been in a sauna. His back was soaked with sweat. He was unable to bear the bloating sensation he felt—as if poison had permeated every crevice of his body, rejecting every single thing about the men. As the police chief had said, it was indeed "the start of a new history in Jeju." Seven or eight police officers were sitting with tense expressions at the table behind the counter outside the room. They kept one eye on their documents and one eye on Gijun, as if they had sniffed something suspicious about him. Gijun leaned against the counter and deliberately asked for a light. He took a drag from his cigarette. For some reason, in that moment Gijun pitied every single one of those police officers. He felt a strange sense of fullness at the fact that everything were now surging toward him and hardening at his feet. He was in the mood to tell a joke. Instead, he simply told the young officer who'd offered him the light that he'd treat him to a drink soon, and left.

As he opened the door and exited onto the stone steps, he was startled by a crow's caw. The murky call sounded oddly insistent in the rain. The snow in the yard had almost completely melted, and the ground had turned into a muddy mess. Five or six corpses had been dumped underneath the cherry blossom trees. He was fairly certain they had not been there when he had passed by earlier. They'd no doubt been thrown out from the jail cells; all that was left was for the truck to transport them away. Caked in mud and drenched in water, the bodies looked like piles of garbage. The arms and legs stiff as ladles, the water-soaked hair spread out like seaweed, the withered bodies . . . they looked so small. Two or three bodies in one of the smaller piles had their arms stretched out as if they'd grasped each other's collars in a fight. Gijun kept watching as the coagulating blood dissolved in the rain, dyeing the clothes and ground a rusty color.

All at once Gijun felt wrung out and depressed. He let out a deep breath and went down the slick stone steps. The crow was still cawing loudly above his head. He glanced up and saw a particularly large one perched high on a withered cherry blossom branch. It bobbed its head as if nodding at him, and its feet were firmly planted on the branch as it looked down with a searching air. The corpse of a young woman was sprawled out underneath the tree. She looked eighteen at most. Her head faced his direction, her thighs were spread, and her chest was thrust forward. Blood flowed down from her swollen, half-open mouth. Her head was twisted so that her chin rested against the top of her shoulder, staining that part of her body as if she'd vomited blood. She probably hadn't been dead for long. Her exposed breasts gleamed in the rain. They were hard and alive.

The crow suddenly swooped down near the corpse, leaving behind only the sound of its wings flapping in the air. The crow, which was most likely female, had the same sharp eyes, glossy feathers, and large taut body as all the other crows of Jeju. It was clearly trying to alight on the young woman. Gijun found himself stopping to look up at the crow. The crow looked down at him. It calmly pecked at a bare branch, then began cawing again, making clear its animosity towards Gijun, an unwanted intruder. Gijun suddenly recalled the dead crow from the uninhabited village. The sound of the crow's beak pecking at the branch brought back to him the sound of the shoes echoing in the street. Yangsun's white light fluttered over the young woman. His spine crawled.

Gijun's hand unconsciously went to the pistol in his inner pocket. The crow squared its shoulders at the movement and then leisurely stretched its wings. In that instant, a shot rang out. The smell of gunpowder filled his nose; the crow fell. It twitched on the young woman's breast, its black wings wide open and twisted. It struggled to fly for a second. Then it tumbled off the body and into a nearby puddle. Bright red blood—just like that of a human—welled up from the black body.

"Ahh, the crow died! It died!" Gijun muttered deliriously to himself. A startled sentry came running into the yard. Gijun thought he saw Yi Sanggeun next to him.

Director Kim came up behind Gijun and thumped him on the shoulder. "Haha, that was quite *wonderful*," he said, using the English word. Gijun heard the sound of the door creaking open and sensed a noisy crowd of people coming out of the building. He quickly came to his senses. The realization that he'd made an awful mistake struck him like a bolt of lightning.

"That's a fantastic shooting arm you've got there. Just one bullet, eh . . . They do say that crows in the morning are a bad omen. Haha, I hate crows. For one, their color is just wrong. And I can't stand the way they caw . . . like an old woman half in the grave. Y'know, on her deathbed, my mother was terrified of crows. Made a noise just like one—*caw caw* . . . " The director lit up a cigarette. He gave an awkward laugh, a little embarrassed by the sound of his own voice saying *caw caw*.

Gijun knew from the director's voice that the moment of danger had passed. It was an instinctual understanding only; as someone who had to constantly live in front of a mirror and constantly slumber inside one, he didn't have time to even ponder if the director had found him out.

He simply had a visceral sensation that he'd overcome the danger. In that instant, the finger on the trigger of his gun began to twitch and tremble. Rage surged through him. Having now drawn blood, the pistol waited patiently and submissively in its owner's palm. Rain flowed from his hatless head down into his eyes, like wet shards of glass. Beyond the thick veil that obscured his vision, the sodden corpse looked like it was floating in the sea. Gijun could hear surging waves in the distance. The roaring in his ears that had followed his violent headache transformed into the roar of the sea. His body was rigid with chills, and the blood vessels on his forehead pounded against his skull. *I must have a bad fever.* He began to shiver and sway. The rain fell even more heavily into his eyes. The crowd of corpses was borne closer to him by the undulating sea.

In the commotion behind him the director's laugh rang out loud and clear. Gijun was seized with the urge to fire a bullet into his stomach. He turned around to look at the director. Beyond the wet ashen veil, the director's face was lit by a white light. It wavered before his eyes like a brazen mask. All at once the leaden atmosphere tore apart above his head, and white powder glittered all around him. "This bullet is going to tear a hole in your stomach,"

Gijun found himself groaning.

A flash of fireworks, and roaring in his ears.

Gijun took a step forward and even more calmly shot three bullets in quick succession into the innocent young woman's chest. He didn't know why the gun had spat fire at the young woman when it should have been aimed at the director. He simply felt an instinctual relief. Those wretched bullets that felt like they'd been fired at his own chest were lodged deep in her breasts. Blood gushed out from the wounds.

He walked away in a daze, the pistol dangling forgotten from his hand. The rain came down harder, streaming relentlessly down his hair. It was all over, it had all just begun . . . Gijun began to laugh wildly. Wave after wave of sorrow threatened to drown him. He tried to plant his feet firmly on the ground, but still he staggered a little as he passed through the gate. Underneath the wide sky, the streets bustled with the life and vitality of the city. Wagons rumbled past, children ran and played, housewives with children on their back walked in the rain. It was as if he were watching it all through a glass window, this scene that was neither far nor near. It was, in fact, positioned so that he could reach out at any time to embrace it if he wanted to. He pushed aside his loneliness as a sense of fullness overtook him again. He leisurely pulled out a cigarette, not caring if it got soaked by the rain. Old Man Boil was shouting out his announcements from somewhere around the Gwandeokjeong area. It was all over, it had all just begun . . . His life must continue on, he thought to himself. This land was still the most appropriate place for him to carry out his responsibilities, the place he would bury his life when it was all over. He clenched his teeth together as he listened to Old Man Boil's sad voice. *I must not cry.*

Yi Sanggeun looked steadily at Jeong Gijun as he walked away in a cloak of rain. He didn't know what was hidden in the roar of those four shots; what he knew was that he'd unintentionally witnessed Gijun's complex savagery. Sanggeun leaned against the soaked barricade, heedless of the rain, and watched Gijun's receding form until it disappeared.

Gwandeokjeong

1.

You could see the archaic structure of Gwandeokjeong Pavilion from the square in front of the police station.

A jumble of streets radiated out in all directions from the square, weaving their way through various government offices and small shops with low-hanging eaves. Almost all of the buildings, even those owned by the government, were only one story tall. The main road that ran through the old downtown area was the most "road"-like of those streets, but it would be more accurate to say that it, too, originated from the plaza and stretched out east and west from there.

The square in front of the police station: in the past, people called it Gwandeokjeong Square. The police station and Gwandeokjeong Pavilion were situated diagonally across from each other in the square, but even now "Gwandeokjeong Square" sounded more natural to people, whether because of its history or because of the air of dignity the pavilion still had. If you were to tell that name to one of the visitors disembarking at the harbor in the *seongnae* (old city area), for example, chances were he'd immediately understand. Once he arrived at the center of the city—which was the square—the first thing he'd see is Gwandeokjeong, its presence immediately eclipsing his own. If the gentleman came from the much larger cities of Seoul, Busan, or Mokpo, he would no doubt take note of the wonderstruck gazes of the country bumpkins who had traveled here by bus from other parts of the island. Though he might dismiss them with a glance, the city gentleman, too, would eventually find himself staring up with awe at the roof of the pavilion.

Long ago, this square had also been known as "the garden of Gwandeokjeong." A lone elderly man was currently sitting on the broad stone steps of the square. He was one of the individuals who still thought of the place in that way.

The man was wearing an unpleasantly smug

expression. Because of his quite noticeable attempts to hide his overbite, his mouth protruded out more than his nose, or at least that's the impression it gave. People could tell at a glance it was Old Man Boil.

He was alone. There was a time when you could always find Old Man Boil at the center of a crowd, but he appeared to have recently lost the ability to draw people to him; in any case, he was alone. Careful observation would no doubt reveal that his smug expression contained a sense of purpose that had lately been absent in him.

The eyes that usually darted about in his wrinkled face were, today, quietly calm. He sat with his elbows on his knees as he puffed on a very long, narrow pipe. A wrapped parcel sat off to the side. For a while neither he nor his shadow moved from their position on the stone steps, like a dragonfly submerging itself in the shimmering heat of spring sunlight. The bamboo pipe gleamed, most likely because of all the handling it had endured over these many years. But his breath easily passed through the long pipe—because the bowl was in fact completely empty. Even so, he kept his gaze trained upon the pipe's end even as he leisurely began to shut his wrinkly, sleepy-looking eyes.

All of a sudden, the old man turned his attention to the stone police gate across the street while giving his armpits a vigorous scratching. A sentry was standing by the barricade. Just a moment before, the old man had exposed his naked upper body to the sun and begun hunting for lice when a voice abruptly rang out above him. The owner of the voice had to shout "Oi!" around three times before the old man noticed. Even then he continued to pick at the lice that crawled over him. The voice scolded him: "What do you think you're doing in such a conspicuous place? The Americans pass by this square all the time!" It was all very confusing. He began to turn around—right as his belt was yanked up from behind by a policeman.

"Where do you think you are?!"

This is the square in front of the police station. That's what he thought but didn't say. Although the other man was dressed in a police uniform, his face was that of a complete rookie. (The old man still considered himself senior in rank, despite having been fired from his job.) "Well, this is Gwandeokjeong Square," he announced. "Where I'm sitting is Gwandeokjeong—my home. Back in the day they used to call this square right here 'the garden of Gwandeokjeong.'" The old man swiftly pulled his *jeogori* (upper garment of a traditional Korean outfit) back on. He then took the young officer's hand, as if inviting him to sit with him on the steps, and said, "Are you, er, still a *chonggak* (unmarried man)?" He proceeded to launch into a long-winded speech about the history of Gwandeokjeong.

The young officer had no desire to listen to the elderly man's ramblings. As is typical behavior in our "Republic of Korea" (if not on this island), the officer grabbed the other man's collar and dragged him forward. The old man clung to the steps and yelled for the police captain. "You're the only idiot who doesn't know who I am!" he told the young officer. "The chief of police knows me. Even the dog that the captain owns knows me. Did you know that one of the dog's back legs is crippled?" Bellowing the captain's name, he began writhing on the steps.

The rookie was flabbergasted. Although it was a spring day, people had begun to gather around the old man from a safe distance. The officer made a strange face—like a man who has unexpectedly achieved enlightenment after having thrown some garbage away—and made a hasty retreat.

"Old Man Boil," someone said in a small voice, after the police officer was safely gone. "You . . . you said Gwandeokjeong Square just now, didn't you?"

Having discovered that he was now surrounded by people, the old man nodded gravely in response to the inquirer's interested gaze. He took up his pipe again and extended it towards the crowd. A cigarette butt that had been on the verge of being thrown to the ground was instead instantly stuffed into the pipe's bowl. The old man squinted and replied solemnly, "Yes, I did say that—"

The crowd buzzed. Gwandeokjeong Square . . . People looked at each other. Immediately after liberation on August 15, 1945, the People's Committee had established a local office inside the pavilion, and a period of great socialist activity had ensued. However, the office was soon shut down by the American military, and the title Gwandeokjeong Square had gradually gone out of use.

The old man looked for a while at the sentry, whom he owed in a way for the crowd around him and for the cigarettes he'd gained. One cigarette in particular caught his attention for the way it resembled a small fish bone in the spring sunlight. The sentry, too, was smoking. The old man took a match from his pocket and used it to light his pipe. He contemplated the bus depot located across from the police station. The mammoth shadow of Gwandeokjeong had shifted quite a bit, and the galvanized iron roof of the depot shimmered in the heat. The old man looked up. The sun was white and bright and ate at the curved lines of Gwandeokjeong's tiled roof that loomed high over his head, blocking the deep azure of the sky. The light was dotted with the black shapes of the crows that had gathered on the roof.

The old man turned his gaze back to the sunny bus depot. He rose. "I have to get going soon," he announced. Chuckling, he scooped up the shabby cloth-wrapped package from the steps and fixed his threadbare felt hat on his head. He guessed from the number of people at the depot that the bus would be leaving soon.

The old man tapped his empty pipe against the edge of the steps and stretched his legs. The children snickered and laughed, watching him. Because he'd been sitting for so long in the sun and because, furthermore, one of his legs was crippled, he staggered and came perilously close to tumbling forward before he could reach the bottom of the steps. Usually he would shake his pipe at the children, but today he ignored them; he wanted to preserve his air of mystery. Even so, the brats swarmed around him, intent on mischief. "C'mon, Old Man Boil!" they cried. "Just let yourself fall forward. Hey, how come you don't got a cane if you're a cripple . . . If you fall, your lame leg will get better, we promise—"

The old man paid them no heed today. Well, he did shout at them and raise his pipe when one of the brats poked a stick through a tear in the back of his *baji* (Korean trousers), but his eyes were laughing when he did so. "I'll use a cane when I really become crippled but not until then, you hear? Go on home now. Old Man Boil's gotta go."

Although the old man would surely have benefited from the luxury of a cane, he didn't use one. He didn't find his condition particularly inconvenient, having been lame from birth, and although it was true that his posture didn't look all that great when he walked, it wasn't as if it impaired him in any significant way. In his mind, therefore, he was different from what he thought of as "normal cripples."

By the time he got to the depot, the bus driver was revving the engine and the passengers were waiting to board. The old man's wrinkles seemed to tauten all at once as soon as he saw the bus. He squatted on the sunniest patch of ground he could find and stealthily took in his surroundings with his pipe in his mouth. In doing so, he discovered that the man who had offered him a cigarette earlier was there, staring at him. In the same instant, he heard a voice: "Old Man Boil—" The old man kept his head down and extended his pipe.

"Where are you headed?"

He was disappointed he wasn't being offered any cigarettes, but the man everyone called Old Man Boil didn't let it get to him. The title itself he saw as a sign of respect, because it did, in fact, describe him well: he made a living sucking the puss out of other people's boils. In other words, he interpreted the title people gave him as proof that he really was the doctor he firmly believed himself to be. The thought gave him great satisfaction.

Before coming to this city, he'd plied his trade in villages that didn't have access to medicine; there, his "treatment" had been able to earn him a glass of soju as payment. He would squeeze out puss from a pimple or cyst by pursing his lips over the protrusion or else sinking his teeth into it (his snaggletooth was ideal for that purpose) with a precision that could rival that of a surgeon. His method might even have been preferable, considering how the villagers broke out in a cold sweat just thinking about the possibility of a gleaming surgeon's scalpel digging into their flesh. To be honest, a subtle pleasure accompanied the intense pain of the old man's method, and he was actually able to make a good living because of it. An added benefit of his profession was that it gave him access to tobacco. He would soften the tobacco (which the patients had to supply themselves) with his saliva and affix the wad to the wound after having sucked out the pus.

In a certain village far from the city, a landowner of some repute had asked Old Man Boil to suck out his pus. The landowner was relatively young and had even received some newfangled education abroad, so for a while people wondered and gossiped about why he didn't go to the modern hospital for treatment. But apparently he'd boasted to others that he'd come to a realization while sitting in the privy. The pigs of Jeju Island were jet black in color, and their main source of food was human feces. Furthermore, they only ate feces that were fresh and warm. The majority of privies on the island also functioned as pigpens; as soon as you straddled the latrine and stared up at the blue sky, the pigs would run sniffing and oinking right up to the privy walls. And then those giant, boar-like black beasts would wait there on high alert, their bright red mouths open wide and their human-like eyes trained on you. The young landowner with his newfangled education came to the conclusion that just as pigs were fed human feces, one had to feed the decompositions of the flesh to others. In doing so he found a way, one could say, to buy the pleasure that comes from feeding human excrement to other humans. But the old man took no notice of such stories. He was a doctor who was carrying on the ancient traditions, after all, and he *was* able to heal his patient's ailments—that was a fact, wasn't it?

He'd recently been fired from his job with the police, but at least he still had his other profession, and it was for that reason—and for a secret purpose only he knew—he was leaving town.

"I'm taking the bus," the old man said as he puffed on his empty pipe.

"You're taking the bus—you? Where are you headed to?"

"I'm taking the bus, see . . . " The old man peered

intently at the other man, as if reluctant to reveal where he was going. Before long he gave him an ingenuous smile. "Hehehe, have you forgotten me already?" He stuck his pipe in his front pocket, plucked out the ticket that had been tucked into the end of the wrapped parcel, and waved it in front of the other man's face.

The young man was a member of the maintenance staff at the depot. He'd stood next to the old man at the ticket booth and mocked him when he bought his ticket.

"Hmm, what's that you're holding there, Gramps?" The young man leaned forward and deliberately feigned interest. He snatched at the ticket with his oil-stained fingers. The old man leaped back in surprise.

"Don't—don't touch it! This is a very important bus ticket. It's the bus ticket I bought at your depot!"

The young man laughed so hard that the smoke from the cigarette in his mouth spewed up into the air. He asked again where the old man was going.

"It's written right here. Are you blind or something?"

The young man didn't let up his teasing. "I was *samdae dokja* (the only son in three generations), but now I'm all alone in the world. Pity me! I was never once given the opportunity to go to school. Can you read it for me?"

The old man brought the ticket up to his nose. With great dignity, he said, "It says 'G. Station' . . . and, er, 'tariff of ninety won' . . . "

The young man burst out laughing. The ticket seller stuck his head out of the booth and joined in the laughter. It was true that "G. Village" was printed on the ticket. The ticket had also been stamped with a red circle that meant "paid." But the old man's mangled use of the word "tariff" was just too much. When the young man pointed out that a "tariff of ninety won" wasn't written anywhere on the ticket, not even on the back, the crowd around him began to laugh as well.

Cigarette smoke danced and swirled in the air. The old man saw the smoke and, through it, the people laughing at him. The young man grabbed his jacket from the counter of the ticket booth and tossed it over his shoulders. He removed a cigarette from his pack and threw it at the old man.

The old man thought he heard a woman's voice among the laughter. He craned his neck in that direction, only to realize that it was not his beautiful Seopun but a country woman who was laughing, her mouth open wide and a wrapped parcel swinging from her hands above her belly.

"Hmph, I'm telling you that this ticket cost me a tariff of ninety won. It's a tariff of ninety won!" The old man walked away with an air of haughty dignity. But his eyes glimmered good-naturedly, and he puffed the cigarette that had been thrown at him, blowing the smoke out from his nose . . .

As the bus pulled out and Gwandeokjeong receded into the distance, the old man looked behind him, deeply moved. Every time the bus swayed, so did Gwandeokjeong. The enormous, moss-covered roof gleamed quiet and graceful in the spring sunlight, contrasting sharply with the white of the stone steps. The vermillion on the wide round pillars and doors was so vivid they lingered in one's vision long after. Although the old man knew it was called Gwandeokjeong Pavilion, he didn't know its exact origins. The building was Confucian in its architecture. Long ago, during the reign of King Sejong, the Jeju *moksa* (regional magistrate) had it built as a martial arts training hall for the purposes of cultivating a "military spirit." Prisoners who had "sinned" against the government were made to kneel on the flagstones in front of the main doors and have their trials right there. The building served as a reminder of the brutal acts of slaughter and savagery by governing officials during the Yi Dynasty. But none of this mattered to the old man. The only thing he knew and took interest in was the fact that in this city—no, in the entire island of Jeju—there was no larger building than Gwandeokjeong, and nothing that better conveyed "the past." One of the reasons his gaze was drawn to it as it drew further away—and why he looked so sad as it did so—was because the old man was the only person in the world who could be said to be a resident of the building. It had no caretaker. He didn't know why, but a massive iron lock dangled from the main doors all year long, left to do nothing but rust red from the slanting rain and wind. The roof had crumbled in places and was missing tiles, and the building itself was in ruins. It was for that reason that he'd decided to live there, soon after getting his job with the police. In the back of Gwandeokjeong (it was crowded with pine trees, and few people passed through there) he'd found a hole that led to a space underneath the flagstone floor of the main hall. In that way, the old man came to occupy the "room" beneath the greenery of Gwandeokjeong.

The old man swallowed his saliva and said farewell to his home: "Oh, Gwandeokjeong . . . I'll return, I promise.

I'll return by winter . . . " But different words of farewell lingered at the back of his throat. The old man's wrinkled cheeks reddened, but he gathered his courage and added in a voiceless murmur, "Oh, my sweet Seopun—I promise I'll return by winter . . . "

One can infer that his yearning for this Seopun woman made his separation from Gwandeokjeong all the more distressing. Right until he boarded the bus, he had maintained his grave manner and filled his heart with a resolve that resembled the great ambition of a hero, but once the bus started up and the city grew smaller and smaller in the rear window, he became overwhelmed with emotion. To save up for the "tariff of ninety won," he hadn't drunk a single glass of soju for many days, no matter how despondent it had made him. It wasn't strictly necessary to take the bus—you could walk to the village in a day—but the old man had decided to ride the bus in the end. The possibility that this vehicle of public transportation called the bus offered convenience and value beyond the merely monetary did not once occur to him. It was his belief that humans were made to walk, from birth until death. He certainly didn't think this contraption was worth forking over so much of his precious money. But today, at last, after many days of dedication and effort, the old man did indeed take the bus. In his sixty years of life, he had only taken the bus—or really, any kind of new-fashioned vehicle—once before. That first time was, you could say, the event that had led him to riding this bus for the "tariff of ninety won" today—the catalyst that had led to the old man's tragic, heroic resolve.

2.

The day that he was fired by the police, the old man left for the police station only after he saw the children who were on their way to the elementary school next to Gwandeokjeong safely pass by.

He went to the gloomy space that used to be a storage room and hung the bamboo basket from his shoulders as always, but it felt oddly light. He thrust his hand into the basket and was astonished to find that it was completely empty. The basket was used to carry the heads of deceased prisoners and partisans. What had happened to the head from yesterday? There was no way it could have come back to life and run away, so where was it? He went to the janitorial closet. The janitor sat there with an air of lofty superiority, but he looked equally worried as he told Old Man Boil that he didn't know what was going on.

The police officer in charge showed up soon thereafter. "You're fired," he said. "Director's orders." He did not give a reason why, only repeated himself two or three times and then asked the old man if he had anything to say for himself. It finally dawned on the old man that the police no longer had a use for him. He thought for a while, peeping up at the police officer's face with a seemingly witless and yet also crafty expression. "Nope, nothing to say," he finally said, and returned to the head storage room without another word. There, he unwound the hemp rope of the basket from his shoulders and looked up at the small transom window near the ceiling. Pure white sunlight suddenly slanted into the room, spilling onto the shelves and making the accumulated dust there look like a thick white membrane. Dried bloodstains had torn through the membrane in places. Up until yesterday, a large number of freshly severed heads had sat on the bottom shelves. The old man sat down in a daze and stuffed some tobacco into his pipe. The room was empty of everything but a thick, sour smell and the weak light from the transom.

Still, you couldn't keep the old man down for long. He took out the envelope of money he'd received from the police officer who was acting as the director's proxy and felt his spirits lift. The fact that they'd given him money made things much clearer. It was probably best if he didn't kick up a fuss (he'd heard of a jailer getting fired without ever receiving a salary!). In any case, what did it matter if he wasn't with the police anymore? Wasn't he still "Old Man Boil," the master of a special technique that guaranteed him at least one glass of soju any time he liked? The old man rose with renewed energy. He placed the basket on his shoulders one final time, then lowered it back to the ground and turned off the lights, even though that wasn't necessary. Even after exiting the room he lingered longingly for a while by the shut door. But eventually he made his way back to the director's proxy and told him, with as much offhanded breeziness as he could muster, "Well, then . . . I suppose it's best if you allow me to quit." With that, he exited the building.

"Hey, Old Man Boil!" A sentry he knew called out to him as he was making his way across the police yard.

"What's going on with you today? Where're you going?"

"You wanna know where I'm going? No need to worry, I'm just popping out to drink some soju. Hehehehe."

"Soju, eh? Hahaha, I'm not worried, I was just wondering what happened to your basket. Did you hear me? Your basket! Do people like you get time off, too?"

"No, it's not that . . . Er, I had the basket, but . . . there's not a single head today."

"Oh, yeah?" The sentry cocked his head. "Ah, I got it. I understand now. The person who walks around with axed heads got axed himself. I'm right, aren't I? Hahaha."

The old man gave a high-pitched laugh. "Why would I be fired?"

The sentry peered at the old man's protruding tooth, which was still firm and strong. "I suppose your tooth will come in handy again. You'll be able to suck out the pus from boils in no time."

"I said, why would I be fired?"

"I doubt you'd understand why, but there's no need to go around trying to identify those heads anymore," the sentry said. "These are the facts. Yesterday they caught a bunch of *ppalgaengi* (Reds) again and tossed them in jail like the trash they are. You remember how his excellency

Mr. President (Syngman Rhee) was here on the island, right? It's probably too complicated for someone like you to understand, but he came with the American general and other bigwigs. Remember? They even brought along their American warships, and those American planes that dropped fireballs—bombs, that is—from the sky . . . The operation was a success. Oh, 'operation' refers to the way that people go about winning battles. Anyway, the result is that the mountain rebels (partisans) were pretty well annihilated."

"Does that mean there's not gonna be any more war?"

The sentry abruptly clicked his heels together and stood rigidly at attention. "The chief's coming!" Then, in a sharp whisper: "You got your money, right?"

The old man straightened his shoulders, looked furtively at the sentry's face, and shook his head sideways. He walked jerkily away towards the main road.

As he exited the police gate, for once without the weight of the basket on his shoulders, the old man felt oddly sad. Usually around this time he would raise his voice, now hoarse and raspy from age, and cry out his usual "pronouncement": "Hey now, hey! Do any of you kind sirs and madams recognize this head? This bastard's head . . . this young handsome head . . . " But today his throat had clamped shut. People would no longer gather to his side. He felt anxious and insecure, like one of his appendages had been torn from his body, and it seemed to the old man that the eyes of those around him were glazed with boredom.

The summer sunlight that had descended all at once upon the city was beating down upon his forehead. The old man looked up at the sky and shook his upper body again and again, as if searching for the basket that was no longer on his shoulders. The sentry had told him that the "operation" had gone well after the arrival of his excellency Mr. President. It now occurred to him that his firing must therefore be the president's fault. *The nerve of the president! That wife of his is one of those big-nosed Americans. If only he hadn't come, I'd still be holding those young men's heads, stroking their black hair with these hands.* Whenever he put the cold heads of the dismembered young men to his cheeks, the old man felt a chill go through his body, followed by a rush of youthful energy that seemed to well up from deep within. Treating the bloodied heads as if they were his own children, the old man would meticulously wipe their faces clean with a wet cloth. For some reason he also loved raking his fingers through their black hair. In the winter he would sometimes go to a place far off in the cliffs, gathering the camellias that bloomed beside a deep pool there to later place inside the basket.

"Hmph, it's Syngman Rhee." He recalled the photo of Rhee that hung inside the police station, and for the first time the image of that stiff, palsy-looking face made him angry. "It's all because of that senile fool's 'operation' . . . " he muttered to himself as he walked along.

He could trace it all back to one summer afternoon last year (1948), just after his arrival in town, when he saw a policeman walking around with a head. Various measures had been taken to identify dead partisans whose names were unknown or who had died from police torture without revealing their origins, all so that the police could then investigate not only the partisans' links to the underground but also their family relations. They even plastered "proclamations" on the round pillars of Gwandeokjeong and put the criminal's head on public display. The head of anyone deemed a possible leader was stuck onto a bamboo spear, with a reward proclamation hung below it; the whole thing was then paraded around the city. Captured partisans were forced to carry the spears as armed policemen followed them from behind. In this way, the immediate and even extended relatives of the partisans were identified and rounded up one and all, and sometimes an entire village was set on fire and reduced to ashes. This was the kind of atmosphere the old man found when he strolled into town at high noon one summer day. He was understandably curious about the head basket being carried by the policeman, and he trailed the officer for some time. That was the chance encounter that eventually led to the old man's obtainment of his "government" job.

By the time the old man left the bar, loudly clearing his throat and parting the door curtain with his pipe, the sun was already high overhead. The light hurt his eyes, but in an agreeable way. He took a step outside but felt unbalanced, still not used to the fact that the only thing in his hand was his narrow pipe and the only thing at his side a phantom gap where the basket used to rest. The ground lurched beneath him with every movement of his mismatched legs and unsteady body. He was a little drunk. The people and buildings around him took on red and yellow tints with every wild lurch. The old man took in his surroundings. Passersby had stopped to stare at him. The old man snickered with laughter and held himself still, looking down at the ground. He began muttering something to himself. And then suddenly, in that peculiar tone of his, he yelled out his old line: "Hey now, hey . . . " The crowd burst into laughter. One woman kept laughing and laughing, her voice high and thin. Even at his age, the old man's ears were finely tuned to women's voices. His *palja* (fate) had kept him a bachelor for the past sixty-odd years and torn apart any bonds that might otherwise have made man and woman—*him* and woman—one flesh. His eyes narrowed with ecstasy as his gaze alit upon a young woman. He chuckled lewdly and gave the woman a sprightly bow. She promptly screamed and fled. Bah, he hadn't even run at her! With a wave of his pipe the old man flounced away in the opposite direction.

A jeep was parked in front of the *gisaeng* house called Nammungwan. The steady sound of drumming was spilling out of the building. Although he hadn't intended to come to the entertainment district, now that he was here he sat in the shadow of a nearby alley and stared at the building. He stayed there for some time, unsure why he'd come but unable to leave.

The old man stayed there for a long time. He later realized it was a long time, indeed, if he could outlast even the echo of the drums and singing voices. At some point he fell asleep. He woke up when two or three flashes of light etched themselves into his eyelids. "Hey! Hey!" a man was yelling. It was an unusually shrill voice for a man. As the old man leapt to his feet, a light flashed again, making his eyes open wide. A group of American soldiers were aiming cameras at him.

The men beckoned him into the sunlight, calling out his name in their mangled American accents. They eagerly gestured at him to make some sort of pose. The fact was, Old Man Boil was "famous" even among the American troops. With the soldiers was a Korean man with a GI haircut who kept to the background, perhaps because he didn't see the need to interpret or perhaps because he privately enjoyed seeing them do pantomimes. The old man retracted his head deep into his shoulders just like a toad but still managed to calmly stare back at the men before him. Suddenly he laughed—*hehehe*—and held out his hand. It was clear he was demanding money. One of the American soldiers cackled and spit out his gum. He withdrew something from his pocket and threw it to the ground. As soon as the old man reached for it, the camera went off again with a flash. It was gum, not cash. The old man let it lie where it was. And then, as if wishing to boast that he too had money, he let them have a glimpse of the bills he'd stashed in the pocket of his pants and retreated with a snicker to the shadow of the alley. The American soldiers seemed to find that even more amusing. They chortled as they climbed into the jeep and threw another piece of gum at him before driving away.

The old man did want to try gum at some point, but not like this. He swept up the gum the Americans had thrown, snapped them into two, and threw the pieces into the gutter. As a resident of the "Eastern Country of Propriety," the old man saw the actions of the *yangnom* (hairy foreigners) to be that of mangy curs that were inferior even to a little child. He didn't know by what means the world had been overturned in this way, but it was improper and indecent how these hairy foreigners waltzed in from their foreign lands and threw their weight around.

The old man was pleased to have finally found more

mangy curs to denigrate. When he turned around, however, his breath caught in his throat. Seopun was standing there, laughing softly. The only reason the old man didn't topple over from astonishment right then and there was because he was bolstered by the fact that he hadn't picked up and eaten the gum that the hairy foreigners had thrown at him. The old man had been waiting for this moment, but now he found himself completely speechless. Why did he, a sixty-year-old man, find himself turning red in front of this woman? He was a gentleman of the "Eastern Country of Propriety," and she was nothing but a *galbo* (prostitute) . . . one of the most ignoble women there was. And yet his heart hollowed out when he saw her, as if she were the Guanyin bodhisattva herself.

"Hehehe, ah, uh, it's right behind you . . . " he finally said, pointing at the gutter. He was referring to the fact that he'd thrown away the gum.

The woman looked intently at the old man one, two, three times. She glanced in the direction he was pointing but then fixed a smile on her lips and pressed some money into his hand. With a wink, she rearranged the bag under her arm and turned towards the sound of approaching footsteps. The gentleman she was with had caught up with her. She went off with him. For a long time afterwards, the fragrance from her cosmetics sat heavily upon him as if pressed there by an invisible palm.

I am not a beggar! He couldn't make himself throw the money into the gutter, but his face crumpled. The old man did take a few steps forward, as if about to run after her, but instead he took a deep breath and lit the end of his pipe.

He caught glimpses of her white rubber shoes peeping out from the swishing hem of her light russet skirt as she walked away. "How pathetic, to follow after a hairy foreigner!" the old man grumbled, looking back at the building she had exited from. "I see you're no different from the others. All young women are the same these days . . . " But for some reason, the hand that gripped her money began to shake uncontrollably. He tapped the end of his pipe against a nearby stone, dislodging the ash. Suddenly he gave out a strange keening wail and began running after the woman. During their encounter the old man had forgotten everything, even the fact that he'd been fired by the police. But now he knew he had to tell her, right or wrong, while the cash was still warm in his hands. He had an intuition that the money was directly related to his "pronouncements."

The old man ran. The way he ran was not much different from the large strides of a normal person in a hurry. There were alleys everywhere, and he couldn't find the woman in any of them. When he finally stopped and took stock of his surroundings, he realized he could see the sunlit tiled roof of Gwandeokjeong and the pine trees that grew beside it, looming at a distance over the low houses of this district. The black dots sitting in a row on the roof were probably crows. Gulls flew past each other in the air but never once settled on the roof. Their white bodies drew beautiful patterns against the backdrop of the mossy green tiles.

"'A pair of gulls, far removed from the sea, frolic on the banks of a lake deep in the mountains . . . '" The old man murmured this line of poetry with all the solemnity of a *seodang* (village school) teacher. When he was younger, he had on numerous occasions asked fortune tellers to consult various divination books in the hopes of escaping his fate as a *chonggak*. The results were always the same: "a pair of gulls, far removed from the sea . . . " Apparently the stars were aligned in his favor, promising something greater than the conventional marriages of the hoi polloi. He didn't really understand how it all worked, but in any case he gladly paid what little money he had to the fortune tellers and entrusted his future to the powers that be. But while August 15, 1945 (the day of Korea's liberation) should have been the start of a new era, the stars only grew duller, not brighter, with the passing of the years, and refused to bestow upon him a mate with whom he could "frolic on the banks of a lake."

The old man watched as the flock of crows took flight. The white gulls continued to swoop through the air. "Heh, maybe I'm a crow," he muttered to himself. And then, inexplicably, he saw Seopun—a different Seopun from the one he'd met earlier. She materialized out of thin air, there on the tiled roof of Gwandeokjeong, only to then vanish behind it . . .

Although his relationship with Seopun would bring nothing but misfortune to the old man, he would never forget the first time he met her. It was the first time in the entirety of his long life that a woman had visited him. That she was a young and beautiful woman only made it that much more memorable.

It happened one evening some time ago, when

the nights were still chilly. He'd been lying in his lair underneath Gwandeokjeong, drinking some alcohol. It was pitch-black. The old man was not asleep, but even with his eyes open he could see nothing. Still, at some point he was able to sense the presence of someone or something nearby. At first he thought it might be the captain's dog, but that didn't make sense; the dog would be able to find him even in total darkness. The sound he was hearing was also not coming from himself. While low and faint, it was undeniably the voice of a woman calling out someone's name. Jeju had long had a reputation for its specters and monsters. If he wasn't just hearing things, the other possibility was that she was a ghost (he was sure now it was female, in any case). But would a ghost bother haunting a man like him? Such a thought never occurred to the old man. He took a match from his pocket and struck it. The area around him instantly grew brighter, as if he'd set fire to the air itself. He used the fire to light the candle beside his pillow. The voice broke off its call for a while, then started up again. The old man went to the entrance of his home. (The "entrance" was a hole in the paving stones that lined the main hall of Gwandeokjeong; it was just big enough for a person to wriggle through with some effort.) If it was a monster, he reasoned to himself, it would probably flee at the sight of the fire. He raised the straw mat that covered the hole and was hit with the thick scent of *gisaeng* makeup. It was coming from a young woman. *If she can give off a smell, she must be human.* The face that wavered in the candlelight was that of a prostitute he'd often seen around town. Instead of letting the old man climb out, the woman climbed in, glancing behind her as she did so.

"It's so cold and windy outside," she said, putting the straw mat back in place. Crouching there beside the old man, she looked around at her surroundings and gave out a deep sigh. The light managed to illuminate the nearby walls, which consisted of the rough underside of the stone paving and some giant wooden beams close overhead, but the candle didn't have the power to banish the darkness that pressed in all around them. The shadows thrown by the two individuals, the stones, and the beams almost looked like alive, and the interplay of movement created an eerie effect. The woman occasionally tipped her head to observe some new discovery. Beneath her makeup, her skin gleamed with nervous sweat. She was not one to usually take notice of her own scent, but faced with this cold air that harbored hundreds of years of history, the smell of her makeup was no doubt more useful than the candle in bolstering her nerves. It was her smell that overwhelmed and intoxicated the old man above all else. To him, it was the uncanny emanation of a divine entity; it was the sublime scent of a lotus in paradise. When he finally returned to reality, he realized that the young woman's eyes were fixed upon him.

"I'm sure this must be the first time for you to get a visitor like me, so late at night," she commented as she took off her neckerchief. "This place is terribly interesting."

"Interesting? Hm, I guess so . . . Hehehe, this is my home—" The old man was quite proud of that fact. In the candlelight, the vague contours of the woman's face looked like a disembodied shadow or picture.

The woman's request was simple: she wanted him to sell her a head. She offered to give him money in exchange for a certain head among the many that he carried around town. She did not tell him the name of the head or its relation to her. It wouldn't have mattered anyway; heads were only "circulated" because the authorities hadn't been able to identify them, either because the individuals refused to reveal anything even under torture or because their origins were obscure for other reasons. By circulating the heads, the authorities tried to find leads that would let them root out their family relations, background, and other relevant information. The woman said the man's age was around twenty-seven. She described his features and told the old man to look for two crowns on his back right teeth and an inch-long scar on the right side of his head, where there was a bald patch. She pressed money into the old man's hand and then covered his hand with her own soft palms. It was her eyes that surprised the old man. Her pleading expression abruptly transformed into a coquettish smile, and in that instant her black eyes gleamed like fathomless pools in her wax-like face. A twisted, dangerous smile hovered on her lips, sending the old man's heart into a frenzy. The pounding of his chest reverberated against the candle holder, and the whole world tilted. The woman released his hands and told him she would do just about anything for him if he found the head for her. Then she left.

Smoking his pipe, the old man kept thinking about what a strange night it had been. He spread the money she'd given him around the candle and counted the bills again and again. There was no doubt about what it was: cold, hard cash. Without the evidence of the cash, he would probably have thought that it was all a dream. Another piece of evidence was the cloying scent that still lingered in the air. The hand that she'd grasped almost seemed to be glowing faintly. To him, that hand was no longer that of a sixty-year-old person but one that belonged to someone else, someone younger. He rubbed his hands together for a long time, then cautiously pressed them to his cheeks. He'd never experienced such a thing in his entire life, not even in his dreams. The old man may have wept, that night. He embraced his own hands.

What would she do with the head she'd bought? It wasn't that difficult to sneak a head out. Each one had a number attached to it, but every couple of days some of them would be carelessly thrown away, once the heads started piling up. On average, around seven or eight people died in the police cells each day. A truck came at dawn to take them away. The heads were loaded onto the same truck and later buried in a mass grave. As long as you properly disposed of it afterwards, one missing head wouldn't be noticed. But what would she do with the head she'd bought? Regardless, the old man had promised her he'd help. He'd taken her money and vowed to keep her secret safe.

This encounter would have been more than enough to forever enshrine the woman in the old man's memories, but afterwards there was another incident—this time in broad daylight—to rival the first. To be precise, it was the incident that led him to buy a bus ticket for a "tariff of ninety won" and set out on his current journey.

The old man had decided he must return the money to the woman—to Seopun—at all costs. He climbed to the top of the steps at Gwandeokjeong and looked down at everyone who passed by, but when he was unable to find her that way, he made his way to the wharf. The space below Gwandeokjeong was his home only at night; he had no connection to it during the day, not even as a shelter from the rain or snow.

The old man knew he'd find many friends among the candy peddlers and shoeshine boys who hung out at the wharf. There was a strong wind blowing along the coast. Huge waves crashed against the breakwater, spraying water everywhere, and the air was heavy with the smell of the sea.

The old man stood at one end of the wharf and gazed

at the sea. An ocean liner and a few smaller boats bobbed in the water, but they were dwarfed by an American warship offshore. Far beyond, a mountain of white clouds limned the blue horizon. The harbor was crowded and noisy, and no one paid any attention to the old man. They would have, if only he had his head basket, but unfortunately he did not.

"Hey, Gramps, what's wrong?" a young man called out as he diligently buffed a customer's shoes. "You on vacation today?" The shoeshine boy got along well with the old man, but he took his job very seriously and didn't let the old man distract him. The old man laughed in response and settled down in front of the customer, next to the shoeshine boy. He stole a glance at the customer's face, then at the shoe tips that steadily grew shinier with every movement of the shoeshine boy's hands. He next considered the young man's grubby face.

"You, er . . . you know that whatchamacallit, that rubbery stuff the hairy foreigners eat?"

"Chewing gum, you mean."

"Er, right. Want some?"

"*Hey! Okay!*" the young man said, speaking in English. The old man seemed to grasp that "okay" was an affirmative answer. He went over to one of the boys selling candy on the street and bought some gum from him. The candy peddler followed the old man back, his curiosity piqued, and the old man gave him some gum, too. The three of them popped the gum in their mouths at the same time. The gum tickled the old man's throat, and he giggled. The young men attempted to imitate his lewd giggle, but ended up laughing in earnest themselves.

The shoeshine boy spoke. "You gotta change the way you laugh, Gramps. It's embarrassing." He abruptly leaned forward. "Take a look at that lady over there! She's a real looker." The candy peddler put his fingers to his lips and whistled sharply. The man accompanying the woman turned his head a little at the sound, but the two continued on their way without pause. The old man had been watching the young men with a complacent smile, but all of a sudden he twisted his body and opened his eyes wide. It was Seopun. He leapt up with a gasp, his hands clutching at the air. He nearly tumbled forward in his haste, but finally managed to right himself and grasp the hem of Seopun's skirt just as she was about to be swallowed up by the crowd.

"I-I have something to tell you!"

Seopun wasn't the only one who was surprised. The gentlemanly manner of the man beside her crumbled instantly as he let out a strange piercing scream and stumbled back a few paces. The young men, too, found their mouths agape and their legs frozen at the old man's unexpected behavior. It didn't take too long for Seopun's companion to regain his composure. Upon closer inspection, it was clear that he was a gentleman from the "Republic of Korea," and he responded in exactly the manner one might expect of such a person: he cursed up a blue streak, refusing to give the old man any time at all to explain himself, and then sent the old man flying with a kick. A few of the young men tried to rush the so-called gentleman, but they were thwarted by the crowd. In the "Republic of Korea," all crowds had just as many policemen as they did pickpockets—whether or not the police were there to catch the pickpockets was up for debate, but in any case you could always count on some plainclothes officers to be there.

"The *gae* (dogs) are here!" someone yelled. The young men hastily packed up their tools of trade and scattered. The old man also rose to his feet. As he scooped up his pipe his eyes met those of the person in front of him. He snickered and ran after the young men, but it seemed they were much practiced in the art of vanishing—he couldn't find them anywhere. Someone began to shout "Thief! Thief!" The old man decided that he too should disappear into the crowd.

That evening, the old man stopped by Nammungwan on his way home from a bar, but of course they didn't let him in. He had to find a good pretext for returning the money to Seopun. She'd given him more money, even though he hadn't yet found the head she wanted. At Nammungwan, he insisted that he had business with Seopun. The women who were seated at the entrance laughed themselves silly when he said that.

"How about me, hon?" one of them asked him.

"I have no business with the likes of you."

The women went into hysterics again. The mistress of the house came to the entrance. She too wore a nice perfume, but the old man still refused to move. Eventually the mistress angrily told him that he couldn't meet with any of the women of the house unless he had money. The old man carefully laid out all the money he had on the floor. The mistress's expression changed subtly, and she exchanged a considering look with the woman beside her. But finally she announced, "That's no good. Where do you think you are? If you do have business with her, then you'll need a much larger sum of money than that!"

It was the first time in his life he'd ever stepped inside a *gisaeng* house, and only after a great amount of vacillation. But as soon as he did, he found himself filled with courage. It must also be said that he was drunk. So he persisted, begging the mistress to let him see Seopun for just a little while. Although the mistress continued to refuse him, a part of her must have felt some hesitation given how often she looked at the woman beside her. In the end, the old man became overexcited and lashed out at the women, screaming that he knew the chief of police and lots of other important people and that he was no ordinary man himself. As he ranted, a tough-looking young man emerged from the depths of the house with an impatient look on his face. "How 'bout it, Mr. Hotshot—you know me?" he sneered, and summarily threw him out of the house.

The old man was eventually able to retrieve his money; once he did so, he settled down in the same alley as before and glared at Nammungwan. It was late and the streets were dark. Curfew had started some time ago, and there was no sign of other people outside. There was no way Seopun would come out now. The moon rose above the rooftops. The old man desperately needed to meet with her. He had to see her in order to return her money; or, put another way, he had to return her money in order to see her. His desire to return the money fueled his desire to see her, until all that was left was the simple thought: *I want to see her.* He decided not to go back to Gwandeokjeong.

At some point he noticed a dog sitting nearby, staring patiently at him. It was the captain's crippled dog. It had shaggy fur and a face like a bear, and couldn't run well at all. The dog harbored a particular affection for the old man. The old man scooped the dog to his chest and stroked it all over, from head to crippled leg. The dog licked his face as he petted its head. The old man and the dog were able to fight off their mutual loneliness in this way. The dog kept licking its sticky tongue over the old man's lips until finally the old man stuck out his own tongue and licked the dog back. The old man held the dog's warm body to him and stayed like that for a long time.

The dog finally squirmed and tried to wriggle out of the old man's hands. Seeing that its ears were pricked forward, the old man realized that another dog was keening somewhere nearby. The old man relaxed his grip and the dog instantly leapt forward. It stood poised on the ground, listening attentively to the other dog. Soon the shadow of the other dog emerged from the opposite side of the street. The crippled dog raised its muzzle and howled at the night sky. The second dog moved closer. The old man called out to the crippled dog, his voice filled with sadness, trying to get him to stay. The dog hesitated and looked at the old man's face for some time, but then abruptly ran off in the other direction.

"Heh heh, I guess it's no surprise that you, too, prefer your master . . . " To his own surprise, the old man found he was crying. He watched the two dogs nuzzle each other and then disappear together into the moonlit alley.

The next morning, the old man awoke earlier than anyone else in town and continued his angry vigil on Nammungwan. But even as the sun climbed higher in the sky the woman still did not come out, not even by noon. The old man sat and thought for quite some time. He tapped the ash from his pipe and then gripped it hard. Full of determination, he got up and approached Nammungwan. At the same moment, a man wearing tinted glasses came out of the entrance and looked around him. It was the same horrible young man from last night. Startled, the old man turned on his heels, pretending that nothing had happened, and departed.

But good fortune is a strange thing; one never knows when it may strike a person, however roundabout a manner it takes. After polishing off a glass of soju, the old man returned to Gwandeokjeong in the early afternoon. He sat down on the stone steps with an air of exhaustion, lit his pipe, and looked up at the sky. He noticed, first of all, how wide it was. And then how deep blue and clear. But what of it? What relation did any of that have to the affairs of life? The literati of old might have looked at the fleecy clouds hanging gracefully in the sky and composed a poem in response. Sipping on some alcohol, they would have then ponderously intoned the words aloud. "Things like clouds and moons, what use are they? Even if I could put them in the pocket of my pants, they'd be no help at all . . . "

When the old man finally dropped his gaze from the sky back to the human world, he saw none other than

Seopun in the distance. He couldn't believe his eyes. It was undeniably her. She was carrying some kind of heavy-looking luggage that weighed down her shoulders, and a pretty little frown was on her face. Completely flustered, the old man almost let the situation slip away from him. By the time he regained his composure, she was already flagging down a *jigekkun* (a laborer who wore A-frames on his back to carry things). The old man jumped down the steps and ran towards her. The luggage had already been placed atop the *jige* (A-frame), and the elderly porter was squatting down to pass the *jige* ropes through his arms.

For some reason, the old man was filled with intense jealousy at the sight. It was a feeling he'd never felt towards the various gentlemen who had walked beside Seopun—men who had probably had their way with her. But this was different. The old man had found a nemesis who was on equal footing with him.

"Whaddya think you're doing, huh?" The old man pulled at the *jige* the other man was attempting to raise.

Unbalanced, the elderly *jigekkun* fell on his backside with his legs splayed out before him. "What am I doing . . . ?" he repeated, rising with a wild look on his face.

"I'm the one who's gonna carry this!" the old man asserted firmly. The *jigekkun* stood there dumbly, overwhelmed by the old man's extraordinary expression, as the old man transferred the package to his own shoulders.

The *jigekkun* looked at his young female customer. He let out a sad cry. "Old Man Boil . . . "

"What?"

"Why're you asking what I'm doing . . . Did I do something to offend you?" The *jigekkun* was clearly rattled. His voice had no confidence, perhaps because he thought he'd made some kind of mistake. "What karma is this, for you to interfere in my business?"

"It's not business. I'm doing this for free."

"*Free*?" The *jigekkun* took another good look at the old man's face. He pulled himself together. "I see. You're planning to get in my way, is that it, you bastard?"

"Get in your way? Heh heh. All I'm saying is that I'm free—"

"Nothing's free in this world!"

The people in this "Republic of Korea" of ours, particularly those who are approaching old age, tend to draw out their fights using words instead of fists. In the past, learned men would find ammunition in their *jokbo* (genealogy books) and other materials, tracing their lineage back to the days of ancient Korea and even all the way back to ancient China. Sometimes they'd draw their insults from Confucius and Laozi, sometimes from archaic texts like *Odes to the Red Cliffs* or *Romance of the Three Kingdoms.* They'd argue and eat dinner and keep arguing, and if no resolution was reached, they'd sleep for the night—only to continue on for hours more . . .

Fortunately these two individuals were not as learned as all that. Curious bystanders began to gather around the *jigekkun* and the unemployed old man; as the crowd swelled and the argument intensified, the customer and luggage in question were ignored. In the end, the "free" side won. But by that time, both customer and luggage had vanished.

The old man eventually caught up with Seopun as she was making her way to the bus depot. She told him that she was going to visit her family in T. Village. As they walked the old man forgot all about the luggage on his back.

The old man tried to walk at a distance from the woman. But then he remembered that he had something to tell her, so he was forced to draw closer. His face screwed up like that of a frightened child, he confessed that he'd been fired. Seopun didn't try to drive him away when he said that, so he told himself now was the time to return her money. But he lost his nerve at the last minute and drew back the hand that had been reaching out to her. His expression hardened, and he resolved not to bring up the issue of the head. The woman also seemed to want to avoid the topic; speaking rapidly, she simply told him she knew he'd been fired, and was glad that he was no longer doing that job. She was glad, she repeated. And then she asked him what he was going to do, and where he was going.

"I'm going to G. Village," the old man answered promptly. "G. Village—it's where an old acquaintance of mine lives. Don't worry, miss. Really, miss, it's okay. I'm glad I quit, too . . . It's just that I get a little sad, when I think about how I can't pat the faces of the young people anymore. It felt like they were my own children. Heh heh . . ."

At the depot, Seopun bought a ticket for herself as well as one for the old man. "Buying a ticket—does that mean riding the bus?" The old man looked down at his palm, at the ticket that had been handed to him, and immediately panicked. He walked close behind her like a flustered schoolboy. When the woman got on the bus, he hurriedly loaded her luggage onto the rack above her, then rushed out as if he'd forgotten something. After that he simply watched in agitation as passenger after passenger boarded the bus. When the engine roared to life, he was the only one left outside. The old man stood there in a daze. The woman stuck one white hand out the window and urged him on, and in that moment—just as he was putting one shaky foot on the first rung of the bus stairs while watching the woman's beautiful face—in that moment, the vehicle began to move. He boarded.

After all that, the old man couldn't just get off at T. Village with Seopun. He tried, telling her he'd bring the luggage to her house, but she gently but firmly refused. Looking like he might cry at any moment, the old man looked out the bus window and stared at Seopun as the bus sped away.

The old man got off at the next bus stop, which was still a long way off from G. Village. He spent almost half a day walking back the way he came. He arrived at the city, right back where he'd started, by nightfall.

3.

The old man's memories and hopes mingled together as the bus rattled over the bumpy rural roads. It was evening when the vehicle reached G. Village.

They arrived later than scheduled. In the middle of the journey, they'd received an official warning that there might be a surprise attack on K. Substation by the partisans—this despite the fact that police headquarters claimed that the partisans had been annihilated. The bus driver and passengers all knew that partisans didn't attack passenger vehicles, but they still had to follow the "considerate" instructions of the police.

In this way, the old man finally completed his journey. Memories of the first time he'd been lured onto the bus by a woman's beauty had combined with his hopes for the future to spontaneously lead him on what could indeed be called a journey. All he had to do now was figure out how to make his hopes come true. Even though those hopes were humble, they still required money. There were no more job prospects for him in town. His last remaining option for earning a living—curing boils—would only work in the more rural areas of the island; city folk were too "civilized," and they had too many of those newfangled clinics to go to. The old man had most likely come to the necessary conclusion that it was much easier to roam around the countryside looking for work. But it must be noted that the old man was different from your garden variety tramp. He was determined to save up the money he earned, and by winter—or so he'd promised Gwandeokjeong as he watched it recede into the distance from the bus window, and so he'd promised Seopun—by winter, he would return to the city.

The old man had once been surprisingly well-known and popular among the residents of G. Village, so when he arrived, he naturally assumed that people would greet him with enthusiasm. *Oh my, it's Old Man Boil!* he imagined they'd say. *It's been too long!*

The place had a permanent place in his heart, all thanks to one intense, unforgettable experience. In the village lived an eccentric middle-aged widow who had been suffering from a boil on her buttocks for some time. She had used a mirror to find the boil and squeeze it with her fingers, but it got infected from her hands and swelled up even more. One languid summer afternoon, this respectable widow secretly called the old man to her room. At first he had confined himself just to the infected area, but as the widow grew more relaxed from the indescribable sensation of his tongue—he was a professional, after all, and *she* was the one who had called *him*—half of her buttocks was laid entirely bare before either of them realized it. The old *chonggak* couldn't believe his own eyes; he had trouble breathing, and he forgot where he was. One can easily imagine the old man's apprehension when he discovered he was cradling the woman's bare buttocks. He squeezed his eyes shut and tried desperately to honor the sanctity of his profession. Frankly, the thin eyelids of a human being are not much use in such times. Two white round mounds emerged from the darkness behind his closed eyelids and drew ever closer to him. The fleshy protuberance inside his mouth was emitting a corona-like light and shooting off hot sparks. He knew if he opened his eyes he would faint. "*Aahh*," the woman breathed. It was the painful moment just before he squeezed the pus out. "That tickles . . . Oh no, oh no." His body felt her body writhing. She moaned. The old man had a pure soul; if it hadn't been for the widow's invitation, he would most likely have contented himself with some money for soju. The old man insisted that the excitement of the moment hadn't been his fault, but the woman never called for his services again. That winter, during one of the coldest days of the year, she passed away from acute pneumonia or something like it. After the widow's death, the old man often found himself thinking about the "pair of gulls, far removed from the sea . . . " fortune he had paid for with his meager savings when he was young. People gossiped that the incident with the widow was one of the indirect reasons why the old man left the village soon after.

But where were those people now? News of Old Man Boil's return had spread throughout the village even before he'd stepped one foot into the village proper (someone had seen him get off the bus), but no one greeted him. In the past, he could have counted on gates immediately being opened for him. Someone would have ushered him to a veranda and let him rest there as they plied him with food. This time, however, the villagers passed by in silence, avoiding him. The atmosphere was chilly.

Just then, he spotted an old acquaintance walking in his direction. "Old Dalsam, it's me! Is young Master Yi doing well?" The elderly Dalsam was on his way home from the fields, hoe in hand. He gave Old Man Boil a curt acknowledgement but continued on his way.

"What's going on with you, Dalsam? Have you completely changed, too?"

"Guess I have," said Dalsam, turning his head. His face was like stone, and only his mouth moved. "But what about you, riding a fancy bus? Either you've changed or the whole village has."

The atmosphere felt even colder and unwelcoming to the old man. Realizing that the doors would be shut against him tonight, he blurted out, "How's Master Yi doing?"

Dalsam had been trying to walk past the old man, but at that question he laughed and turned back to face him. "That's right, I remember you once sucked out his boils. These days he's been killing his pigs right and left and raising a big stink. He's been stuffing himself full, but he's still plagued by boils."

"I didn't 'suck out his boils.'" The old man's small eyes glittered. "Watch your language! As you very well know, I *cured his illness*."

"Same thing, in the end. So, why're you here? You come all the way to this village to find yourself some more heads?"

The old man sighed deeply at the word "heads." His expression turned unexpectedly rapturous. "The thing is . . . " He gave out another sigh, a distant look in his eye. "You have no idea what a young person's head is like. And anyway, back in town there's this young lady—"

"*Aigu,* you crazy old fool!" Dalsam refused to let Old Man Boil finish speaking. "I knew it, I knew it! I knew it wasn't a mistake. You've changed completely!"

The evening breeze stroked the old man's cheeks. Dalsam's furious yells could be heard from several feet away. Dalsam squared his shoulders, upon which his hoe still rested, and left the old man to his sighs.

Twilight dropped down upon the old man like a dusky wall. The frogs in the green paddies began to clamor in chorus, and the crows cawed as they returned to roost. Still, it was terribly quiet. The haze of twilight hung upon Mount Halla far off in the distance, making the mountain look like one of those depthless images from a shadow play. Its peak rose high and sharp into the sky.

The "roads" in the village were no better than the mountain paths that jutted along the rugged cliffs, and there were no streetlamps. The old man picked his way along very carefully, mindful of his lame leg. This place was different from the city. It wouldn't do for a man who had come all the way here from the city, on a bus no less, to spend the night on the roadside. The old man set out for the estate of Master Yi, who he figured would probably be suffering from boils brought on by the approach of summer. They did have a bond from the past, after all, and had even run into each other in the city once (although clearly he'd been quite busy then, as he hadn't paid the old man the slightest attention). Besides, he'd heard that the master was also affiliated with the police in some way.

The old man was easily able to identify Master Yi's giant house. But it had changed quite a lot since his last visit. Earthen walls had replaced the stone fences that were so common on this island. Something was going on; people were scurrying in and out of the new gate, which had been left open. Seeing how much had changed, he knew he would have to reformulate his strategy on how to ask for a place to sleep for the night. The smell of the new wooden gate, the earthen walls that had replaced the stone—all of it bothered him.

He was still loitering when a burly manservant stepped

outside the gate. Without missing a beat, the old man looked at the manservant and murmured, "Er . . . long time no see. This is all quite impressive. Uh, I arrived just a little while ago, from the city. I'm Old Man Boil. Old Man Boil, from police headquarters."

The manservant glanced down at the old man. He didn't let the old man finish; instead, he silently grabbed his hand and pulled him through the gate. The old man hesitated a little, but the other man was so strong that he was able to pull him along like a balloon. Night had fallen. It was strange—he had succeeded, but it felt all too easy. And the manservant hadn't reacted at all to the news that he'd come from the city. Still silent, the manservant now extended a meaty arm and gestured at the main building. *Go there*, he seemed to be saying. The old man looked up and down at the manservant, but hurriedly walked away upon seeing the annoyed expression on his face. He could see it clearly thanks to the lamp that hung from the gatepost. But then he soon returned, with the air of someone who had just remembered something. "You're deaf, aren't you?" he said with a laugh. "Haha, thanks for the hard work." He then proceeded on his way once again. He was surprised to see that the area around the main building was bustling with people, their upper bodies lit by the light of the lamps. From the veranda, the old man peered into the house. An enticing aroma cut through the commotion to rouse his appetite, and he heard the sound of meat and *jeon* (Korean pancakes) sizzling on the stove somewhere. Now that he'd managed to step through the gate, he knew he'd be able to find a place to sleep inside the estate. Even if it was just the shed, or out in the courtyard underneath the moon—even so, he could say that he'd stayed at young Master Yi's home.

It looked like they were getting ready for *jesa* (memorial services for one's ancestors) tonight. The women were bustling about with their skirts bound up with string they had wound around their waists. He didn't see the young master, but some older people who may have been his relatives were huddled together in some sort of discussion. He looked over their shoulders and saw that the *jesang* (memorial table) had been set up in the back of the room. This was quite fortuitous indeed. He would only have to put up with his empty stomach for a little while longer.

The number of people in the house increased as the night wore on. Straw mats were placed in the courtyard, and latecomers were put there to hold court with the moon. There was even a *seonbi* (classical scholar) who used the opportunity to declaim his views on the arts, pausing occasionally to give an old-fashioned, haughty cough. The moonlight poured down like silver over the edges of the gathering clouds, and the flowing white clothes of the people in the courtyard were pale and ethereal in the darkness. With great composure, the old man joined the group of individuals sitting on the straw mats. But he still made sure to keep one cautious ear on the squabbles around him.

Their conversations swayed like balancing scales across the fulcrum of their family relations. *I'm the thirteenth* chon *of the head of the family* (a *chon* is a unit that expresses the kinship distance between relatives. For example, three *chon* is the distance between uncle and niece; four *chon*, the distance between cousins) someone would say, prompting another person to claim that they were thirty *chon* because they'd shared the same ancestor sixteen generations ago, during King So-and-So's reign in the Yi Dynasty. As one might expect, those who could prove their kinship through the *jokbo* and those who engaged in these *chon* debates with the most ease and authority were the close relatives of the young master.

"Huh, what's my *chon* number again . . . ?" At some point, the old man had fallen into the delusion that he too was a distant relation. At that moment, the courtyard suddenly flooded with light, and several lamps were hung from the eaves of the house. All the doors were thrown open. A single cough sounded against the expectant silence. The entire house fell still.

An elderly man with a long, dignified beard entered the room and greeted first the guests there, then those in the courtyard. This was the uncle of the young master.

The uncle began his speech by proclaiming that all those gathered here before the ghosts of the family's ancestors were not "guests" at all but family, in both name and reality, and should therefore feel completely at home. He then said some confusing things about how it would soon become clear that people who they didn't know were relatives would become their relatives soon.

Even though the ancestor they were honoring tonight had, according to the *jokbo*, over a thousand descendants left on Jeju Island, his *sanso* (grave) had fallen into utter neglect and the proper rites had failed to be observed for all too long. It went without saying, the uncle continued, that this state of affairs was harming our illustrious clan and, by extension, going against the fine customs of our "Country of Propriety."

And then: "Before their arrival on Jeju, the Yis of Jeonju birthed countless noble men, from prime ministers to other leaders of governance. Our ancestor of the sixteenth generation whom we are honoring today through *jesa* was himself a high-ranking official from the Yi Dynasty, as you know . . . " He continued in this vein for some time, all the while combing his fingers through his long beard. None of it was of much interest to the old man.

Master Yi finally entered the room, drawing everyone's attention. He wore mourning attire over his white clothes. First he put a hand to his hip and looked up at the moon for a while, then swept his gaze through the crowd in the courtyard. He gave a deep bow of his head. When he did so, he put a finger to the bridge of his glasses to keep them in place, but still they slipped forward. No one did anything as modern as clapping, of course, but the people in the courtyard began bobbing their heads up and down and whispering together. The old man craned his neck. The lamplight caught on the newfangled glasses on the young man's beefy face and exposed his glossy, silken skin. There was no indication that he was suffering from boils of any kind. "Hm, maybe they've formed on his bottom?" A man who was sitting in front of the old man turned around and glared at him.

Although he was a young man of the modern world, the master's way of speaking was rather old-fashioned, anachronistic, and hard to follow. This was the twenty-sixth year of the sexagenary cycle, he declared, and therefore we must strive all the more to honor the name of our clan. Our revered ancestor passed his higher civil service exams during such a year, and the clan's *samcheon* (star fortune; a superstitious way of selecting grave sites according to the principles of feng shui) had revealed an auspicious omen for prosperity . . . Essentially, the young master was making an election speech about how they *must* get one of their own elected to the National Assembly in the next by-election, no matter what. He was mobilizing all his relatives to vote for him and to devote themselves to his campaign.

It was hard to fault his logic. As the hundreds of years of history contained in the *jokbo* showed, in this "Republic of Korea" some people drove away even their own beloved wives in order to maintain the "harmonious union" of their *jongsi* (relatives). Given that, it was not a bad idea at all to have a "great dignitary" in one's family. *If I can't achieve fame, then at least my relative . . .* Uncles, siblings, nephews, grandchildren—the sacred book that was the *jokbo* silently attested to these kinships. An elderly man might point to a "great dignitary" and proudly boast that the man was his nephew (even if he was in fact several dozen *chon* removed). If one's nephew was great, the logic went, then that meant the uncle must be great, too.

This logic was not limited to familial relations. If the village produced even a single "great dignitary" or even someone like a lawyer, from that day onwards the tax burden would ease at least for a while; the villagers could also look forward to fewer odious visits from the police. That's why it was such a big deal when a village produced someone of importance. The police and tax collectors who had previously hounded the village would instead descend upon the neighboring villages like a swarm of mosquitos.

It was for this reason that one could hear the ceaseless sound of hammering in the homes of those "families of note" who were vying for a government post. Carpenters went in and out of their homes on a daily basis. Wobbly *jesa* tables that had been relegated to the storage shed were unearthed and repaired. It was something of a fad these days to call forth the spirits of ancient ancestors who had previously been utterly forgotten and declare "filial piety" to them. Family members would gather many times a year to perform *jesa*, all for the sake of a "harmonious union."

As it turns out, the ostracism that our Old Man Boil had faced earlier that evening was a blessing in disguise. While tomorrow was still anyone's guess, for today at least he would be able to eat, drink, and sleep to his heart's content. A lavish feast was already being brought into the room. One by one, relatives came into the room and performed the usual rite: crouching down on their hands and knees in front of the *jibang* (paper Buddhist mortuary tablet) upon which the name of their ancestor had been written in calligraphic ink, they struck their forehead to the floor and intoned their gratitude. The old man used the opportunity to fill his belly. Once the *paje* (the last rites of the memorial service) had concluded, more food was brought in and another round of campaign speeches commenced, delivered with antiquated flourishes that felt musty and disused. By that point the old man had become pleasantly intoxicated. The last thing he saw before he fell into a deep sleep was the moon shining above him.

The next day, the old man finally ran into Master Yi. He was quite surprised to see that the young master was smiling and in an obliging mood. As the old man fidgeted and squirmed, the master told him he knew he'd been fired, and that he was grateful for his attendance at his ancestor's *jesa*. Then: "How would you feel about joining the clan of the Jeonju Yis? You'd be my relative, in other words. You're not getting any younger, and if you're not entered in a family registry there will be no one to perform the rites for you after you die." That certainly made sense. And he couldn't ask for better than to become a member of young Master Yi's family, could he? The old man readily consented. He knew that his family name was Jeong, although he wasn't sure how to write it. Well, now it didn't matter; he threw away that old name with alacrity.

The young master explained to Old Man Boil that because he was elderly, it wouldn't do to make him a younger sibling, nor would it do for him to join the uncles he already had. "Be my nephew," was the conclusion. The old man looked for a while at the eyes that glittered with a cold light behind the young master's glasses. No one would have blamed the old man for feeling dissatisfied at having such a pup of a man as an "uncle," but what was genealogy anyway but a collection of lines drawn out of the blood relations of unknown ancestors? At any rate, that wasn't the old man's fault. "Nephew, grandson—it's all the same to me," he said. He agreed to be recorded in the family register.

The next task was to christen him. The young master's *hangnyeolja* (a shared sinograph that was used in the given names of siblings and cousins, in order to indicate that one was part of the same bloodline and same generation) was *hae*, the sinograph for "ocean" (representing the element of water). *Tong*, the sinograph for "barrel" (representing the element of wood), had been selected for the names of the next generation. In this way, Old Man Boil was reborn as Yi Baektong.

The young master's adolescent daughter wasted no time in coming up with a new nickname for the old man, teasingly calling him "Little Cousin Old Man Boil." It was not just her. The other children began referring to him as "Big Bro," and not in a respectful way. He didn't mind when the young master's daughter called him such things, but to be called "Big Bro" by those runny-nosed brats was too much. As he argued back and forth with the brats by the earthen fence, this time it was the young mistress's turn to scold him: "Baektong, enough! Bring over some firewood right now!" Then there was the young master's uncle, who called him "grandson" while stroking that long beard of his, even though they were nearly the same age. To add salt to the wound, he was forbidden from smoking anywhere near the uncle.

In time, the old man found himself with a number of new "younger brothers." A man who used to loiter around the police substation on the main road showed up one day with the rather pompous name "Yi Cheontong." Two or three others swiftly followed. Naturally, the old man took it upon himself to play the older brother. But one of the men, a seedy-looking person with a twitchy eye, put it plainly: "You're nothing but a senile fool. There's no way I can accept you as an older brother." His twitchy eye fixed itself upon his fellow brothers. "We've already decided who to listen to—and it ain't you, old dolt."

The old man told himself that it didn't matter in the end whether he was a younger brother or a grandson or great-grandson. His most pressing goal was to make some money and then return to the city. Although the old man was the oldest among the "brothers," the young master had already decided that the twitchy-eyed man was to be the leader of the group. The young master would give orders to Twitchy Eye, and Twitchy Eye would then pass them on to the master's underlings, the old man included. The orders included registering more people into the Yi clan, using whatever enticements—including free food, money, merchandise, etc.—were necessary to get them to sign up. In this country, once someone was added to a family registry (with the cooperation of the local authorities, of course) they were given voting rights. Their "votes" could then be manipulated freely by the political candidates.

The old man took a break for the time being from his career as Old Man Boil and set out on the campaign trail. That is, he went out looking for potential targets for registration. He was given some money as "capital" for this venture and was told that he'd receive a commission if he obtained good results.

But this seemingly simple task turned out to be harder than he thought. For one, there was a lot of competition among the "families of note" in this part of Jeju, which didn't have as many beggars and vagrants as the big cities on the mainland. For another, the people here didn't really respect the candidates of the "families of note," perhaps due to the influence of the partisans who had made Mount Halla their main base of operations.

He therefore found himself returning to Master Yi's home only once every three or four days. Most of his time was spent roaming remote villages, searching for potential clients for his patented boil remedy. He did manage to earn some cash that way. He knew he'd be berated by Twitchy Eye as soon as he returned, so he decided to only return after he'd managed to register even a single person.

One late fall day, the old man found himself walking along a road in a village that was far inland. The wind was gusting noisily through the poplar trees. The old man sat beneath one of the trees and puffed a bit on his pipe, but his thirst distracted him. Because the village was situated near the mountains, he knew he could easily find some rainwater or pond water to filter and drink. He set off to find a pond, but his search was interrupted by the sound of shouting. He headed in the direction of the voices and soon arrived at a pond that was tinted a muddy yellow by the sun. At the edge of the small pond was a large angry mob of people who had formed a circle around something. A handful of them were waving long poles over everyone's heads.

Once you reach the age of sixty, you may find that your priorities change. The old man was less interested in joining angry mobs and rubbernecking than he was in relieving his thirst. He got down on his belly and started to drink from the pond.

"Hey, Gramps!" someone yelled. "Don't do it! Don't drink the water!" A farmer ran over and roughly pulled the old man back from the pond, just as his mouth grazed the surface.

"But I'm dying of thirst!"

"I said you can't drink it!"

The farmer dragged the old man into the crowd. The old man waved his pipe at everyone, just as he used to do with the children in the city. By the time he realized that waving his pipe had accomplished nothing, he was surrounded by villagers. The farmer silently pushed his way through the human wall and pointed at what that human wall had been encircling. It was a single man, crouched low on the ground, bracing himself against the wave of anger directed at him.

"Who's that old guy?" someone asked.

"No need to worry," the farmer declared. "This here is a good citizen who wanted to drink some water."

The man on the ground was in bad shape; it looked like he'd been tossed around and punished in some way. His clothes were even more ragged than the ones the old man had worn during his rounds as a head circulator. They were so soiled with blood and pus and dirt that you couldn't even tell they'd originally been white. The rips exposed bluish black bruises on the skin. Bald patches the shape of copper coins dotted his head. One of the men in the mob was resting his chin on a long pole with his lower lip stuck out. He looked like he was at a loss as to what to do next, perhaps because he'd already gotten his punches in. The mob waved their arms around and yelled at the man on the ground to speak, but they got no response. The man kept his arms clutched around his head, his elbows planted firmly in the dirt. He was shivering. The mob didn't attempt to close in on him; no one seemed to know what to do.

"I know—" said the owner of the long pole, suddenly turning towards the old man. "Let's ask this stranger. We've got ourselves a problem here. Got any wisdom for us, Gramps?"

"—Wisdom? What kind of wisdom?"

"This man has leprosy . . . "

The old man gasped. "Leprosy!"

The farmer spoke. "The thing is . . . You tried to drink from the pond water just now, didn't you? This leper bathed in the water. Our priceless drinking water . . . "

The old man gasped even louder.

Coming up with some wisdom required hearing the whole story first. It was true that the leper had recently arrived at the village, but no one knew from where. The villagers couldn't possibly be expected to play nice to a leper that even the government had abandoned, could they? So it was also true that they'd bullied him. One moonlit evening, the leper waited until everyone had fallen asleep and then entered the pond that was the source of the village's drinking water. He bathed himself in the water in retaliation. The wife of O-seobang (a form of address that used to be attached to the family name of individuals without civil service positions) had discovered him there. There was a great uproar, naturally. The villagers had leapt out of their beds and homes. Here was the strange thing, though: even when they hit him and yelled at him, the leper remained silent, crouched there on the ground. He stayed in the same spot all through the night. The villagers were stymied. It would take half a day to contact the substation that was located on the main road near the coast, and in any case the police were likely too busy with their primary occupation of hunting down the "Reds."

The old man tried to squeeze out some "wisdom" for the occasion, but wisdom wasn't something one could suck out like a boil, and even the old man knew better than to try. He finally decided he would bring the leper back with him. For some reason, he was hit by a surge of sympathy. The man was most likely unregistered, anyhow, which meant that the young master would surely welcome him. There was no way they'd let him sleep in the house, but that would be the case no matter where the leper went, so he might as well let the master's village take care of him. Who knew what would happen if he was left here? These villagers were desperate for his help, and the ocean water was better for bathing, anyway.

"Right. People of the village, I have some good wisdom for you . . . I'll take him off your hands." The villagers were stunned. "I'll take 'em away."

"—What kind of wisdom is that?"

"Take *what* away?"

Everyone looked at each other in bewilderment. Then they turned their gaze towards the old man with their mouths agape. The old man's mouth, meanwhile, was firmly shut. Wild joy warred with keen, cold suspicion in the villagers' eyes.

Once they realized he wasn't lying, however, the villagers began to cheer. What a miracle this was! No one knew how and where this shabby old man, who had chosen to drink their muddy pond water instead of begging for a cup of water at one of the farms, had come to have the wisdom he did. *Just who are you, sir?* the villagers asked. "I'm Old Man Boil," the old man proclaimed proudly.

That answer got an audible response from the crowd, particularly from the awestruck wives. "You're *that* Mr. Old Man Boil?" The old man was an instant hero. He was ushered into house after house, followed by a long line of admirers, and plied with alcohol from day to night. And the patients, oh yes—he gained many patients. It didn't end there. To have a leper as a companion on the road . . . well, that meant that the villagers were eager to collect donations for their traveling expenses. The old man was given a fat drawstring purse filled with cash. The old man was greatly pleased by all of this. Puffing contentedly on his pipe, he accepted everything that was offered to him.

The old man kept a tight grip on the money. But then, Seopun's smiling face flashed like a ghostly superimposition over the face of the farmer's wife who was pouring him alcohol. He looked down at his bowl and saw Seopun's face wavering there, too. So that was that. After promising some that he would visit again soon and promising others that he might even settle down there permanently one day, he took the leper and left the village.

The leper was quite docile. Although the old man didn't ask him to, the leper made sure to keep a few paces away as they made their way back to the young master's home. For those who belonged to the lowest classes (and this included the old man), the only means of transportation was their own two feet, and home was where you made it. But just as the old man had predicted, the young master didn't allow them to make his home their own. As the old man described what had happened, the color drained from the young master's face and the muscles on his forehead began to twitch. He yelled for the manservant and had him throw the old man out. His companion was waiting outside the gate. The young master's parting words were shouted at the manservant, behind the old man's back: "Don't—don't touch him!"

The sun had set. When the two reached the main road, the old man asked, "What will you do? Where are you gonna go?"

"You don't need to worry about me," said his companion. "With my condition, no one will dare hit me, and anyway this seems like a nice village. And if I do get beat up, then I'll just go somewhere else. Where're you gonna go, Gramps?"

"Heh, I'll be fine. It may be hard for someone like you to understand, but I've got an important job to do. I need to return to the city."

"The city!" His companion sounded impressed. "You really are an important man."

"Oh, well . . . I don't wanna brag, but I'm pretty well

connected with the police." The old man suddenly slapped his knee. "That's right! I've got some good wisdom. Lots of wisdom!" It appeared that he'd become quite enamored with the word "wisdom."

The old man told his companion that he should loiter in the area for a while and find a place to sleep next to the substation once it got dark. When the police found him, they'd no doubt be surprised and try to drive him away. But not to worry; the angry villagers would take him back to the substation. Better not to use the silent treatment then! In the end, the substation was sure to contact the city. "That way, we'll be able to see each other again in the city for sure," the old man concluded, bidding a fond farewell to his friend.

4.

The farewell was quick. Upon parting, the old man gave the leper some of the money he had gotten from the villagers, telling him that he deserved it. And then he treated himself to a drink, as he was wont to do.

On his way back to the city, he ran into someone

who had recently joined the ranks of the young master's family. "Where're you going, Old Man Boil?" the man called out. "You look like you're in a good mood. But you're going the wrong way—the house is in the opposite direction." He quickened his pace to catch up with the old man.

"Say—have you ever slept with a woman?" It was not a slip of the tongue; the old man had pensively given voice to an issue that had been haunting him for some time.

The other man was forced into silence by this strange, unexpected question. "I dunno what games you're playing," he said finally, "but if you were worried I was gonna ask you for a drink, well, I wasn't."

The old man sat on a nearby boulder with a brooding air. "Do women ever listen to what a man says?" he mused, packing some tobacco into his pipe. "The young master once told me that you could do anything in the world, as long as you had money."

"What's up with you today, Gramps?" The other man moved back a little and peered at the old man. In the dimness, all he could see was the red glow of the pipe. "Heh, with enough money even I could become a bigshot lawyer like the young master. Women, hah! That's easy.

You know what women are like . . . Heh heh, with enough money someone like you could even nab the daughter of that sardine catcher Ko."

The old man let out a *hehehe* of laughter. "You just don't understand . . . It's about my son. No way you can understand." He leisurely rose to his feet. "I'll be off now."

The other man had been chuckling to himself in a strange manner, perhaps because he was still thinking about Ko's daughter, but now he gripped the old man's arm. "Where're you going? We can talk things over tonight, for the sake of this son of yours . . . Wait a minute. You have children? I thought you were a *chonggak*."

"You wouldn't be able to understand. Hehehe, it may surprise you to know that I've got a woman . . . She's much, much prettier than the young master's missus." Here, it became hard to follow the old man's ramblings. He launched into a rant while the other man was still trying to figure out whether the woman in question was the son's wife or not. "I'm going to the city! There's nothing for me in this backwater town." The old man had completely forgotten about how he'd boasted about having a son; the thought of Seopun had loosened his lips (already loose from drinking) despite himself. "I'll never lay a hand on the missus. I'm gonna worship her from afar!" His hoarse voice climbed higher and higher as he babbled on, until he was almost yelling. Capping his speech with a final twisted laugh, he ran off into the darkness, towards the main road.

"Hey, Old Man Boil! You're not gonna buy me a drink?" The other man started to chase after him for a bit but soon gave up. He stood there on the road and blew his nose through his fingers. "Bah. Good riddance, you senile old *chonggak*! Pervert! Bet you saw the young master havin' a good time with the missus, and it finally drove you mad. Heh heh, guess what, I've seen 'em going at it, too. But as you can see, my mind's still all there!" He flicked his head with his fingers as if it were a watermelon.

The old man reached the outskirts of the city by noon the next day. He had spent the previous night under the eaves of some farmhouse in a neighboring village. He hadn't been able to sleep well, back in the young master's village; people had remained chilly towards the old man, and it wouldn't have done for him to be caught sleeping outdoors there. He had set out for the city early in the morning. A bus would have only taken a few hours, and it wasn't as if he didn't have the money to buy a ticket, but still the old man walked. It was not just because he was something of a cheapskate. He believed that humans, by nature, were meant to walk. Walking settled him. Taking the bus would separate his feet from the ground, make him feel like he were separated from Jeju and even from himself. Not only that, it would unmoor him from the city and everything it held—namely, Gwandeokjeong and Seopun. Planting his feet firmly on the ground bolstered his heart. To walk was to be connected to the earth, and by extension to the people of the island, to Seopun. Walking had always given him a way to escape the loneliness of his life. It was natural that he sometimes suffered from aching feet, but the ache was proof that you were alive. If you became too tired to walk on, well, all you had to do was rest on a boulder by the side of the road until you were ready to move on.

The old man did just that: he took a short rest atop a boulder that was positioned near the road, underneath the shade of a young pine tree. But his rest was rudely interrupted when some bird droppings from a crow splattered the surface of the rock right beside him. The offending crow then flew off, followed by two or three of its companions. Black crows had been cawing and circling above him for a while. He spotted a line of black dots far off in the distance, in the direction of the city; they were probably more crows. The road was deserted. The wind began to howl. A massive crown of clouds had settled upon Mount Halla, covering it from peak to bottom and turning the surrounding ground a hazy milky color. Small droplets of rain fell from the sky. The sea was dark and rough and full of glimmering, roiling, large white-capped waves.

But the western sky near the city was strangely clear, even as the clouds rapidly moved ever closer. The old man hurried his pace. The wind was blowing from behind him, urging him forward. The crows flew high above the old man's head, leaving behind only the echo of their caws. The sun suddenly peeped through a tear in the black clouds gathering in the distance, spooling down golden beams of light that swallowed up the crows.

The closer he got to the city, the more his uneasiness grew. So did the number of crows winging their way westward, their pitch-black shadows a heavy weight over his head. It was too early for the crows to be returning to their nests. One bird leisurely flew down a few feet in front of the old man. It hopped around for a bit, stole a glance at the human, then abruptly gave out a caw and took to the air again.

"That crow's got some nerve. I'm not dead yet."

The rain continued to fall. It also appeared to be raining over the city, and the clouds that had released that beautiful weave of light just a moment ago were now ragged around their edges and hanging low in the sky.

The situation became clearer once he reached the outer edge of the city. Armed police and mounted soldiers were scattered among crowds of people—no, they were *scattering* the crowds that choked the streets. The atmosphere ached with ponderous silence as the rain beat down. Armed cavalrymen were bellowing at people to hurry forward. The old man knew exactly what was happening: "forced spectatorship." Whenever you saw policemen or the army herding people along on this island, it could mean only one of two things. Either the people were going to be massacred or else they were going to be forced to watch a massacre. The old man saw a dense swirling eddy of crows above Gwandeokjeong. There were so many of them that it was as if a raucous jet-black cloud had settled over the building. The old man waited for the policemen to pass him before turning to a nearby passerby. "Is there some big 'incident' or something happening today?" he asked. The stranger glared at the old man with sullen contempt but didn't say anything. "Heads! They're parading around the heads!" someone else explained. After that, he didn't hear anything else but the sound of feet being dragged along the wet road.

They were in the heart of the city now. Gwandeokjeong Square was already crammed with rows and rows of people. Some had umbrellas open; others who looked like farmers shrugged on straw raincoats while the women tucked their skirts over their heads, exposing their Korean undergarments. Others were cramming themselves under building eaves and choking the alleys and straining the rope barriers to their limits. The old man bent forward and deftly pushed his body through the crowd. He eventually managed to make his way to the very front.

On the other side of the square, his beloved Gwandeokjeong stood murky in the rain. But soon a bizarre spectacle was to unfold before his eyes, making Gwandeokjeong recede into the distance like a phantasmal backdrop. Behind the rope, inside

Gwandeokjeong Square itself, he saw a military procession—no, wait. What was taking place there made even the old man open his eyes wide as he brushed aside the rain that streamed down his felt hat. Even if he'd been completely intoxicated, he would still have reeled from the sight. It was a procession of death that was happening, under that sky that was roiling with crows. The old man could tell from their clothes that the procession was composed of partisans. Four columns of captured partisans, numbering several dozen in total, were being marched around the square before the stone steps of Gwandeokjeong. "Procession" was perhaps too generous a word to describe how ragged the march had become. The partisans' steps were disordered and slow, as if the earth itself was attempting to cling fast to their feet, and they looked like prisoners who were on the verge of collapsing after having been force-marched for countless miles. On their shoulders hung not rifles but freshly severed heads that had been speared onto bamboo poles like meat on skewers. Rain, blood, and dirt mixed together and ran down the poles and the chins of the starkly pale heads, soaking the marchers in red. The green color of the fresh bamboo stood out starkly against the thick dark blood.

A large "proclamation" dangled from the neck of every partisan like a dog tag. The rain blurred the words that were written on the proclamation. The old man wouldn't have been able to decipher the words in any case, but based on past experiences he could easily guess what they said. It wasn't just the old man; every single person in the city, even those who were completely illiterate, could "read" the runny ink of the proclamation. *I am an insurrectionist. I am an insurrectionist who has violated the national policies of the sacred Republic of Korea. I am a hateful insurrectionist and evil human being who went against the welfare and interests of the public and who murdered innocent citizens.* It was this kind of message that was now being dirtied and washed away by the rain.

A few crows broke away from the black swirling mass overhead and swooped down to where the humans were gathered. They began to peck at the heads that were speared on the ends of the poles. An unearthly sound arose from somewhere in the crowd. It was a grating, almost lewd-sounding voice, not quite a laugh and more like a scornful jeer. The heavy silence suddenly seemed to grow and then tighten around the area of the crowd where the voice had come from. Crows hung from the disheveled hair of the severed heads and writhed above the heads of the living partisans. It was as if the crows had formed their own procession to mirror the humans. The old man, who had sincerely and deeply loved the heads of the youths that had come to him, was filled with an unbearable sadness at the sight of the crows snaring their beaks in the tangled hair and flesh of the severed heads. One particularly brazen creature had flown down among the partisans and was busy attacking the humans who were still alive and walking. Crows. They had eyes like a cat but were more relentless than any cat ever was, and a cowardice that was somehow savage. As they flapped their wings, driving away the rain, they let out a series of caws that rang with an eerie pathos. The captured partisans continued their forced march. Shaking their poles on occasion—only then would the crows teeter from their perch, their wings flapping—but not bothering to ward off the ones that attacked them, the partisans walked and walked.

Whenever the crows got too boisterous, a pistol shot would ring out. The birds nearby would take off at once in a clamor. The soldiers continued to fire their guns. Sometimes a shot would pierce the wings of one of the birds overhead, and a black mass of feathers would plummet to the ground. Its companions would soon swoop down nearby, as if pursuing its fall.

The national defense forces and police officers that were gathered upon the stone steps of Gwandeokjeong and around the police barricade had their guns pointed at both the marching partisans and the rope barrier that held back the crowd. There was no sign of the military police, the cavalrymen, or the American soldiers—or really any Americans at all, even though this was all the result of the operations of the American army. The old man was not the sort of person who could grasp the politics of it, but even he found it strange how the American soldiers who usually rode around in their jeeps and cars every day were absent today of all days. It was exactly during such times that one expected to see a tall American soldier with a big, long nose like a pole on those stone steps, hands stuck in his pockets as he looked down at the scene below. Why? Because the old man knew that American soldiers hated the "Reds" above all else.

Near the police station, flashes like far-off bolts of lightning occasionally pierced the deepening dusk. Someone was taking flash photos. "Shh, quiet!" was the response the old man got from a nearby stranger when he asked about the Americans. "They're watching us from somewhere!" The old man later learned that the events of the day were a result of the "returning allegiance tactics" (a calculated military plan to eradicate the Jeju partisans that was carried out through the combined forces of Syngman Rhee and the American army in 1949). Despite an initial "declaration" promising otherwise, the partisans who had "returned to allegiance" (surrendered) were in the end treated the same as those who had refused to capitulate; not only that, they were forced to parade around before the crowds while carrying the severed heads of their former comrades who had been killed for their defiance.

The rain continued to fall and the march continued on, churning the ground into slop. People began to stumble over the mud-plastered corpses of the crows that had been shot down. Some partisans collapsed on the ground like limp dishrags, and they too got covered in mud—but they were still human beings. Everything looked weirdly white: the bamboo poles that were thrown to the side after people lost their balance, the soles of the partisans' bare feet as they were washed by the muddy water and rain. "This is wrong, this is wrong . . . " The old man's mutterings gave voice to the nameless groaning thing that had been constricting his chest ever since his arrival. Confronted with that parade of heads, he finally realized for the very first time just how grotesque he himself must have looked, circulating heads around the city. The march continued on. Several more people pitched forward. Once they fell, they didn't try to get up again; they could barely manage to even move their heads.

A cry broke the silence. A young woman was scrambling over the rope barrier. The old man watched as she leapt into the center of the square. She managed to run five or six paces before stumbling and pitching face first into the ground. Her pure white clothes were transformed into mud instantly. Wailing, the woman scrambled to her feet with violent desperation. The agitated crowd moved forward like a surging wave against the rope barrier, which looked like it might snap at any minute. A startled constable jabbed his gun muzzle into the crowd.

The long hem of the woman's skirt kept tangling around her ankles, but still she rose and ran towards where the partisans marched. "*Oppa* (big brother)*! Oppa!*"

she shouted, in between her wails of sorrow. The falling rain muffled her voice. But, ah! That young woman, she was—By the time the old man figured it out, it was already too late. *That woman reminds me of Seopun.* Even as the old man thought this, he realized that it *was* her. Shock struck him with the force of an earthquake. By the time he came to, the "spectators" had already pinned down his arms and put a hand to his mouth. They all knew what would happen. Still, the eyes of the crowd couldn't help following the figure of the woman who was flying forward like a great white bird with its wings spread wide. With a roar—a roar that could not be mistaken for anything other than what it was—and with great deliberation, a gun went off. A few steps short of reaching the partisans, the woman's body gave a savage jolt. The body fell with a thud to the ground and rolled over once. Two police officers grabbed one leg each and dragged the woman over the mud, into the police compound. The hem of her skirt was dragged further and further up her body, like a great rind being peeled. An ornate hairpin fell out of her loosened hair and glittered there in the rain. The march continued on.

That evening, the city felt as oppressive and quiet as

the bottom of the deep sea. The silence weighed down the gait of the people as they left and seeped into every last crevice of their homes. The usually garrulous old man didn't speak to a single person that evening, nor did he listen to anyone, either. Talking now felt like a terrible, shameful, awkward thing. He'd wanted to see for himself that the great white bird that had fallen into the mud wasn't Seopun, but that was the one thing he was unable to do. Rumors were already starting to circulate, and the doors of the Nammungwan were firmly shut. It was most likely the first time the old man had ever witnessed a person get shot to death in front of his own eyes. His usual bar had closed its doors for the day, but the old man shoved some money at the owner and forced his way in. The owner was quite surprised to see that the old man had finally gotten his hands on "lots of cash," as he'd always boasted he'd do. Unusually for him, the old man didn't try to engage in any conversation. "Poor thing . . . " he simply said, knowing then too that Seopun was dead. The old man didn't drink much. As he warmed himself at the bar, he sank into a deeply pensive mood. He was still pensive and extremely subdued when he left. It was dark outside, and the streets were deserted.

It was still raining, and the wind was sending water into the air. The old man wiped away the slanting rain from his face with his sleeve and made his way to the square in front of Gwandeokjeong. The crowd was gone. Sentries were posted on either side of the stone gate to the police station, their guns readied and their steel helmets gleaming. The old man stealthily tried to check if the sentries were people he knew. But the gate lamps reflected off the rain in a white dazzle, obscuring his vision, and the helmets made it hard for him to see their faces. From the sound of it, the sea was rough tonight; he could faintly hear the roar of the surging waves as they crashed against the shore. Drizzle continued to patter to the ground. Everything was calm and still. The old man leisurely walked beside the barricade, towards the gate. Abruptly, he let out a bear-like growl that made the sentries whip around. That meant that their guns ended up aimed at each other. It was a bizarre sight.

"W-what was that?" they said simultaneously, their voices shaking and their guns at the ready. And then: "Uh . . . Er, guess it was nothing." Once again, they expressed their relief at almost the same time.

"That was strange. I got a bad feeling, just now . . .

Thought I heard something, but must have been my imagination."

"No, I also felt the same thing . . . Hey! You weren't thinking of killing me, were you?"

"Don't be ridiculous—you're giving me the creeps . . . Though a-actually, I was wondering the same thing about you."

"You're nuts. Bah, it's the heads' fault. It's all because of the heads . . . You see this? They've made me break out in an actual cold sweat." The sentry who was closest to the old man rubbed the back of his neck with his hand. He then took out a cigarette and offered another one to his partner. "Even the dead bodies inside the gate are giving me the creeps tonight."

The sentry lit the cigarette. But as he did so, the other man suddenly swung up his gun again in a wild panic. The sentry with the lit cigarette jumped back and glared at his partner, but soon he too turned and readied his gun. "W-who's there?"

The old man calmly materialized before them. He doffed his hat and gave a quick bow of the head. He had recognized the voice of the sentry. "It's me—Old Man Boil."

"Oh, it's only you!" the sentry said with a relieved laugh, though he didn't lower his gun. "Hahaha, I see you're still alive and kicking, then. B-but what're you doing here at this hour?"

The old man flashed some money at the two men. It was more than enough to allow a policeman to drink well for the next few days and even buy something nice for his wife. The sentry whom the old man knew, the one who'd lit the match, ushered the old man through the barricade. The old man told them he'd give them all the money he had in return for letting him take away Seopun, whose corpse had most likely been thrown somewhere inside the police grounds. Both sentries were astonished once again. To use all that money to buy a corpse, when corpses were so abundant these days that even the crows of the island didn't know what to do with them all—! The bodies would be loaded onto a truck at daybreak tomorrow and either buried in a mass grave or else weighted down with rocks and tossed into the sea anyway. As long as no one else knew, what was the harm in taking away a single body? All the higher-ups at police headquarters knew that the female corpse was Seopun of Nammungwan. The two sentries stood by the gatepost in a huddle, but eventually the one who knew the old man returned and asked him where he'd be taking the corpse. He was relieved when he heard the answer: beneath the floors of Gwandeokjeong. The old man then answered his next question by saying that Seopun was a distant relation of his and he wanted to give her a decent burial. The policemen agreed to take the money. And then they told the old man what he himself had been meaning to ask—namely, that all this be kept secret. As to the old man's final request, well, it wouldn't do for them to go around looking for the head of Seopun's brother, but they agreed to let him take away one of the heads that was lying around instead.

The policemen put a man's head inside the straw bag that covered Seopun's corpse and carried them both to the barricade. The old man tearfully thanked them. He slowly and painfully carried his bounty back to Gwandeokjeong, crippled leg and all. Underneath the floors of Gwandeokjeong, he gently hugged the body and then laid it on its side.

The next day, finding Old Man Boil back in town after such a long absence, the people of the city amused themselves in swapping stories and rumors. The old man had his long pipe in hand as always, but something had caused him to age terribly. His back was bent and stooped, perhaps because of the cane he now sported. The children immediately spotted the bamboo cane, which looked like something he might have picked up after someone else had already discarded it in the street. The children followed him around and told him he was a "real" cripple now. The old man simply gave them a sad smile, as if agreeing with them; he was finally acting his age. People recalled that the old man had been away for a while, maybe several months or so, and explained away his sudden transformation by assuming he must have experienced a terrible hardship in some far-away place. They didn't know that the old man had only recently begun to use a cane. It wasn't just the cane that was different; the old man had completely lost his former cheer and no longer bothered to make conversation with people. Even if you tried talking to him, his only response was to give you a sad smile. He spent his days squatting on the broad stone steps of Gwandeokjeong, bathed by the rays of the late autumn sunlight. At times he would let out a hard cough, but otherwise he sat there unmoving and mute all day. His gaze was always fixed upon the dusty white earth of Gwandeokjeong Square. He cut a sad, lonely figure on the chilly stone steps, decrepit and ugly with age, his cane and pipe his only companions. He did sometimes still smoke tobacco with his pipe, but even the smoke was lethargic and meager.

How many days continued in this way? No one bothered to count. At any rate, a while later—people could not be entirely sure how many days later—the old man completely disappeared from Gwandeokjeong. It was true that the sight of the old man crouched silent and mobile in front of the pavilion gave people a sad impression. But seeing those white steps completely deserted made people feel truly sad and empty, as if something important had broken free from the city. Most likely he'd gone off on another journey—or so people told each other, even though no one had seen him get on a bus. Or maybe he had come down with a cold—there was that terrible cough he had, remember—and was sleeping it off underneath Gwandeokjeong.

To the people of this city, the world beneath Gwandeokjeong had no connection to the world above it at all.

One wintry day, an American general and some of

his soldiers were given a tour of Gwandeokjeong by a government official and some policemen. The huge rusted lock was taken off, the bolt was pulled out, and the great vermillion doors were slowly opened for the first time in years. The American soldiers pointed their cameras and snapped photos as they always did. The residents of the city watched at a distance as several packed crates were carefully brought out over the course of the next several hours.

It was then that people thought again of Old Man Boil. It had been a while. There were some who firmly believed that he'd died underneath Gwandeokjeong, but another, more plausible rumor emerged from the crowd that day. The rumor was that the old man was now on the other side of Mount Halla, in the warmer climes of Seogwipo in the south. It was said that as he plied his trade as "Old Man Boil" there, he would tell anyone who'd listen that being human meant never, ever working for the police, no matter what.

Feces and Freedom

1.

One person. When the roll call was repeated, it was discovered that one person was missing out of the hundreds that should have been there. A ripple immediately went through the rows of labor conscripts that packed the training grounds at the news, and a low clamor arose. The air itself seemed to waver violently around the laborers' shoulders.

Come to think of it, he hadn't seen Myeongsik for a while now.—*No, it can't be . . . He couldn't have . . .*—Seong Taeil searched the other rows as a heavy weight settled on his shoulders. He slowly grew more agitated at the thought that Myeongsik was missing. His knees shook, sending strange chills through the rest of his frozen body.

He was seized with a feeling like fear, as if his was the name that had been called, and the absurd, uneasy protest in his heart—*It can't be . . .* —instantly fell apart when confronted with the scene before him.

The Korean overseer who was the "work leader" in charge of their group showed up in a panic. He ran between the rows of laborers, checking to see if the missing person had gotten himself mixed into another row. His face was a mask of impatience, but his eyes were hard with hatred, and he glared at the laborers as if it were their fault. As soon as he moved away, all the laborers threw scornful mutters at his retreating back. But the work leader's gaze lingered the longest on Taeil.

The laborers stood in the open space by the boarding house that served as their training grounds, arranged in six rows of fifty people each. Taeil was in one of the back rows. He hadn't noticed at first that Myeongsik wasn't among them. He had looked around, but it was impossible to immediately spot one person among the three hundred. Still, it did appear that he was missing, especially given the overseer's actions. It was clear at least that Myeongsik was not in Taeil's row, though he normally stood at the end of the line to his right. Taeil could see the worksite in the distance. He knew that Myeongsik had been at the worksite just a few hours ago. He'd driven a pickaxe down into the ground over and over, greasy sweat flying from his body the whole time. The skin on the tough palms that gripped the pickaxe was torn and bloody, and the handle had bitten into his flesh. *Run. Run far away. It doesn't matter anymore. If we're gonna die here, might as well die running . . .*

The harsh intersecting cadence of flesh and pickaxe had stopped, and all you could see as the sun sank behind the mountain mine was the black soil they'd dug up. Chromite ore made the dark clods of soil glitter with a translucent light. If you fixed your gaze on it, after a while the whole area would suddenly look brighter. To Taeil, it shone a spotlight on the keening emptiness he felt at having been abandoned.

Someone in the last row behind him blew his nose through his fingers. Just as Taeil realized that it was a signal, the atmosphere became suddenly strained and—

"Hey, you!" A hand slapped Taeil's right cheek. The overseer was gripping a white birch pole about three feet in length. "Idiot, look straight ahead!" he shouted in Japanese—or tried to. He stumbled over his words at first, and his pronunciation was garbled. But there was no mistaking the anger in his voice.

Taeil tried massaging his cheek with his palm, but the overseer wrenched his hand away and grabbed his collar. "What happened to Rimoto—Rimoto Meishoku?" he stammered out, using the Japanized name that had been given to Myeongsik. His voice was oddly wan. Taeil's body had automatically gone rigid. He lowered his chin and replied that he'd like to know the answer to that, too. The overseer's face immediately twisted into an expression of startled offense; in the same moment, a man in the last row facetiously offered in Korean to help look for him. There was laughter. Someone in one of the front rows whistled. The overseer's arm, which was still pressed against Taeil's throat, spasmed at the sound and finally dropped away. The overseer, whose Japanized name was Yasukawa, swiveled his head uncertainly, looking both grim and perplexed. He ran off in silence. Yasukawa had been conscripted about half a year ago not in Korea but in Tokyo. When he arrived here, he had with him a recommendation or something from the Harmonization Association (an extra-governmental organization of the Special Higher Police with branches in every prefecture, formed in 1936 through the auspices of the Japanese government with the goal of assimilating Koreans residing in Japan). A hard worker, he'd been "promoted" to the role of work leader within a month.

Yasukawa paused for a moment to kowtow to the Japanese leader who was positioned in the front row. Still kowtowing, he ran on. Two or three of the other overseers were already huddled together in front of the outhouses lined up by the building where the ore got sorted, next to the watchtower. As Yasukawa hastily shouldered his way into the group, the light reflected strangely off the long white birch pole he was still holding. Myeongsik was not in any of the outhouses, and in any case guards always followed the laborers to the toilet. It was clear what had happened. One person missing: it could only mean that one person had run away.

"Be careful, Taeil. Your partner's gone."

Taeil's voice was stuck in his throat. He didn't turn around to address the person who had spoken.

The roll call took longer than usual. The laborers were already like limp rags, fatigued from a long day of work, and the extra time only made them even more exhausted. Even putting aside the uncertainties of success or failure that an escape engendered, the mere fact that someone had indeed escaped gave them a dizzying shock. Stepping a single foot outside the designated area which the laborers derogatorily called the "semi-octopus room" was already to enjoy success in a way, to enjoy freedom. But the catch was that the moment you did so, you were almost always caught. Rather than pondering what might become of the fugitive—the escapee, that is—the laborers couldn't help but think of Yi Myeongsik's fate as their own. And imagining that fate further strained their nerves and wasted even more of their energy.

"Pah, that bastard is such an idiot!" one of the men snarled. He spat on the ground. Behind his boozy voice of despair hid an impotent envy: *Goddamn it, he really did it!* Underneath the shadow of the great boundless wings of freedom—of flight, of escape—the laborers could do nothing but wait. A foreman from the Labor Section arrived just as the sun was setting. His feet trod over the spindly, slanting shadows cast by the laborers in the front rows. The foreman, who acted as the general supervisor of the mining operations, was a short but burly man. He had sturdy wide shoulders and was built like a tank. The subsection chief for the Labor Section, in contrast, was a pale, thin man who looked like he'd be more comfortable in an office than at the mine—the type of person who looked better in a suit than in the wartime civilian uniform he was currently wearing. He puffed on a cigarette with an air of unconcern about him, giving the laborers the strong impression that he ranked above the foreman.

A Japanese work leader walked briskly over to the foreman and saluted. "One person from Group Three, Squad Five has deserted. The other 295 individuals are all accounted for, sir!"

Yasukawa stood at attention as the Japanese leader gave his report. Just moments before, the Japanese man had slapped his face and censured him. Yasukawa seemed unable to look at the foreman directly. He fixed his gaze instead on the top gold button of the man's uniform with a solemn expression that suited the contours of his Korean face quite well. The gold button shone persistently in the twilight, but as the sun sank lower it began to lose its luster, as if its gilt were being peeled off.

"No irregularities to report from the other leaders?"

There were around sixty Korean leaders—overseers in charge of driving the laborers to work ever harder—who were each in charge of multiple laborers. Above them were a number of Japanese leaders who were nicknamed "the big shots." In all, there were almost a hundred people with white birch poles now encircling the laborers. Hearing that there were no other reports, the foreman jerked his chin at the leaders. He then spit some gobs of phlegm to the ground and turned his glare to the laborers.

"Listen up!" he yelled in a raspy voice. "You lot should already know what's coming. Anyone nods off, we're gonna knock you awake. Remember what the warden told you when you first arrived? Use those words to shake yourselves awake. The new members in Group Three need to clean out your ears and pay extra attention to what I'm saying. It's been a few days since you started work, but there's still so much left to be done. You should be ashamed to call yourselves imperial subjects. Remember, your spade and pickaxe aren't just for appearances. They're your substitutes for guns and swords!"

The foreman leisurely clasped his hands behind his back. The person next to him shouted a ten-hut order. But the laborers actually fell even more out of step, and their movements were sluggish. The man in front of Taeil stood with his legs spread wide and the cuffs of his shirt rolled up; he was pulling his shirt away from his sweat-soaked skin to get some air flow. Looking at him, Taeil thought suddenly of Korea. The local authorities had leveled some farmland in his village and turned it into a large training ground with the Shinto sun goddess Amaterasu Omikami enshrined in the eastern corner. Every morning, they rounded up the people of the village—young and old, man and woman—and forced them to pay obeisance to the East, which meant worshipping the Imperial Palace from afar. The Japanese chief of police and Korean village head would turn to the eastern sky and conduct a ceremony wherein everyone chanted the Japanese "Oath of Imperial Subjects" in unison. He remembered seeing one old woman in white Korean clothes who couldn't possibly have understood the Japanese. She was worried about the exorbitant amount of rice they were obliged to supply to the government and about the farm work she had to do.

"As you were!" Then the command came again: "Attention!" All of a sudden a grim silence settled upon the training grounds. The foreman straightened his posture and changed his tone. "As imperial subjects, you enjoy the benefits of 'mainland Japan and Korea as one body' and 'impartial and universal brotherhood' through the gracious will of the Emperor. Labor conscription is second only to military conscription and is a boon His Majesty the Emperor has given you, his children of the empire, in his infinite benevolence. You must not forget that running away is an unpatriotic and traitorous act. Being unpatriotic is unacceptable! Think carefully about what I've said tonight. Got it? Starting tomorrow, you must all do better!"

The foreman twisted around to look at the subsection chief of the Labor Section, seemingly checking to see if anything else needed to be said. The subsection chief simply gave a casual nod of his head. The nod was not just a formality; when he nodded, an alarm began to blare from the top of the watchtower.

A Korean leader had climbed the watchtower while no one was looking and was now assiduously ringing the alarm bell. The pealing of the bell was soon picked up by the rising wind. It rippled through the clear, empty air, echoed around the mines, and rained down shards of noise upon the laborers, shattering the silence. Two German shepherds let out a howl, and the horses all began to neigh. The laborers heard the harsh grating of wheelbarrows crashing against each other inside the carriage shed, followed by a driver bringing his whip down on his horse, the snapping voice of the foreman, the clattering of hoofs, and the metallic creaking of the cart as it jolted over the ruts in the road. The noise was completely different from the usual din of the workplace in the afternoon. It could drive a man mad. The alarm was still sounding above them from the watchtower. Puffs of dust rose up from the far road, resembling a string of white clouds in the twilight. The laborers stood in their rows and watched the scene, silent statues all.

The boarding house was like a jail; once you entered, you were completely cut off from the outside world. The main entrance was bolted, and a few steps beyond that was a steel door that was watched over by a Japanese guard. Beyond that was a concrete hallway around eight yards in length that stretched all the way to the end of the building. To the right of the hallway were two rooms for the laborers; between the rooms was another hallway that led to the bathrooms. On the left side was the sickroom, a room for the work leaders, and the cafeteria. The laborers gathered there now. The leaders monitored them along the perimeter of the room, still carrying their white birch poles. The atmosphere was as severe as a Zen monastery; no talking was allowed during meals, nor any joking after. There were, of course, guards there as well. Each of the two doors to the building had locks on them, but guards were still stationed in the hallways near the laborers' rooms, the toilets, the corners, and other such places, and every single move the laborers made was observed.

The clock on the cafeteria wall struck seven. Dinner was an hour later than usual. The acetylene lamps flickered a few times and then turned on all at once, emitting a blueish white light that did little to alleviate the pressing darkness outside. Like a child, Taeil had to clumsily clasp his chopsticks with his fists as he ate. The skin on his fingertips and palms was torn, bloody, and blistered, and his fingers were stiff and unwieldy. The empty seat where Myeongsik usually sat diagonally across from him looked like a strange deep chasm. Taeil's heart jumped in his chest every time he swallowed the coarse rice. Even now he felt a pressure that was close to fear, an unsettling paranoia that the empty seat would crack clean into two and a horse would leap out with a clatter of hooves, dragging a cart behind it. Envy mixed with worry over Myeongsik's fate, and a fierce hope that his friend would find the stunning, breathtakingly beautiful freedom he sought. The more intense Taeil's emotions grew, the more he struggled to breathe under the suffocating tension weighing down upon him. He gripped his chopsticks and bowl, knowing that the tension might take some clearer form at any moment—such as through the hands of the work leader stretching out to tap him on the shoulder. A cold sweat broke out on his forehead when the person sitting next to him—a middle-aged man called Harimoto, if his memory served him right—began jostling Taeil's foot with his own. He didn't know what the gesture meant, but he did know it meant something. Taeil tried responding in kind, pretending to know more than he did. With his mouth still crammed with food, Harimoto twisted his lips and gave an unpleasant, muffled laugh. The moment Taeil felt Harimoto's tough, leathery feet knock against his own, he knew in his gut it was urgently important he prepare himself for what was to come. Taeil could be considered Myeongsik's "partner," after all. Each laborer was required to share a futon with one other person, and Taeil had been paired with Myeongsik. Even just that fact would have been enough to trap Taeil in the helpless sensation that he was, if not the missing person himself, then his alter ego or shadow.

But the meal ended without any mishap. As soon as mealtime was over, the laborers formed orderly rows and marched in military formation back to their rooms. The room monitor who sat at the desk by the entrance glared at them as they poured into the tiny room. The men were given a thirty-minute break after mealtime; after that, they would be ordered to go to bed.

The filthy, sweaty bodies of the laborers created an almost tangible odor that filled the packed room like a hot wind. *Aigo*—careless sighs of relief spread across the room, joining the noises that rose up from the ground to the very ceiling: people cleared their throats, blew their noses, and hummed in a surprisingly cheerful manner as they threw themselves down on their futons. The room was soon filled with a dense cloud of cigarette smoke, as if the noise had somehow transmuted into something tangible. The laborers were allotted five Kinshi cigarettes per day. Taeil stretched out under the window and took one of the two cigarettes that still remained in his upper pocket. Turning to his neighbor to ask for a light, he saw that it was Harimoto lying on the futon next to him. Harimoto thrust his already half-smoked cigarette towards Taeil. The laborers were not allowed to carry their own matches. A handful of people were allowed to get their cigarettes lit by the monitor at the entrance, and the rest of the cigarettes were then lit in a relay fashion.

"Hey." Harimoto blew out several smoke rings, opening and closing his mouth just like a fish. "The way you smoke is no good. It's a waste, dontcha think? It's better to slowly pass the smoke through your nose, like this." He half closed his eyes. Two white lines of smoke were boldly expelled from his nostrils. Behind the curtain of dissipating smoke, Harimoto was smirking. "Your way of smoking is a waste," he repeated. "I bet you still can't appreciate the taste of a cigarette." He suddenly lowered his voice. "The guy who ran away—was he a pal of yours?"

Taeil refused to turn around. He shifted his gaze to the myriad stars that glittered in the clear autumn sky. Five bars roughly two and half inches thick had been nailed across the window, which was furthermore covered by a wire mesh. Taeil felt something flash through his heart, but he kept his gaze trained on the window. "Aren't we all pals?" he replied carelessly.

Harimoto snickered. "Ha. You're a young'un, aren't

you . . . I bet you miss your hometown, eh? It's not just you. Everyone here feels the same, even me. Well, working hard is for your own good, as they say." He kept puffing his cigarette until all that could be seen was the ash at his fingertips. "Listen here. Let's make a bet, you and me. Cards are forbidden, of course, and we don't have any matches. But how 'bout it?"

Taeil kept looking at the sky that unfurled endlessly beyond the window bars. His hands and joints were on fire with pain, and his whole body ached with a terrible chronic fatigue. But even more persistent than that was the creeping mental strain that turned his fatigue into a thorny curse. Taeil began to involuntarily murmur to himself, like someone counting stars. "Bet? . . . Bet? . . . What would we bet with? What would we bet on?"

The other man turned over on his futon and thrust his large, square, deeply sunburnt face towards Taeil. "Don't you get it? We're betting on your pal."

"He's not my pal."

"Heh, that's a cold thing to say, considering you two slept on the same futon . . . " He giggled. "Men can become pals, just like women. So how 'bout it? Do you think he'll escape or not?"

"I can't possibly know a thing like that."

"Haha, that's the spirit. That's what it means to bet. You know, I understand what you're going through. I really do. That's why I'm betting you."

"Just because we slept on the same futon doesn't mean I know the inner workings of his mind. It's not like any of us sleep this way because we want to. Anyway, I'm not interested. You should find another person to play your game."

"I see . . . The thing is, though, that you're just about the only person who doesn't appreciate the taste of tobacco."

The person who won the bet would be able to take the other person's cigarette allotment for the day. Five cigarettes was by no means enough for Taeil, but he had no desire to get an additional five cigarettes if it meant taking them away from someone else. He realized that Harimoto's foot nudging in the cafeteria must have been in preparation for this bet. Oddly enough, he was unable to shake his sense of disappointment. He had to admit that he felt a simple desire to know which way Harimoto would bet. *Who knows, this might even be some sort of initiation.*

Taeil nodded, knowing that he was at an important crossroads right now. Although it was ridiculous, he couldn't help but feel that Myeongsik's fate would be decided here and now, in one stroke. Myeongsik *must* keep running, to the very end, until he reached his newfound freedom. But a haze slowly filled Taeil's boundless vision. If Myeongsik happened to fail—even then, Taeil decided, he must place his bet on the exact opposite option. So he prayed: *He must not fail.* He sat up abruptly. Harimoto decided that a closed fist would indicate success and that a closed fist with the thumb stuck out would indicate failure. If the fists matched, the outcome was even; if not, the outcome was odd. It was a rather unusual code, but Taeil agreed to it. A group of laborers had formed a circle around the two of them without Taeil realizing it. There were some who wiggled their closed fists with a chuckle, some who stuck out their thumbs and moved their arms about like a snake, and others who jeered and spread out their palms in a gesture only they understood. There were also those who pounded Taeil encouragingly on the shoulder with a low laugh. But no one else volunteered to join the bet.

"Alright, here we go. Will it be even, or will it be odd . . .

Even or odd?"

Taeil tried his best to conjure up a splendid vision of Myeongsik continuing his successful escape. But like a filmstrip that's been cut, that vision abruptly broke off in the middle and reeled back into itself, stuttering to a halt in front of a blurry wall. It was an unexpectedly painful battle. He had no way of knowing for sure, but still he prepared a fist. He would bet on even.

The laborer acting as the referee knelt on one knee, stretched out his arm, and planted it straight up like a knife on the tatami floor. Why did the laborers take this foolish game so seriously? Smiles suddenly vanished from the faces that surrounded them. A thick silence took their place. The silence settled over the space like a snug hat, keeping everyone at bay. Taeil's heartbeat thundered in his ears so loudly he was half afraid others might be able to hear it. His blood fizzed and rushed through his veins. At that moment, a shadowy unease raced through those same veins like an electric spark. It was like . . . like what he had felt when Harimoto had said *Isn't he your pal?*

The man in question was sitting cross-legged, his back bent and both fists thrust into the hollow between his legs. But no, the man was now standing before him. He was just like a fish in an aquarium, opening and shutting his mouth to create frothy rings. He was muttering something. The words he was saying swayed through the aquarium water like seaweed. *I bet you miss your hometown, eh? It's not just you. Everyone here feels the same, even me . . . Don't you get it? We're betting on your pal.* Taeil's eyes were downcast, and his arms were folded. His gaze settled precisely over the referee's large, meaty hand.

But what was this? The fists that clashed together both had their thumbs stuck out. *Even.* The other man's expression changed in a flash. Cold sweat clung to Taeil's forehead, and he felt like he had been wrung dry. Laughing through his nose, Harimoto rubbed his thumb against Taeil's. He forced Taeil's thumb back into his fist.

"You meant to bet that. It's the nature of the game—like being pulled deep into a mountain in the middle of nowhere by some no-name gambling *gwisin* (demon), only to be abandoned there. I hate that feeling."

Taeil felt, if nothing else, an immediate sense of relief at what his own thumb indicated. He had wanted to boldly stick out a fist. But a fist—perhaps that was just nothing more than a form of resistance. Right now he was unable to move his thumb, pinned down as it was by Harimoto's large, tense finger. His bet may have been the result of the lie he had been telling himself being overturned in an instant. But what kind of lie could exist in this place? He wanted things to remain as they were, and in any case none of it really mattered anymore.

But then an unexpected wave of anger struck Taeil, and not just because of the pain Harimoto was causing him. Taeil knocked Harimoto's fist away. He knocked his fist away and gave the man an unwavering glare. The eager, nervous expression slipped off Harimoto's face. Taeil's actions were accompanied by an obstinate sense of resistance, similar to the feeling one gets when prying out a nail. He thought he heard Harimoto give out a low strangled growl, but in the next moment he swiftly reached out to grip Taeil's wrist.

"That's cheating, you know," drawled a man called Nishihara, speaking in Korean. He was sitting behind Taeil with his arms crossed, swaying his upper body back and forth. "Suppose the best thing to do is just call it quits."

"What? Cheating? . . . I didn't know you'd be presiding over this affair, Teach." Nishihara had earned the nickname "Teach" because he had a habit of rocking his upper body while he sat with his legs crossed like a Zen priest, as was the custom of *seodang* (village school) teachers. Taeil pulled his arm out of Harimoto's grasp while keeping his eyes trained on the other man's face. He knew without looking that the owner of the voice was the man who had spoken to him in the bathroom the first night he arrived (also the first night he was struck by a work leader).

Harimoto gave Taeil's arm a final twist before rising to his feet. At that moment, the door to the entrance opened and a work leader stepped inside the room.

2.

The work leader took Taeil to the execution room inside the cafeteria. With the exception of an old but sturdy desk with worn edges, the room was mostly empty of furniture. A beam had been fixed just high enough so that your toes wouldn't reach the floor when you were hung from it. The thirty-minute break was over. In the hallway he heard the Japanese guard giving out the order to go to bed, his voice sharper and tenser than usual.

The cafeteria was deserted. From the kitchen came the busy sound of dishware clattering together. One of the cooks—the one whose food always tasted like sand—was still clearing the tables. He gave Taeil a sidelong glance as Taeil walked across the cafeteria. His eyes were cold and unwelcoming. *Fucking waenom* (Japs) . . . Taeil was conscious of the "*waenom*" even as the Korean work leader ushered him through the cafeteria.

As soon as he entered the execution room, he was made to recite the Oath of Imperial Subjects. The two other people in the room were both Koreans. Faced with Koreans, Taeil managed to get through the first line of the Oath: "1. We are imperial subjects . . . " The one who was sitting behind the desk nodded in satisfaction and asked him for his name. This same man had, just a few moments ago, called out *Nariyama Taiichi*—the Japanese name assigned to him—at the entrance of the laborers' room. He then told Taeil that his group leader, Yasukawa, was currently away but would probably return soon with Myeongsik in hand.

Why should Taeil give these men what they wanted? *There's only one possible reason why they brought me to the execution room.* If the other men had been Japanese, Taeil might have eventually been able to spit out the name *Nariyama Taiichi* with relative ease, as if it were some other person's name. After all, a name wasn't something that one chose for oneself; even if it were, it still wouldn't be a big deal. Taeil had thought so even during the campaign for Koreans to adopt Japanese-style names. When threatened with the possibility of prison, he didn't have the strength or courage to refuse the "establishment of a family name." Like many others, he was called to the local government office again and again until he finally signed the papers. While tragicomedies are inevitable in such cases, many of his young colleagues had actually thrown away their "moldy, old-fashioned" colonial surnames with alacrity, replacing them with awkward two-sinograph surnames in the Japanese fashion. A name wasn't a big deal—or so he told himself when his surname was erased even from the family registry. A name, in the end, was nothing more than a rhetorical question for him. Nothing more than a warped reflection of his resistance against his own powerless self. He had a thorough and intense attachment to his moldy, old-fashioned surname, the surname that had persisted for centuries on that dreary peninsula stuck in a corner of the Orient. *After all, the family registry is one the Japanese made, not us . . . But then where in the world is ours?*

Names were apparently so plentiful that a country like Japan could forcibly export surnames to other countries. How could names matter if that were the case? To cling to a surname . . . Without resistance, there was no way the Korean people could forge self-identities.

Seong Taeil, Seong Taeil—Or, to pronounce it in the Sino-Japanese way, Sei Taiichi . . . But Taeil gave the following blithe response: "Nariyama Taiichi." He felt himself rise and fall, rise and fall through a dark cave as if he were in an elevator.

"What? *Nariyama Taiichi—*" The work leader put his hands on the edge of the table and deliberately rose to his feet. Suddenly he leaned forward and struck Taeil's cheek with his palm. Taeil understood why. It was because he hadn't answered politely enough. "Where do you think you are?"

Maintaining silence, Taeil felt a stinging pain in his cheek—not because of the slap, but because of the humiliation he felt. Sadness shook his young soul. Taeil took a good look at the other man's face. The work leader looked steadily back, his eyes like that of a hunter aiming at his prey. He would probably spring on him the moment he averted his gaze. Taeil refrained from putting his hand to his cheek. His cheeks had been hit countless times before: during the first evening he arrived, on the training grounds, at a dozen other locations. The dark cave abruptly expanded out from the bottom of his ears and rang with the echo of a memory: *It's better to get hit; when you get hit, you get tougher. If you're too scared of getting hit, it's your spirit that will suffer.* The work leader's eyes moved restlessly, as if his aim had gone wide. Taeil's upper body swayed a little from the impact of the palm to his face, but still he stood straight. The elevator rose up the dark cave and then shuddered to a stop within him.

The problem was not that he couldn't speak politely in Japanese. The problem was that he couldn't bring himself to speak politely in Japanese to a fellow Korean. "My name is Nariyama Taiichi, sir"—why was he unable to say such an easy thing?

The thick walls closed in on the two living Koreans in the room, urging them to talk. The walls were alive, too. They collapsed into an ooze that seeped into his mouth and then his stomach, only to gradually rise up again and fill his throat like bile.

"I don't know anything about Rimoto."

He deliberately didn't use the name "Yi," with a cunning that the heavens can sometimes bestow upon humans in such moments. But how much of a difference was there between saying "Nariyama, sir" and saying "Rimoto"?

"You don't know?" The work leader moved his cigarette to the ashtray. Rather unexpectedly, the polite language he hadn't used earlier had transferred in a leap towards Rimoto. "Anticipating our questions, I see."

The work leader planted his elbows on the desk, folded his hands together, placed his chin on his hands, and let his gaze move down towards Taeil's feet. His big toe was sticking out from a hole in his military-grade socks. He had planted his feet in such a way that his body was firmly supported by his legs, even as his legs tensed for flight. The fists at his sides shook a little, as if reverberating to the pulse of the blood vessels on either side of his forehead that was half hidden by shaggy hair. Taeil moved his small, deep-set eyes from the work leader's face to the table. The lingering smoke from the cigarette in the ashtray wafted up to his face, mocking him. He desperately wanted a cigarette himself.

Although he tried to suppress the desire, Taeil found his hand creeping up to his upper pocket anyway. He might get hit again for that. He swallowed down the bloody saliva in his mouth. Most likely there was a cut on the inside of his mouth. *If they're going to hit me anyway, might as well give them a reason sooner rather than later.*

"Excuse me, but could you lend me a light?"

"A light?" repeated the man behind the desk.

"I want to smoke a cigarette."

"A cigarette! You've got some nerve." From the corner of his eyes, Taeil saw the second Korean man approach, the white birch pole in his hand. The sharp sound of his footsteps pierced through his clothes like thorns, stabbing the skin all over the left side of his body.

"How old are you?"

This unexpected question from the man behind the desk was enough to erase the sound of the footsteps. Taeil answered that he was nineteen. He estimated that the other man was probably a decade or so older than he was. Many of the work leaders were around that age.

"Nineteen, eh? I see . . . I started smoking at fifteen."

What was even more unexpected was how readily

the other man lent him a light. It may have just been the opening salvo for an interrogation, but Taeil responded as artlessly as he could, making a sound of polite interest. He took out the one cigarette he had left. As soon as the cigarette was lit for him, his puffy cheeks sensed an unprovoked impact coming and began spasming.

Taeil inhaled the smoke deep into his lungs and then exhaled it again in a great sigh. Until he was given a reason why he'd been brought into the execution room, he had no way of predicting what might happen. But his heart had calmed. His eyelids drooped as the effect of the tobacco leisurely wound its way through his system. Night seemed to have arrived all at once. He stood frozen where he stood, illuminated by the acetylene lamp that swayed within the boundless night—while far beyond the darkness of Hokkaido, Korea appeared before his eyes: now as a panoramic landscape, now as a map.

Taeil endured three more hits (all to the cheek this time) before he was allowed to return to the laborers' room. He was hit because he couldn't tell them what they wanted to hear about Myeongsik's escape. Taeil didn't know much about the escape to begin with, and he was able to act as if he knew nothing at all.

As he entered the laborers' room, he saw some people already yawning, their mouths open wide as if they were trying to expel their fatigue with their breath; others surreptitiously watched Taeil's return. It was quiet. Inside the dim room, only Taeil stood. The tatami floor was completely buried under several dozen futon laid out in four rows, with two people crammed onto each futon. Taeil stepped onto his own futon, which someone (most likely the person next to him) had already laid out for him, and began removing his clothes. It felt like the air had been sucked out of the space around him. Several people were tossing and turning. When he finally realized that meant they were still awake, he quickly stripped off the rest of his clothes. He took a quick glance at the entrance and saw that the monitor stationed there was watching his every movement. Stripping down to his underwear made the room feel cavernous, and he had goosebumps from the cold. Taeil knelt down and massaged his arms with his blistered hands. He could tell that he'd lost a lot of weight just from this past week. His palms were too gnarled to register any goosebumps. The scar that ran along one of his palms turned white, then red. And then came the moment when the room became even more cavernous, the moment that Taeil was still not used to. Now was the time for him to take off his underwear.

In this place, the order to sleep meant, first of all, that you had to strip off *all* your clothes. Only once you had shown them you were naked were you allowed to get into bed. It was a deterrent against escape. Taeil hasn't been able to take off his underwear at first. Myeongsik too had stood there in a daze, until suddenly he gave a chuckle and boldly threw off his clothes. With another chuckle, he crawled under the covers. *It's not like we're in a public bathhouse,* Taeil thought to himself. *How can they expect us to endure such absurd orders?* He stood there in bewilderment, surrounded by naked bodies. He attempted to crawl into bed first and then take off his clothes, but the fractious work leader called Yasukawa made a big scene about it and struck him right then and there. At the time, the other laborers had done nothing but watch as he got hit. Was the key to escaping humiliation the ability to endure being naked? But if you got used to being naked, didn't that mean you were already steeped in humiliation? To become accustomed to nakedness, and to stop feeling humiliation . . . Taeil couldn't stand it.

It had been more comical than tragic at first. Whenever they went to the bathroom they did so stark naked, their penises dangling in full view as they walked down the long hallway. Some men would wake up in the morning with cocks that were filled with the intense urge to urinate; others would brazenly grip their cocks or press them down or expose their erections to the air with a terrible, unnatural calmness. All this was a shock to the newly arrived Taeil, but in time he was able to recover. Just like the hundreds of naked men lying idly on their side like green wood cut down from the mountains, he too learned that you couldn't survive unless you submitted to the order of this foreign world. But on that first night, tears had come to his eyes. Surprised by his own tears, he had for a moment looked closely at his own groin. Taeil felt a sense of discomfort even when looking at a statue of a naked man. How much stranger it was that his groin still lived and moved in this environment where they were treated like slaves. That first evening, images of those countless naked bodies—actually, of only that particular area—wriggled like alien reptiles through his sleep-deprived brain, worming into every crevice of his head and gnawing holes deep into the tissue. He couldn't laugh away the dog's life that had been cast upon them the way Myeongsik had. *We're dogs, aren't we?*

The next morning, someone had spoken to him in the bathroom. "Sleep well?" teased a man with a long face and thickset body as he went about doing his business. "You took a punch yesterday, I know, but it's better to get hit. When you get hit, you get tougher. If you're too scared of getting hit, it's your spirit that'll suffer."

"I dreamt all through the night," Taeil said without thinking, then wished he could take back his words. "It's a 'time of emergency,' as they say, so we've just got to tough it out."

Back in the present, Taeil turned his back to the monitor, mechanically tucked his underwear in between his clothes, and crawled into bed. There was really no difference between taking off your clothes one by one and stripping them off all at once; after a week here, Taeil no longer thought of it as anything but the pretense of choice.

The room was large and cold. The futon was heavy and shiny with black grime. Although Taeil had positioned himself in the middle of the mat, his body gravitated to its usual position at the edge, making room for a sleeping partner who was no longer there. But it was not just because of that. He had deliberately filled Myeongsik's spot in order to convince himself of his escape; similarly, leaving space open meant that some part of him was anticipating his friend's "return" via arrest.

Myeongsik's body warmth hadn't just disappeared; it seemed to have taken away his own body heat with it, leaving behind only an empty hollow. He could hear the sound of trees bending against the gusty wind outside, and the cry of insects saturating the stillness of the night. The laborers' beds were probably all reflected in the barred window glass. Silence spilled through the room—no, the entire building. Even the loud snores of the sleeping men did nothing but accentuate the stifling silence. Not a single murmur arose from the futons. The men sometimes pulled the covers over themselves and whispered about all sorts of things: their hometown; their wife and children if they were married, or their lover if they were a *chonggak* (bachelor); their parents . . . Some of them may even have talked about the independence of their fatherland, which seemed to be steadily approaching, drawing closer day by day. In any case, they all feared being overheard by others. Or, to be more precise, they feared that they would be suspected of plotting an escape together. Last night, with the tension thick in the air, Myeongsik cautiously confessed to him that he was planning an escape. His big body had trembled as he talked about how he'd wanted to escape since the very first day; after a week of thinking it over, he'd finally decided to go through with it. Among other things, he said he couldn't take a single more day of this hell. Taeil urged him to endure it for just a little longer. In the meantime, he should do more research about the surrounding geography and conditions. It wasn't just about escaping from this place; if he was going to succeed, he would have to keep running to the very end. He told Myeongsik that he too had been preparing and waiting for a chance to escape, but they couldn't afford to be hasty. Right? Taeil was fiercely opposed to the idea, in short. Arguing that they should wait for an opportunity to flee together, he did his best to dissuade Myeongsik from leaving. Myeongsik was as immobile as green wood as he listened. In the end, he sighed and said, "I'll think it over again," and that was the end of that.

Taeil looked over to Nishihara, the man who was

nicknamed "Teach." He was the man who'd spoken to Taeil that first morning. He was probably sleeping; he wasn't moving, at any rate. Taeil couldn't see his face very well, whether because of the dimness or because he had laid out his futon in a different spot than usual. During their break period at 3 p.m., he would leisurely gnaw on a piece of dried herring and ask Taeil questions about what he'd seen in Korea and Japan before arriving here. Almost everyone responded eagerly to newcomers because they brought with them the fresh atmosphere of the outside world and possibly even news about things back home. But Nishihara was different, more concerned with general issues than with personal matters. He had a cheerful and humorous disposition. During their breaks, he would often gather the other laborers together and there, underneath the blue sky, he would dance to the sound of the Korean folk songs sung by his friends by nodding his horselike face that was oddly out of proportion to his short but sturdy body, gripping his compatriots' hands and swinging them about, and moving merrily in time with the music. His actions would inevitably make the other men laugh. In those moments Taeil suspected that he and Nishihara were thinking the same thing: hidden in that laughter was a grim endurance, an acknowledgement that the only path for completely escaping their fates as "octopuses" lay in Japan's (surely inevitable) defeat in the war and Korea's subsequent independence.

Beyond the barred window, an endless black night. A window that reflected only bars and darkness, a window that moved not one fraction of an inch against a howling wind that bent the tree branches so wildly one could almost feel the tension in one's skin. He didn't know when, but surely one day—one day soon—this window too would smash to smithereens. Surely then the order of things would completely reverse, screams turning into roars of laughter. Like most Koreans who kept up with the news, Taeil knew in a vague way that the outbreak of World War II was an unparalleled opportunity for Korea to gain its independence. A certain Japanese professor at the "imperial university" in Keijo had lamented that all Koreans were already ideologues by the time they were eight—which was not necessarily much of an exaggeration. Taeil didn't know how one might set about on the national task of gaining independence. The only path he could think of was escaping even Korea, occupied as it was by the Japanese, and crossing over into China, Russia, or some other foreign country. He had heard that Koreans were already leading pro-independence movements there. But those movements were plural and diverse, and Taeil didn't have the ability or the qualifications to adequately understand them. You could say that he was nothing more than one of those quasi-nationalists who didn't belong to any particular organization. Unlike the majority of the labor conscripts who came from farming families and lacked even rudimentary elementary school education or the ability to speak Japanese, he had at least managed to enter middle school in Japan through sheer dint of effort and hard work. But a Korean history book found in his possession had led to his expulsion from the school. After that, he worked for a few years before returning to Korea. Soon after that his mother had died, leaving him alone in the world. He was still in mourning when he was forcibly conscripted and brought to this place, the complete opposite of everything he'd intended for his life. He didn't even know there was an organization called the "Association for the Restoration of the Fatherland" (an anti-Japanese national liberation front formed in

1936 under the leadership of then General Kim Il-sung) that was active even within Korea. Still in his customary Korean mourning clothes, he'd searched for the means and opportunity to escape the peninsula through just such a movement or organization. By that point the so-called military volunteer system for Koreans had already been implemented, and speculation was rampant among Koreans that a conscription system "as willed by the Emperor" would soon follow. Taeil was just around the target age.

He knew that the heavy oppressive weight in his heart was not the fault of the futon, but still he pushed aside the covers and let the cold air wash over him. He couldn't keep his eyes shut. Whenever he blinked, the light from the acetylene lamp went straight into his eyes for some reason. The lamp spouted out white haloed flames and an intense, headache-inducing smell. How much longer would it continue to burn? The more time that passed, the higher the probability that Myeongsik would succeed. The thought was a dizzying beam of light that set Taeil's brain on fire. The god of fate was always a bystander. The neighing of the horse, the creaking of the wagon as it passed over a rut, the white cloud of dust that rose in the twilight to conceal the wagon, the escape Myeongsik had carried out without anyone's knowledge just a few hours before . . . All of these things were like moves on a chessboard. Knowing how it would end, fate declined to get involved in the battle.

—He awoke. He'd instinctively kicked the covers aside even though he didn't have any idea what was going on yet. A sharp scream immediately pierced his ears, as if it had been waiting all this time for him to wake up. The scream transformed into a groan that set his teeth on edge, then again into a high-pitched cry that reverberated along the hallway. Taeil was now completely awake.

He realized he'd been in a deep sleep. A headache was pounding against his skull, and his body felt like candy that had melted onto the futon. With great effort, Taeil crawled out of bed. The other laborers were already silently dressing. The room monitor was in the hallway, talking with the other Japanese men. Yasukawa was also there, nodding along, his face quite pale. He stuck out like a sore thumb. It was still dark outside the window. The laborers' reflections were trapped there in the glass, their images broken up by the black window bars. They'd turned their backs to each other. Taeil began to shiver.

The long, trailing, heartbreaking moan struck directly at his heart and choked his breath. He put on his clothes as if he were grasping paper.

The voice was unmistakably that of Yi Myeongsik, and the voice was unmistakably coming from the execution room in the cafeteria. Every laborer's face was hard and black. Some sat cross-legged on their futon, staring into space with eyes that were empty from tension and lack of sleep; others looked steadily at the entrance with eyes that were like that of a cat.

Yasukawa stood at the door. The entrance was blocked by the monitor and the other work leaders. It might have been the fault of the acetylene lamp or his imagination, but Yasukawa still looked quite pale. His face was tinged with the telltale redness that signaled he'd been drinking. His voice was hoarse and low—the result, it appeared, of quite a lot of alcohol. He announced that the time was just a little past 3:37 a.m. The schedule would proceed as usual until 4—an orderly washing of the face, tidying of the room—at which point everyone was required to gather in the cafeteria. Yasukawa looked down at his wristwatch again as he finished his announcements. He pointed towards the cafeteria with his wristwatch arm, no doubt intending to give a speech, but his palm accidentally hit the face of the monitor next to him. Startled, Yasukawa hastily bowed his head and extended his opposite arm instead. The monitor seemed even more startled than Yasukawa. Once he'd recovered from his surprise he stepped back and grabbed Yasukawa's arm. Of course the misunderstanding was soon cleared up, but people were already starting to laugh. Taeil too found himself laughing.

Having blundered his opening salvo, Yasukawa had to extend his arm once again in order to salvage the situation. He prefaced his speech by saying they should listen carefully to the pitiful voice of that unpatriotic soul. *How could any of you be so stupid as to think you could escape, despite all evidence to the contrary? As your fellow compatriot, I cannot help but feel ashamed.* Both his almond-shaped eyes and his small, thin nose (which strangely and strikingly balanced out the rest of his face) were twitching. *Why not focus instead on working hard and saving up as much as you can? Not only will you benefit, you'll also fulfill your duties to the Empire as a person from the peninsula.* He spoke standard Japanese well, though his voice trembled a little. Taeil recalled how dismayed Yasukawa had looked on the training grounds yesterday. But even if Yasukawa's voice did sound pitiful, Taeil could not ignore the evidence before him: Myeongsik had been captured. After the laughter died down, the laborers could do nothing else but expend their energies wondering what connection existed between the designated hour, still shrouded in darkness, and his clairvoyant eyes. And listen again to those cries.

In the bathroom Taeil found himself next to Harimoto. "You laughed the loudest, didn't you?" Harimoto said, peering at Taeil's yellowish reflection in the small mirror. Instead of looking at himself, Taeil looked at the reflection of Harimoto looking at him. It was an unpleasant face.

"Didn't you laugh, too? I saw you."

"Well, yeah. But my laughter meant something different from yours. If I were the work leader, I wouldn't make such a stupid mistake."

"I'm sure. I look forward to the day you become our great leader and work me to the bone." Harimoto was unbelievable. Still, Taeil regretted what he had just said. *If he really does want to become the next work leader, he'll have to sell someone out—maybe even me.* An indefinable wave of nausea welled up inside him, alongside an anger so thick and hard it gave him goosebumps.

"You young'uns are so full of energy . . . What, you think I can't become a work leader?"

With his toothbrush in his mouth, Taeil shook his head to indicate that he couldn't speak at the moment.

"Remember, you lost our bet. I knew what would happen. And I know what you're thinking, deep down." Harimoto spoke with great confidence, not caring how loud his voice was. The monitor who was stationed at the other end of the bathroom yelled at them to be quiet. Harimoto snickered and scratched his head. "Yessirree. As you well know, I'm quite serious. I think of this place as my home . . . So when I see someone wanting to run out of my warm, welcoming home and into the cold night—and, well, the war situation being what it is—I just get so angry . . . "

They trooped to the cafeteria. A phlegmatic nausea rose up in Taeil once again, but he managed with some difficulty to keep the blood from draining from his face. For some reason, he could not avert his gaze from the terrible sight before him. It was like his neck had been nailed in place. He planted his feet firmly on the floor and tried to keep his composure amidst his rising vertigo. The air in the cavernous room coagulated and wavered before his eyes like a silk curtain.

Myeongsik had already been brought to the cafeteria. Or no—most likely he'd been tortured there. The tables and chairs had been cleared away, leaving a space as wide and empty as a dance hall. Myeongsik's arms were tied to a rope that hung from the ceiling. Although his feet just about touched the floor, he no longer had the strength to support himself, so his body dangled limp and unmoving from the rope. It looked like they'd focused their blows on his head: his face was mangled, his eyes were swollen, and a thick clotted line of blood ran red from his nose to his neck. A handful of men slumped in chairs at the end of the row of laborers. You could tell at a glance that they were patients from the sickroom. As one might expect, the laborers were unified in their silence. The silence went on and on, unbroken even by a single cough.

Just what kind of admonitory speech were they planning to give in front of these living corpses? Taeil waited, hoping for a quick resolution. How naïve he was. The resolution—or, to be more precise, the prelude to that resolution—that he hoped would come swiftly because he couldn't stand the cruel weight of time . . . it came all too soon. It came and materialized an entirely different kind of world order right before his eyes, one that was so utterly unexpected that it transcended the words "unexpected" and "cruel." Surely *this* must be a dream, he said to himself. A dream that had been plunged into a primal hell. Some instinctive part of himself noted the length of the line he stood in, and his position towards the front of the line. Hokkaido nights were long. The light from the acetylene lamp was pale. It washed out all the colors in the room—except for the red of Myeongsik's blood. Why did it stand out in that way, as vivid and insistent as the shine of enamel? The three hundred laborers stood in single file like pilgrims. They were told that they had to take up the same white birch pole that tormented them during working hours and use it to cane Myeongsik—their fellow Korean, their colleague, their friend—twice each.

Taeil and Myeongsik had been conscripted at the same time. They first met on the boat over. Then they'd been seated nearly on top of each other on the train and then, by coincidence, had ended up sharing the same futon. Myeongsik was four or five years older than Taeil and bigger, too, with eyes like an elephant and a face that often smiled. He'd been smiling when he told Taeil that despite the hassle of boarding the enormous ship and taking the lengthy train ride here, you could still earn more money working in a factory for two or three years than you could laboring as a *jigekkun* (laborers who wore A-frames on their backs to carry things) on the dusty, parched streets of Busan. He was one of the men who hadn't been "forcibly" conscripted but rather duped into signing up for work by the Busan branch of the recruiting office for the company that managed the mines. For that reason, he'd arrived at this place in Hokkaido with some amount of hope, hope that would already start to crumble by day one. He was an optimistic person by nature, but even he couldn't forget the conscripts who'd managed to evade the watchful eyes of the monitors and make their escape on the journey over. And then there were the words that greeted the workers, after a long half-day on the train from Hakodate to Asahikawa and from there to the mines buried deep to the north of the island: "Congratulations. You've finally reached hell."

Soon enough, they all learned the lesson that the "rugged manpower" of Hokkaido owed everything to the octopus rooms.

"You might think you can earn some cash, eat well, and make a good living, maybe even find yourself a wife here. Ha! You'll eat your own arms and legs before any of that happens, even eat your own guts . . . and then you'll die. That's what an octopus does. We're no better than octopuses, you hear? That's why this is the octopus room. You're not human any more—you're all octopuses!"

After a full day of backbreaking labor, they were shut up in this prison with an iron door. But there were even worse places than their "half-octopus room." To Myeongsik, all of Hokkaido was a horrible hell. It was utterly different from Busan, a place where one could ply one's trade freely as a *jigekkun* while gazing at the sea from underneath a wide blue sky, seeing all sorts of Korean faces, and even occasionally enjoying the scent of a beautiful young woman.

If he were only a little more cautious and a little less trusting, he might have succeeded in his escape. It probably would have helped if he knew more about Hokkaido, too.

Myeongsik had taken advantage of the fact that he was at the foot of the mountain during the 3 p.m. break. He'd used the cover of the trees to stealthily make his way across the mountain. The "mountain" was actually only around four hundred yards tall, but it was still densely covered with oak and cedar trees that blocked out the sun. The mine itself was located at the base of the mountain. They had to dig underneath the trees to get at the chromite. Therefore, while the foot of the mountain was heavily guarded, there were gaps here and there in the barbed wire that encircled the mine area due to the constant digging the laborers had to do around and under the trees. The mountain too acted as a kind of barrier.

Myeongsik fled wildly through the woods, refusing to look back until he'd crossed the mountain and reached the valley. Although he didn't hear any blasts from a hunting rifle or angry shouts, he couldn't shake the feeling that he was being pursued. He hid in the shadow of a nearby boulder and peered around him, but it looked like his escape was a success. At that realization, he broke out in a cold sweat that flowed down his spine. Although the valley was full of the clear, high warbling of the birds in the treetops, an eerie silence seemed to rise up like steam from the mountain surface.

Myeongsik set off again late at night, after first throwing away his hat and work gaiters. It was September, but already the starlight was like cold ice shards falling through the dew-soaked trees, and the ground quickly grew hard and frozen. He stuffed pebbles into his pockets and found a sturdy tree branch to grip in his hand. He could barely see, so he groped his way along using only his sense of touch, like a blind insect. When he finally emerged from the dense tunnel of trees his vision immediately expanded, even in the dark. The atmosphere was stagnant and heavy and shot through with pale silver, as if the air itself had oxidized. He felt a sudden stab of hunger, and tears came to his eyes as he thought of home. He crouched there at the foot of the mountain for some time. What should he do next? He had successfully escaped from the mines, but without any sort of plan. He could make out a road up ahead, but he didn't know where he was or how far he'd come or in which direction he should go or in what direction he was facing. Based on his gnawing hunger and the fact that he couldn't hear a single train whistle, he guessed it was quite late. He remembered that when they first arrived at this place, they'd walked quite a while from the station to the mines, but he didn't know how to figure out his current location. He did sense, however, that he'd come quite far. He was abruptly seized with the fear that the night would soon give way to dawn. He had to get on a train as soon as he could, one that was going towards Asahikawa and not away from it. If he could just find the station—once he did that, he was prepared to do anything, even crawl underneath one of the train cars and cling there like a grasshopper. He waited for the train whistle to sound.

But before that could happen, he heard a person's voice. It was such a strange, lulling voice that he wasn't even startled by it. It drifted towards him like a song, carried along by the wind, and tangled itself in his memories. Myeongsik sprang to his feet. It was not a dream. Someone was singing. It was a Korean song. The voice was getting louder. Soon two long shadows emerged, and a small red ember that might have been the end of a lit cigarette bobbed around in the darkness. The men were walking along while loudly crooning a Korean folk song. Myeongsik was so overwhelmed with nostalgia that he nearly ran to them. Ah, who knew that his Korean brethren could be found even here! They were probably returning from *jesa* (memorial rites) or something like it. He felt like a man encountering people in the desert.

Once Myeongsik confirmed that they were indeed

Koreans—and, based on their dialect, even from the same province as him—he approached them. The two men stopped in their tracks in apparent surprise, and the one who'd been smoking swiftly dropped his cigarette to the ground and rubbed it out with his feet for some reason. Myeongsik spoke to them in his Gyeongsang Province dialect, first apologizing for accosting them at this late hour and then asking if they could point him in the direction of the station. The men—silent shadows, really— peered at Myeongsik's clothes. Even in the dark you could tell they were the clothes of a conscripted laborer. The silence stretched out. Suddenly one of them (not the one who'd snuffed out the cigarette) said cheerfully, "Sorry for our rudeness! We were caught off guard, seeing as it's the middle of the night . . ." And then, in a solicitous voice: "You look like you need help. Where in the world did you come from?" Although Myeongsik couldn't make out their faces, he was excited by the warmth of the man's tone and confessed everything.

"This is a nice coincidence. The station is on our way home, so we can take you there. But I've got to warn you, the next train probably won't arrive until the morning . . . Still, let's hurry to the station. You never know, there might be another train."

Poor Yi Myeongsik. He'd walked himself into a trap. Once he saw the faces of the two men illuminated by the electric lamps at the station, he finally realized why the person with the cigarette hadn't said a single word. It was because he was Yasukawa, the work leader. What awaited them at the station was not a train but the empty two-wheeled cart that had carried the two overseers there and a second, empty wagon. Myeongsik was trussed up like a pig and thrown into the back of the wagon. From inside the wagon, Myeongsik heard the far-off whistle of the dawn train. The elderly station attendant looked long and hard at the wagon as it departed. The station was H. Station, one stop north of the N. Station that serviced the mines.

3.

The foreman stood before the gathered laborers, his attitude stern and uncompromising while his victim bled behind him. He had the air of either a hero or a devil—or a hero who might or might not fall into the role of a devil by seizing power or else dancing on its wicked edge. In any case, the squeak of his boots as he paced in front of the line of bare-footed laborers was as sharp as a blade to the ear. The silence was suffocating. Before long, everyone was made to chant the Oath of Imperial Subjects in unison. Taeil actually welcomed the order. It meant liberation from the silence, as well as the freedom to cough or sniffle if necessary.

"The Oath of Imperial Subjects: 1. We are the subjects of Imperial Japan, and we will loyally serve the Emperor. 2. We imperial subjects will unite together through love and mutual cooperation. 3. We imperial subjects will cultivate endurance, discipline, and strength so that we may exalt the Imperial Way."

The work leaders recited the Oath with the earnestness of obedient elementary school children. They even managed to convey the impression that they would have willingly cheered "*Banzai* to His Majesty the Emperor!" if given the chance. After the recitation of the Oath, the foreman turned to the work leaders and gave his thanks to them, particularly to the two men who'd apprehended the "traitor." He then gave the two men envelopes of money, telling them that they'd also get a full day of paid leave. Each envelope contained an award of twenty yen. Considering that one bag of rice cost twelve or thirteen yen, twenty yen was not an insignificant amount. It was more than enough to buy a train ticket into the nearest city, some alcohol, and a prostitute. It was even enough for a successful escape, although these men were like pet dogs who could be counted on to faithfully return to their masters. Japanese work leaders also got a day of paid leave if they caught an escapee, but their reward money was set at thirty yen.

Once this little ceremony was over, a handful of overseers arranged themselves next to Myeongsik, while one Japanese person stood behind him. Guards with hunting rifles lined one whole side of the room. The straight line of laborers had already begun to bend and fray. A young man in his twenties from the other laborers' room was the first to hold the white birch pole. Taeil wondered why it wasn't him standing at the head of the line, in place of that man. His thoughts were clinical and distant, as if all this were happening to someone else. He even tried imagining that he was the one gripping the pole. It was clammy with sweat. Did "that man" really intend to strike Myeongsik? No doubt he would, and with force . . . Taeil explored the sensation of the handle clinging to his sweaty palms, the handle that looked almost like a woman's slender neck or even, if you squinted hard enough, like a sculpture of a woman's naked torso. At some point Yasukawa had come over to his side with a rare smile on his face. He was prattling on about how much he wanted to return to his home in Tokyo once his term was over, and how he'd been entrusted with a subcontract for a chrome munitions factory, and how this was his big chance to show the bosses what he was worth . . . Really, he was nothing more than a petty man with small ambitions. Taeil surreptitiously touched the white birch pole Yasukawa always used on the laborers in the mines. He discovered that notches had been carved into the handle. But at that moment Yasukawa's slanted eyes sharpened, and he snatched the pole away.

The sticky pole would never break. The wood used was plentiful in Hokkaido, but that wasn't the only reason why it was popular; it was strong and tough because of its fat content, and its bark let off a long-lasting black flame when peeled and lit. It was with such a pole that they were expected to administer a blow to Myeongsik's naked torso. The first man dangled the pole from his hands like a baseball bat. He raised his gaze slowly to Myeongsik's face and looked at him for some time with harsh, hard eyes. As one might expect of this portentous moment, even the work leaders and foreman were silent as they watched over the scene. Did Myeongsik already realize his own death was near? Tears leaked from eyes that twitched within swollen, bruised flesh. For a while his tears gathered in the creases of his skin, then spilled all at once down his face. Behind the first laborer stood an overseer with an evergreen oak pole gripped in his hands, waiting to bring that pole down on the laborer's head if necessary; and behind *him* stood a Japanese man, blocking any chance of escape. It required great animosity to view an escapee as an "unpatriotic soul." If your loyalty towards the emperor and empire was strong, would you find yourself able to strike an enemy? This was the question demanded by "patriotism."

In the end, the man struck him. He struck him as if he were striking a dog. When the foreman silently approached him, red boots squeaking, he raised his arms and brought the pole down as hard as he could. Myeongsik cried out and began to struggle violently against his restraints. He was clearly conscious. He cursed and cried and screamed at the people who caned him one after another. Those tears from before had been the tears of a submissive animal. Now he was a human battling death itself. Every time he thrashed, the rope tensed with an audible creak. The pole bit down with a thwack into the raised muscles on his back over and over, until soon the whole area was swollen and blue like a giant earthworm. His flayed skin began to stick messily to the pole, and blood gushed from his wounds. By the fifth or sixth person, the pole was bright red with his blood. If it continued on like this, no doubt the flesh would come off entirely, exposing the bone underneath; perhaps even the bones would crack and begin gushing out marrow. The rope quietly grew taut. The body dangled heavily from it, no longer thrashing. Ragged breaths escaped from the gaping hole of the man's mouth, as did a trickle of blood that dripped down slowly to the floor.

It was around this time that several laborers got hit in the head from behind with the oak pole because their blows were deemed "insincere" or weak. One by one, the laborers paid their dues. Taeil knew that during the Edo period, some Japanese had been forced to tread upon an image of Jesus or the Virgin Mary to prove that they weren't part of the forbidden Christian faith. The Japanese forced Koreans to learn about such things at school even as they also forced upon them their own terrible crimes. As the line grew steadily shorter, Taeil found himself growing accustomed to the sight of blood. His fear was replaced by an icy conviction that he would indeed be able to bring the pole down upon his friend's head when it was his turn. But it was the self-confidence of another person. Another, truer part of him hoped against hope that some miracle would occur. Why was everyone so deadly silent? *There are three hundred of us, and only one hundred of them. And some of those one hundred are our fellow Koreans. If we were to all rise up at once . . .* Would they shoot everyone immediately? Kneading his sweaty palms with his fingers, Taeil stole a glance behind him. An older man was standing there, looking at him suspiciously. The man slowly shook his head at Taeil. His eyes were gleaming. Taeil quickly shifted his gaze to the rest of the human wall that stretched out behind him, searching for Nishihara, but he couldn't find him.

The night was steadily giving way to dawn. The cafeteria window revealed a darkness that melted into a wave of indigo, then a deep blue, then finally a beautiful, translucent aqua. The acetylene lamp continued to flicker its bluish-white light. The color inside the room began to match the color outside the room. There wasn't anything clear or definite about the transition; like Taeil's own self-confidence, the light that filled the room was vague, obscure, and dim. Against the gentle backdrop of the light, Myeongsik's blood changed by the minute into a vivid but also deeply sedate color.

That color was clearly rejecting Taeil. Taeil closed his eyes and inhaled, opened his eyes and exhaled. The line had completely frayed in formation, and there was no longer anyone in front of Taeil. Taeil told himself he mustn't panic. He'd meant to grasp the white birch pole with a firm hand when it was finally passed to him, but instead it slid out of his grasp onto the floor. He was angry at himself. *Calm down, calm down* he repeated to himself as he bent down to pick up the pole. But he was unable to calm down, and his actions betrayed the cries of an unmoored heart. The moment his palm touched the sticky pole, he remembered how he'd imagined what it might feel like, to be the first man to strike a blow. The face of the man who'd shaken his head at Taeil now appeared to him as an expression of sad resignation, and the dense human wall that stretched behind him was blown down and scattered to pieces. For the first time, he became deeply aware of reality—of the reality he was in. The pole clung to his palm, red and heavy from all the blood and sweat it had absorbed. In the one or two minutes that passed, a long reel of overlapping but clear images of everything that had happened up to this point spooled through Taeil's brain.

A certain youth disappeared from the Busan ferry. A roll call was ordered as the boat approached Shimonoseki, and it was discovered then that one person was missing. The surprised company officials swiftly notified the Special Higher Police that were on board as well as the Coast Guard. The missing man was finally caught on the ramp trying to disembark with the general Japanese passengers. Rain was falling on the pier. The man had somehow gotten his hands on a raincoat and an umbrella and even some eyeglasses, a hat, and a leather bag. He used these accessories to pass himself off as a Japanese man. After he was captured by the police that was the end of it, so no one was able to confirm if he'd stolen the items while on board or if he'd entrusted them to a general Korean passenger who possessed a valid travel certificate, having planned from the beginning to make his escape that way. Labor conscripts weren't issued travel certificates, and neither were the Japanese, but any Korean seeking to board a boat as a general passenger was required to get a travel certificate in advance.

At a lodging for laborers in Shimonoseki, the following incident also occurred. A group leader and assistant group leader had been chosen among the ninety-some conscripts while they were boarding the ferry in Busan. The group leader was a man in his forties who'd previously worked in a coal mine in Hokkaido. He prided himself on being an "industrial soldier on the home front," or so it seemed from all the grand speeches he gave on the subject, so the conscripts had no reason to suspect him. When it was discovered that one of the conscripts was missing on the boat, he'd taken it upon himself as group leader to be the first person to go looking for him. (Though in the end, it hadn't been him but the police who'd captured the missing conscript.) The company was delighted to have found such a reliable group leader. Even after they disembarked at Shimonoseki and settled into their lodgings, he continued to spout zealous patriotic speeches about "bringing the holy war to a successful conclusion" and "fulfilling our duties as loyal imperial subjects." *While the imperial army is out there fighting on the battlefronts,* he'd say, *we must fight here on the home front with our shovels and pickaxes instead of swords!* It wasn't just the company that was impressed; some of the laborers couldn't help but admire his silver tongue. One evening, while everyone was relaxing, he set out with the assistant group leader with money he'd persuaded the company to fork over for the purpose of buying two bottles of unfiltered sake. He'd been to Shimonoseki before, so he was familiar with the layout of the city and knew a Korean neighborhood where one could get cheap sake and some nice giblets. Sometimes, he told the company, leaders just needed a night to themselves. The company let them go, trusting that during this time of war, when even alcohol was in short supply, the cheap unfiltered stuff would be good enough for the Koreans. The two men never returned. They'd managed to find a way to cross over to mainland Japan without the need of travel certificates.

Another incident: a young man had sat across from Taeil on the train, smirking as he read a book. His seat was in the middle of the car. The young man told him that while he'd graduated from a trade school in Keijo, he was also a gymnast who specialized in the horizontal bar. The young man must have trusted Taeil for some reason, because as the train approached Kobe he confessed to Taeil that he was planning to make a run for it by jumping out the window. He asked Taeil if he could throw his bag to him after he jumped. Taeil thought it was a joke at first. Muttering about how hot it was, the young man opened the window as wide as it would go. He then sat in his seat for a while, wiping away his sweat. Then he went to the bathroom. His expression when he reemerged had transformed completely into a hard mask with eyes as sharp as arrows. He'd stuffed his shirt into his pants. It was obvious even to Taeil how he was taking large, deep breaths—preparing for his leap, no doubt. He walked slowly back to his seat, alternating his gaze from the aisle to the window as he did so. Suddenly he bent his knees and broke out into a trot. And then with a great burst of energy he grabbed the overhead rack as if it were a horizontal bar and in one smooth motion leapt out of the window as if he were a gust of wind. It was an incredible moment that was over in a flash. The young man made one elegant, soaring circumvolution in the air, landed on his feet on the roadside opposite the train, and waved his white hands at Taeil. Taeil stealthily dropped the bag from the window. Even though he'd been forewarned, the young man's actions had so astonished him that he'd almost forgotten about the bag. The gymnast's figure was rapidly receding into the distance. He leisurely picked up his bag and gave a final wave at the train. And then he disappeared into the fields . . .

The fragments of these memories of escape flapped about him like black birds. Afraid of moving forward, his heart spewed wave after wave of fragments, until they surrounded him like a dark heaving sea of remorse.

Taeil gripped the pole with both hands and looked directly at Myeongsik's corpse. The body dangled so heavily from the rope that its toes now reached the floor. As he looked, he simultaneously took in the sight of the people who surrounded his dead friend. He could distinctly feel the sweat flowing down his back and pooling into the hollows of his belted waist, and knew that the sweat was there because he was going to calmly step over—and thereby get over—the body of the dead man. If he couldn't strike the corpse that was Yi

Myeongsik with all the force he had now, he would never be able to gain the strength to live on and endure. *I have to hit this guy and step over his body. I have to step on that face that's staring at the steward and the monitors and the taskmasters and step over to the other side.* There was a sharp whispering in Taeil's ears. Taeil wasn't actually afraid of the work leader who was even now standing behind him, his oak pole poised to strike. He was afraid of making a misstep. Taeil raised his hands, his eyes fixed on the corpse that dangled ponderous and motionless from the rope. He was faintly aware of how the blood was pulsing through the veins in his temples. He discovered himself in that moment: a self that was completely isolated, hemmed in on all sides by black walls that were rapidly closing in upon him. A self that stood atop a desolate, rocky mountain, whip in hand, faced with the specter of a man who held an awful thunderous power.

Oh, God! Why couldn't he turn around and use this whip of blood to strike down the enemies that were behind him? He struck a blow. The pole embedded itself deep into flesh that was nothing more than ragged chunks. Out of some wild impulse he wrenched the pole out from the groove it had gouged, struck the body once more, then threw the bloody, flesh-encrusted white birch pole to the ground instead of handing it over to the next person in line, who was even now shaking his head with a sad, resigned expression on his face. And then he shoved the work leaders aside and left the line. The leaders opened up a path for him.

Taeil blindly exited the cafeteria. He had done it: he'd stepped over him. Somewhere, a person was dead. Dead once again. Somewhere, someone was groaning softly. The entire area around him, from the walls to the floor, was lit up in red as if engulfed by flames. Taeil returned to the laborers' room and lay facedown on his futon. A sadness tinged with the white light of dawn pierced his body all over. And a voice, a voice that refused to be suppressed, this voice was crawling up from the bottom of the hollow cave in his body, its claws scrabbling up and up through the walls of his throat. He wept.

But it wasn't over yet. It wasn't over yet because Yongbaek ended it once and for all—Yongbaek and then Nishihara. Yongbaek was the one person who refused to hit Yi Myeongsik. Back in Korea, he'd served at a mountainside temple as the young monk in charge of meals. He was tall and amiable by nature, a person who worked hard and never had a bad word to say about anyone. It was this man who delivered the final blow to Seong Taeil after he stepped over the corpse of Yi Myeongsik.

Yongbaek had gripped the bloody pole with both hands, just as everyone else had done. He looked down at his hands. People held their breath, wondering how hard of a blow he'd deliver. He rocked his massive body back and forth a bit, then abruptly turned around and silently thrust the pole at the nearest work leader. In his confusion the leader automatically found himself reaching for the pole, as if preparing for punishment, but soon roused himself.

"What the hell is this?"

"I am return this to you, sir," said Yongbaek in broken Japanese.

"*What?*"

"I am return this to you, sir."

"…*What??*" The leader appeared to be completely at a loss at Yongbaek's words. He readied his pole as he shouted. "I d-dare you to say that again!"

"I, I am return this pole to you, sir. I do not want hit him."

A restless, unsettling atmosphere immediately rose up in the room. The line began to waver and clamor. The work leaders were murderous. An oak pole crashed down onto Yongbaek's head. Hunting rifles materialized before the laborers' eyes. Yongbaek screamed.

"*Aigo*, why you hit me, what I do wrong? I won't hit my brothers. Even if I die, too. I won't!"

The line of agitated laborers broke apart then, forming instead into surging chaotic clumps.

"This is cruel! You're all cruel!" The laborers finally tore the door of silence down.

"Let him go! Just let Yongbaek go already!" Some people were shouting in Korean and some in Japanese, but still they shouted the same thing. One particularly loud voice shouted in Korean from the back: "Let's beat the bastard to death! Hey, you shithead, you call yourself a Korean?!"

One of the work leaders had leapt at Yongbaek when he fell on his back. It was then that Nishihara, who happened to be next in line after Yongbaek, took action. Bending down like a bull charging a predator, he ran forward and headbutted the leader in the chest. The crowd scattered left and right, as if the chaotic clumps of men had sprouted wings, then pressed forward ever closer. One could say they were being reckless, but it was too late to stop now.

A rifle spouted fire, and a bullet pierced the ceiling. Another bullet tore a hole into another part of the ceiling further away, towards a corner of the room. The gunman's hand had probably shook when he fired. The window glass rattled.

"Everyone be quiet and listen to me!" yelled the foreman, emerging from behind his hunting rifle. He shot a contemptuous look at Yongbaek, who was now sitting on the floor, and flicked his index finger like a store clerk organizing merchandise. "That's enough. Let both of them go."

Startled by the sound of gunshots, Taeil had run back to the cafeteria with the other laborers. He tried to push his way through the wall of human bodies, but the wall refused to let him in. The deep voice of the foreman ringing over the laborers' head sounded shaky, even broken.

"You work leaders are, well . . . hahaha, you're not murderers. You're the shepherds of your fellow brethren. You must take good care of them. Good care." That was to the Korean work leaders. "As for you lot, rebellion is useless. Calm down and listen carefully . . . I don't want a repeat of what happened last year. I'll tell you: the imperial army can get here in twenty minutes. What do you think will happen if they come? Although it's my responsibility to see things through, I too wish to avoid that outcome if possible. We can't mobilize the imperial army on a whim. But they will come. Once they've been deployed, there's no going back—you understand that, right? Nothing good will come out of you making fools of yourselves. Calm down and really think about this."

He then glanced at the body of Yi Myeongsik, which was hanging limp and broken between the arms that were suspended from the rope.

"This one here—he was called Rimoto or something like that, yes? Well, he's been dead and gone for a while now. That's enough. Release Rimoto from the ropes."

And then it was over. Yongbaek was carried to the sickroom. The crown of his head had been cracked open to the point where you could see the soft tissue underneath. Someone had wrapped a towel around the wound, but it soon became bright red and sticky and sopping with his blood.

Taeil was utterly defeated. He could no longer give himself any kind of excuse for having brought the whip of death down upon Myeongsik. Yongbaek had completely destroyed all possible excuses down to the very root. After that day, Yongbaek buried himself into Taeil's heart as a more terrible and sometimes even more hateful presence than Myeongsik. Nishihara's actions only poured salt on the wound. Taeil felt like he was being pursued by Yongbaek as Nishihara spurred him on. He was being pursued—he saw himself falling deeper and deeper into the abyss. Waiting in that abyss was the simple, artless power of Yongbaek and the others. He felt that power wash over him.

Taeil recalled—too late—the day that Yongbaek first arrived. With no time to even put their luggage down, the conscripts had been forced to stand in a strange unfamiliar square and listen to the strange unfamiliar speech of the Japanese warden. Before that, there had been a roll call—a roll call repeated over and over again. Only Yongbaek had neglected to respond. The company men grew panicked: *Oh no, yet another person missing!* But when they counted the number of conscripts, the number matched the number they had.

"Oyama Ryuhaku!" shouted a Japanese commander, finding Yongbaek at last. "You're Oyama Ryuhaku. How many times do we have to say it? I can't count how often we've reminded you of your name since you boarded the ship. You simpleton!" One of the overseers for the mine translated the Japanese commander's words, mimicking his angry tone as he did so.

The answer was always the same, no matter how many times he was asked: "I'm Yongbaek the *kongyangju* (monk who prepares meals). Yongbaek is the precious name that was given to me by the head monk. I never knew my ma or pa, so my only name is the one I got when I entered the temple. It's Yongbaek."

The Japanese commander explained that the new surname Oyama had been established for him when he was conscripted. "That's strange," Yongbaek said in response. "I never had a surname to begin with (not knowing who his parents were, there was no way he could know his name), so how could a new one be 'established' for me?" No matter what anyone said, his answer was always the same.

4.

The dead Myeongsik was stuffed into a straw bag and placed inside the sickroom, next to the "good-for-nothing old-timers" with persistent chest problems who were still clinging to life, then thrown into a nearby pond sometime in the middle of the night.

No particular action was taken that evening regarding the "commotion" that had occurred. The next afternoon, however, as the laborers were in the cafeteria eating their lunch, Nishihara was called to the office in the main building. He never returned. Two or three days later, one of the work leaders came to the laborers' rooms, bundled up Nishihara's things, and left. Most likely he'd been transferred to another mine or handed over to the police, but the laborers never heard anything more about him.

On the day that the "commotion" happened, the imperial army did come. Two trucks of infantrymen arrived in the afternoon, but all the soldiers did was parade around the main gate for about half an hour.

Yongbaek steadily recovered with an unearthly vitality. But he was completely mentally incapacitated, and had lost the ability to speak.

Eventually he was sent out to work. Yongbaek had always liked working. That was probably why he was allowed to live. He pushed the mine cart. At first he stared hard at the cart and gently stroked the boxes in the cart with his palm. He then spit on the wheel axles, perhaps thinking to oil them. That made people laugh hard. Hearing their laughter, Yongbaek grinned and pushed the cart forward at full speed. There were seven or eight tracks laid out from the ore processing station to each of the mining sites, with each path an average of about two or three hundred yards in length. The eighty yards around the mining sites were the most arduous to navigate. Because they had to dig down into the mountain for the ore, the area was steeply sloped even after leveling the ground. Two laborers pushed one cart, and four carts made up one troop. The sturdiest and most skilled laborers were placed at the head of the procession. Naturally, their cart tended to be the fastest. The other laborers had to push their carts with desperate speed and energy in order to keep up. They could not afford to fall behind, as a work leader always followed them. The work leader assigned to the troop would jab his white birch pole (the end of which was affixed with a nail) into the laborers' backs to spur them on. The laborers' pants would steadily become stained with blood in a suggestive way. The laborers were driven like cattle from the moment they began work to the moment they ended, not only by the leaders but also by themselves. As they pushed the cart, they had to be mindful of those both before and behind them. Still, getting yelled at as a nail stabbed you in the behind was better than getting stabbed with no warning at all, as sometimes happened with the more malicious leaders. The laborers tried to counter by stuffing things in their pants, but the leaders could always tell by the nail's response when they did that, and punishment swiftly followed.

Yongbaek was assigned the front cart. He worked even harder than before. Even so, there were times when he would get yelled at for making a mistake. Whenever that happened, Yongbaek would flinch and clap his hands over his ears like a child trying to drive away the sound of thunder. Wordless moans would escape from his mouth. At other times, he was like an obedient dog: as soon as a pole was raised threateningly over his head, he would crouch on the floor and whine. For some reason he always covered his ears then, too, and his fearful eyes roamed restlessly like those of a blind man. People saw it as an expression of supplication. Taeil watched the new Yongbaek constantly. He hadn't been able to witness Yongbaek's ordeal that fateful day, but it hardly seemed to matter: even when squatting in the bright light of the afternoon sun, Yongbaek's body bore its own witness to the events of that dark morning as clearly as a photograph. Taeil found it unbearable.

Taeil's job was to shovel the chromite soil that others had unearthed with their pickaxes onto the mine cart. The laborers were forbidden from bending their waists when they dug, even when driving their pickaxes deep into the soil or when scooping the soil up with their shovels. Instead they were forced to stand ramrod straight, moving only their arms as they mechanically dug up the soil without pause. Bending down or doing anything that required a return action was seen as a waste of time. And so they worked and worked without pause, swinging their arms like the pendulum of a clock, until it felt like the bones in their hips and arms would break apart. Because of that, their torsos remained as rigid as if they'd been corseted with a medical brace even at night. But the old-timers learned to endure it. Even if there was no possible way to endure such a hell, still you had to endure it. The proprietors of the company that owned the mines didn't just profit from linking their operations to the national policies of Japan; they also profited by using the same methods as the imperial army and taking extreme advantage of humans' ability to adapt to their environment.

No Korean laborers were assigned to the fairly easy job of sorting the ore. Chromite soil contained mineral dust that was more valuable than even gold. That was one of the reasons why only the Japanese workers, which included three young women who commuted from the nearby village, were allowed to handle the ore. The laborers would listen to the young women's raucous laughter as they went to and from the factory, note the sashay of their curves in their wartime pants, hear the overlapping laughter of the Japanese men. There was freedom there. Even the mere smell of the women's face powder was enough to give the laborers the feeling that the building where the ore was sorted was its own special world.

Every time Yongbaek's empty cart rattled down the tracks, Taeil would reflexively look back at Yongbaek.

Baring his yellow teeth and laughing gaily like a child, Yongbaek would climb onto one end of the cart and wave his hand at him. And then he would croon a peculiar melody that was not quite speech, not quite song. Outside, in the shadow of the green mountains that enclosed them on all sides and underneath a sky that was as clear and wide as the skies of Korea, he became particularly merry—one might even say he frolicked. Yes, it was true that he brightened the work environment. Even the "big shots" treated him with some kindness, giving him caramels as a treat during the 3:00 p.m. break. While sucking on his caramel, Yongbaek would point to the Japanese person who had given him the treat with an innocent expression on his face. (Was that his way of thanking him?) He had no interest in the dried Pacific herring that was allotted as a snack and always gave the fish away to his fellow laborers. Sometimes, as he clambered off his cart, Yongbaek would bow his head to Taeil, his gentle eyes narrow and a soft smile on his face. Taeil was always startled when that happened, and his chest would tighten with emotion. Although such moments were painful, they were also a rare and heartwarming diversion, and so Taeil treasured them.

What really broke Taeil's heart, though, was Yongbaek's use of cigarettes. Like the other laborers, he smoked his allocated five cigarettes during the breaks. His expression as he inhaled the smoke was so comically serious that it always made the people around him laugh. The sight of him choking on the smoke got even more laughs. The laughter seemed to delight Yongbaek. And so it was through laughter that the repercussions of Myeongsik's escape—which included Yongbaek becoming disabled, Myeongsik dying, and Nishihara getting taken away by the police—gradually faded into the background. Everyone understood how twisted their own laughter was. Still they laughed. They protected and treasured Yongbaek's laughter by folding his laughter into their own. Taeil also laughed, even as anguish tore at his heart. But there was nothing that could be done. The more Yongbaek laughed, the more Taeil was chained to the ghost of Yi Myeongsik. Although Nishihara was no longer there, he too raised his long thin face and laughed.

When Yongbaek smiled, the smiling face of the good-natured Myeongsik also revealed itself. Taeil knew that Myeongsik had been beaten to death. And yet there he was, clinging to Yongbaek's back like a coward, merging their two bodies into one single disabled body that hounded Taeil always. Hitting Yi had split him into two warring factions: a Taeil filled with self-remorse and a Taeil who was acutely aware that *he had been able to hit him* in order to step over him and move on. But even these conflicting sides of himself threatened to collapse before this new creature that was Yongbaek. *Yi, I wasn't able to refuse their order the way Yongbaek did. But what would have happened to me if I hadn't struck you as hard as I could? It was my own choice to strike you, and it was for my own sake that I struck you so mercilessly. My body sprang into action, trying to find a way I could live with a self that had struck you, and it wasn't the white birch pole but my palm that came crashing down upon your flayed flesh. When my palm confirmed the blow, I think I might have gone mad with joy. I broke your back, and I broke down the wall that stood in my way.* Well, Seong, there really was a wall in you. The wall pressed down and squeezed out the rotting pus inside you, which you then spewed out at me. I wasn't the wall. That's why it's not true that you chose that other path of your own volition. Having succumbed to your fear, you were chosen by the wall. From the time I was caught at N. Station and brought here to die, I was struck over one hundred times. One fifth of my compatriots whipped me before Yongbaek made it all disappear. But even so, it was still around a hundred strokes. But Taeil—yours was the most relentless of them all, like you wanted to saw through my flesh. I was already dead by then, so I didn't feel anything, but I watched from beside my own corpse. You were so enthusiastic about hitting me. That's why that damn work leader didn't bring his oak pole down on your head. The fierceness of your apparent sincerity took even him aback. I'm not blaming you. But what's with this lip service of yours? You won't be able to fool yourself with that dithering nonsense. *I know, Yi. But—but—I just can't feel remorse over this one thing, the fact that I struck you as hard as I could . . .*

Yongbaek lay on the futon across from him, his expression a blank Noh mask. The mask slipped off Yongbaek's face and stealthily crept towards Taeil like an apparition or an assassin intent on strangling his victim with a silk rope under the cover of night. It was heavier than anything he'd ever known, a heavy presence that made him feel like his exhausted flesh was being injected with some spiritual toxin meant to turn him into a living corpse—or no, to make him inexplicably disintegrate into a viscous mess of liquids right there on the futon.

More and more people became sick. The labor demanded of everyone else became more and more intense as a result.

Taeil watched for an opportunity to escape, having strengthened his resolve to flee this place. He knew in the end he would have to do it alone.

The company intensified its surveillance efforts. Barbed wire couldn't be placed around the mining area due to all the tree chopping and digging that had to be done there, so overseers with hunting rifles were stationed every 160 feet or so around the perimeter instead. Even the laborers' hopes of reaching the outside world were completely snatched away. There was no hope of a miracle, either. No miracles could occur in a place that had eliminated every risk. They had to either endure living in this hell until they cannibalized themselves like octopuses, or else they must rise up—but insurrection, if not impossible, offered no hope of survival. The imperial army was lying in wait in the city, not that far away. Something had to happen by the time they reached the point of self-cannibalization, and until then there was nothing to do but wait. But even as surveillance intensified and the worksite became one big cage, cutting the laborers off from the outside world with a line of rifles, a whispered rumor began to circulate in the wake of Japan's humiliating defeat and withdrawal from Guadalcanal Island: Japan would soon lose the war, and Korea would be liberated.

Taeil had a strong interest in how things were going with the war, but the only way he could satisfy his interest (they weren't allowed any newspapers; instead, they were subjected to bimonthly propaganda lectures) was by smoothing out old newspaper sheets that had been thrown away in the toilets.

And then it happened. It was a day when work clothes were being distributed to the laborers from the leaders' rooms. A headline from an old newspaper that had been carelessly tossed among the clothes caught Taeil's eye. He managed to smuggle the newspaper out by surreptitiously tucking it in his bundle of clothes. When he finished reading the newspaper, he threw it into the toilet. The newspaper told him of the surrender of Italy, one of the so-called Axis Powers. The enemy stronghold had begun to crumble. Taeil relayed the information to one of the laborers. Rumors had already been circulating in various other ways, sometimes even accidentally slipping out of the leaders' mouths, but this latest news reinvigorated the men, giving them the strength to endure.

But still they were made to labor day after day, and their "octopus" limbs were torn away one by one. As always, the most effective (but also negative) means of saving oneself was to be promoted to the position of work leader. The vast majority, however, would remain octopuses. Within this environment, Harimoto did manage to separate himself from the other octopuses, just as he said he would. When one of the work leaders was assigned to guard duty, Harimoto took his place as troop leader at the mines.

On a day that began just like any other, a green truck arrived at the compound, its bed loaded with large tanks. The truck drove through the entrance next to the watchtower, rounded the corner of the dormitory building, and then came to stop beside the annex that contained the toilets. Taeil could just make out the front of the truck. Light refracted off the windshield directly into his eyes, obscuring his view, but still he could tell it was the night soil truck. It had come to "scoop up" the excrement from the toilets. Come to think of it, the toilets did seem like they were dangerously full lately. In Taeil's mind rose up an image of the toilets clogged with human waste, toilet paper, and dark urine. He'd never tried peering down into the pit below, but he knew that unlike the world above it was as deep and wide as a pool. A certain idea pierced his brain with all the force of an auger. It was such a sudden and unexpected idea that for a while all he could do was stand there in a daze, unable to understand his own thinking. He was seized with the urge to cast aside his shovel right there and then and dash to the toilets. Moving out of the persistent glare of the sun, Taeil tried to calm his rapidly beating heart and put his thoughts in order even as he continued his work, his fatigue having vanished from the excitement of his shocking discovery.

As soon as dinner was over, he went as calmly as he could to the bathroom. The toilets were located in an annex that was connected to the main building by a narrow passage between the two laborers' rooms. Inside the annex were eight partitioned stalls (used for feces) in two rows back to back and two troughs for urinating that faced the stalls. Each stall door only went up to one's waist, giving you a full view of the buttocks of the people who were urinating. The floors and stall walls had been constructed with wooden boards. A rectangular hole was cut into the floorboards inside each stall, revealing a pit that was dark and deep. Taeil stuck his head down the hole and saw the lingering light of dusk glimmering through the filthy aperture that was used to draw up the night soil, called the scoop opening. There was still feces and urine down there, as not all of it had fit in the tanks in the night soil truck. The stall hole was big enough for his head but obviously not big enough for his body. Taeil quickly examined the floorboards. He had crouched over these shit-stained boards countless times but had been too anguished about other things to really notice them. Who could have predicted that he would find such significance in them now? Was it just coincidence, or had fate finally opened up a path for Taeil? The boards seemed fully willing to accept their new role for his sake. They had lain there patiently, waiting for his gentle hands to shake them awake. In each stall, three boards had been placed to the left and right of the rectangular hole, with another board placed at a perpendicular angle both above and below the hole. The boards were nailed down, but in a rather perfunctory fashion. If he could manage to pry up one of the planks to the left or right, his body could probably fall straight down. Having ascertained this much, Taeil deliberately crumpled the old newspaper that served as their toilet paper as loud as he could, coughed, and spit into the hole. He then opened the door, reconfirming with some satisfaction that he was in the second stall from the end, at a fair distance from the guards. As he returned to his room he told himself he needed to remember the faces of the guards (there were two inside the building and one at the corner of the passage that led to the main hallway).

Having set his mind on escape, he was filled with a restlessness that filled his every waking moment. It was a terrifying risk that might end in death, so how strange it was that he felt more hope than fear. If he planned it carefully enough, he might just succeed. He'd thought about escaping before, of course, but he'd always reached the same conclusion: rather than what happened after the escape, the question of how to get out of the building was the first priority and the decisive factor in determining if one succeeded or not. It was also no easy matter to get to Asahikawa. But he knew there was a Korean neighborhood in the city, and he even knew where it was; if he could just make it there, he'd be okay. Taeil proceeded with his plans with the utmost caution, even as the sad spirit of Yi Myeongsik from that fateful night—as rigid as green wood, as silent as a rock—came back to haunt him.

Taeil went to the bathroom late one night, after he'd already stripped naked. His stomach was roiling. But now was the perfect time to go: the guards were changing shifts.

He was unexpectedly accosted by one of the guards. "What's wrong with you—your stomach hurt or something?" Taeil pressed his hands against his stomach and nodded. He told the guard it might be diarrhea.

"Diarrhea? Ugh." The guard knit his brows, then gave him a wry grin. "Try not to be so noisy . . . "

"No problem," said Taeil, smiling back more than was necessary. "I'll try my best."

Taeil entered the stall next to the one he'd used before. The boards there were nailed down in the same way. His diarrhea was unexpectedly loud. There was no doubt the guards could hear it. Taeil squatted there for some time, straining as hard as he could. *How fortunate. Oh, wonderful diarrhea! Please make even more noise!* He pulled at a board at the edge of the hole, but it refused to budge. He refrained from exerting his full strength, of course. It would be better to make use of the breaktime after meals, when there was a lot of coming and going. Right now, even the slightest sound might disturb the slumbering air.

The stink of the board lingered on his hand even after he'd crawled back into bed. Afraid of rousing suspicion, he'd washed his hands for only a short time. He turned his back to the laborers, all of whom were in a deep sleep. He couldn't trust any of them very much. Taeil brought his hand to his nose and sniffed deeply, as if trying to recall what he'd forgotten.

What can I do to loosen the boards—how can I take out those nails? That was the first task. The second was to wait for the human waste to accumulate until it nearly reached the scoop opening. Because the pit was so deep, there was no way he could reach the opening without relying upon the buoyancy power of accumulated human waste. Finally, he had to figure out what to do if the iron grill over the opening was locked from the outside . . . He had to check it out. And he had to prepare a change of clothes and shoes at the very least, in order to make a full-speed escape. Those were Taeil's own personal conditions. On top of those grimly awaited the conditions of the outside world, which he had no ability to predict. When he thought calmly about it, he realized there were any number of barriers blocking his way. Like terrible giant birds, stretching out black wings that reached all the way to the horizon. Was this no more than a fleeting fever dream, in the end? . . . The thought drew Taeil into a deep sea of despair. Waiting in the sea like giant undulating strands of seaweed were two creatures with the faces of Myeongsik and Yongbaek. Snores pitched both high and low hummed around him, creating a strangely harmonious rhythm, but one particularly loud snore rose up from a short distance away. It was Yongbaek. Since his brain injury, he'd become a person who drooled and snored as he slept.

5.

October came. Yellow flooded the nearby mountains and fields, although the mountain range in the distance remained the same. There were many days when it rained, but as long as the rain wasn't heavy the laborers continued their work in their rain gear. The blistering winds grew even fiercer and drove the chilly rain into every pore of the laborers' bodies. A persistent cough made its rounds among the men. There were no doctors permanently stationed at the mine, but at least they had access to some medicine. Taeil asked for medicine whenever he could; he needed to take scrupulous care of his body, in preparation for his eventual escape.

The digging had expanded to quite an extensive area by then, reaching the space around the buildings and even extending behind the lodgings. The wire fences were removed, and trolley tracks were laid out connecting the main line directly to the ore sorting station. Work was begun on driving railroad ties into the ground near the annex that housed the toilets. By a stroke of good fortune, Taeil was part of the squad that was responsible for laying down the new tracks, giving him an unexpected opportunity to inspect the scoop opening. He excitedly imagined himself crawling through the shit-filled hole. *Okay, let's say you were able to break free. Will you be able to run up the tree-stripped base of this mountain that's now at my back? Will you be able to find your way through the forest at night? As long as you etch the lay of the land deep into your memory, it shouldn't take you more than ten minutes to reach the cover of the forest, even if it's dark. And then . . .* That had been the path chosen by Myeongsik; it was by far the fastest path to escape. The scoop opening was wide enough to allow a human body to pass through. It was fitted with a cover made of a steel frame, wire mesh, and plate glass. Just as he'd suspected, the cover had a lock on it, but it was designed to simply latch onto the steel frame. The lock looked rusty and scuffed, but even so he would have to use some kind of sturdy instrument to wrench it open.

The rainy days continued. Fortunately for him, all the rain caused the human waste in the pit to expand. He hoped the water would also help dilute the smell. Roughly half a month of careful preparation passed. Every day Taeil gazed down at the mound of human waste that swelled from the contributions of four hundred humans while patiently working at the nails that held down the boards. His fingernails became ragged and torn. He couldn't very well justify going into the stalls all the time, so he tried as much as possible to go during breaktime, or in other words while he was wearing clothes, in order to use the metal fittings on his belt to pry at the nails. At night, when he was naked, he used his fingers. Each board was nailed down in multiple places. Extracting the nails without making a sound, with his bare hands, and in the limited amount of time available to him was even more difficult than he'd imagined. First he would grip the edge of a board firmly but carefully and wriggle it around for some time. A small gap would open up between the boards. If you trod down on that space, the head of the nail would eventually poke up. He'd then work at the nail with the edge of the metal fastenings on his belt. Then he'd use his fingernails to move the nail about, trying to pry it out. The nails were badly rusted and refused to move easily. He'd periodically look over the door and make a motion of wiping his (clean) ass with paper. And then he'd push the nail back down and return the board to its original position.

After ten days of this, he was finally able to gain control of one nail. Using his fingernails, he was able to pull the nail out with ease; to return the board to its normal position, all he had to do was push the nail back in. He rubbed some dirt onto the nail head with his fingertip. With that, and with the dim lighting, no one would be able to see the difference at a glance. Now, finally, he'd be able to slip the nail in and out as easily as a blade in a sheath. The second and third nails weren't as arduous as the first one, but since he worked at them not one by one but in equal measures, it was still painstaking work. The only tools at his disposal were the metal fastenings on his belt—and, even more than that, his half-torn fingernails.

Due to the rain, the feces and urine accumulated faster than anticipated, and he worried that he wouldn't be able to finish his preparations in time. In order to avoid suspicion, he didn't always use the same stall, and there were days when his stall was occupied by someone else. When that happened, Taeil always went into the next stall over, but he often found it difficult to do his business due to his nerves. Instead he eavesdropped as best he could, wondering if all his efforts would be overturned by a single incident beyond the wooden wall.

Pressed for time, Taeil anxiously threw himself into this lonely work. The night soil truck would most likely arrive in the near future. If he missed this opportunity, he'd be faced with a Hokkaido winter that was as severe as that of Korea. The fields, mountains, and roads would get buried in deep white snow. A benefit was that the human waste would freeze over with a thick layer of ice. But the outside world posed a big problem.

These thoughts spurred Taeil on. He finally got the nails to move exactly as he wished. All that remained was to get his hands on a small crowbar of sorts (though how to hide it was another problem) and to stash a change of clothes somewhere outside.

The fateful day arrived swiftly. It was a rainy day, rainy enough to make the laborers rejoice. Gusting winds drove heavy sheets of rain up into the air and then back down to the ground in thunderous white plumes. The horizon was nothing but a hazy mist of gray. The water accumulated against the slopes of the worksite, steadily eating away at the earth. The laborers enjoyed their temporary reprieve from work. Some raucously played Korean chess on boards they'd made with cardboard, some sang popular melodies from Korea or Japan, and others gazed out the window and talked about how they'd no doubt be made to do extra work when the rain stopped. Taeil looked on as the rain exploded onto the ground in smoky white sprays. He had goosebumps and couldn't stop shivering. If he were to escape on this kind of day, the rain would at least wash the filth from his body, though it would be a shower as cold and hard as ice. Before this, Taeil had thought about making use of a rainy night. He didn't yet realize that today was to be the fateful day. Shall we call what happened coincidence? By coincidence, he found and stole a crowbar.

That afternoon, a lecture on the "current situation" was held in the laborers' room. In preparation, the room was thoroughly cleaned and then set up with a lectern, some flowers, and a curtain. Nails and tools were employed in the process. Taeil volunteered himself and did his best to blend into the environment, all the while choosing work that required hammers and other such implements. Many tools were thrown carelessly into the toolbox or even left scattered on the floor. To Taeil, it was like finding an alleyway lined with gold. It wasn't a difficult task to use the cover of the crowd to steal one of the tools. Taeil walked around the room as bold as brass. But his mind was already breaking through that dark hole, hurtling forward towards the road to escape.

A middle-aged Korean man with good complexion and a receding hairline stood patiently at the lectern, the Japanese flag behind him, as some last-minute participants arrived at the lecture. He was apparently an advisor for the Asahikawa chapter of the Harmonization Association and the manager of a munitions factory. Rumor had it that he'd conscripted every last Korean youth in Hokkaido to do construction work on the Paramushir Airfield on the Kuril Islands, something which the man himself seemed to take great pride in. He hinted as much in his speech. As he spoke, jeers rose from the crowd. *We don't understand Japanese, so speak in Korean, why dontcha? We really, really wanna listen to your talk, Teach, but we can't follow along in Japanese.*

The speaker took a sip of water and stuck his hand into the upper right pocket of his civilian uniform with a priggish air. "Gentlemen!" he said in Japanese, his words stiff and fussy. "This thing you call the Korean language no longer exists. You must be cognizant of the motto 'habitual use of the national language.' You gentlemen need to learn the national language—Japanese—in that spirit. The Korean language is now a relic of the past. It is my dearest wish that you will be able to understand the gist of what I am saying by the time I give my next lecture on the current state of affairs."

In the rest of his speech, he expounded on the

"invincibility of the land of Gods"; declared that the "people of the peninsula" would finally become one of the leading powers of the East once the "holy war" was won; and insisted that this was all quite justifiable and natural, considering that "the mainland and Korea" were of common ancestry. He then emphasized the roles and responsibilities of the "people of the peninsula" three times and declared that their function as "industrial soldiers" was a very important one. "In order that I too may better serve the Emperor," he concluded, "I have decided to become the first person from the peninsula to run for the Hokkaido Prefectural Assembly." The work leaders began to applaud. Harimoto, who was seated in the front row, enthusiastically joined in. A few scattered claps sounded around the room, but that was it.

After the lecture, Harimoto approached the speaker and asked him for a handshake. Delighted at having found this apparently ardent and noble supporter, the Harmonization Association advisor seized Harimoto's hand with both of his own as if he were an old, trusted friend. The scene was so cloyingly patriotic that even the Japanese people next to them felt vaguely guilty. The advisor flashed a wide smile that caused his pearly-white skin to shine even more. Turning to the laborers, he raised one hand and shrilly proclaimed, "I will do my utmost. Gentlemen, I expect you to do the same. For His Majesty's Empire!"

Taeil took his time eating his last meal. He would have to leave this place within the next thirty minutes. Although he'd joined Harimoto's fervent applause at the end of the lecture, the thought never left his mind that everything was now over; all his preparations were done (although in reality Taeil still hadn't been able to prepare a change of clothes). He waited for the moment when he could make his "departure," all the while telling himself over and over that he mustn't forget even the slightest detail of this "half-octopus room," or even a single scrap of memory of this life. Concentrating his entire being on the feel of the rigid crowbar against his thigh, he tried hard to suppress the wild beating of his heart. But as he left the cafeteria and entered the laborers' room, he began to hesitate. *Today isn't the only day I've got. There's also tomorrow, right?* whispered a voice inside him. *If I don't go through with my plan today, there's always tomorrow, and the day after tomorrow . . .* To take action in the face of adversity, to leap into an unknown world—Taeil was afraid. He was haunted by the feeling that the amorphous shadow of death would swallow him whole.

It wasn't just that. As he left the cafeteria, he saw Harimoto, who was still tailing after the Harmonization Association advisor, make his way to the building entrance with some of the work leaders. But then Harimoto abruptly turned around and gave Taeil a broad, devilish grin. It was an off-putting grin, to be sure. Why would he smile like that at Taeil, today of all days? His eyebrows were raised in a normal fashion, but his lips were drawn back in a half-snarl that seemed full of hidden meaning. His face was divided into two very different expressions, in other words. *Has he somehow sniffed out my secret? . . . And what should I do about my clothes? How will I be able to walk along the road without suspicion if I'm smeared in shit?* He'd managed to hide away some old work shoes (they'd been carelessly tossed away outside, near the lodgings) in a stack of lumber next to the annex, but he'd been unable to prepare a change of clothes. *What to do? There's still time to think. Do I wait for the next opportunity or not?* His heart wavered. But no, the crowbar was the final weapon he needed to smash apart the lock to the scoop opening. The crowbar sat heavily against his thigh, ordering Taeil to depart. Where in the world should he hide the crowbar? Would it lie peacefully inside his pocket as he slaved underneath the blue sky tomorrow? What would happen if the rooms were searched while he was at the mines? Would it vanish into thin air for him during the pat-down after work? Forget about the clothes, the rain that was pouring down now like a waterfall would wash him clean—.

Time pressed on. Yongbaek was sitting close by. What was going on in that slow brain of his? He was staring at the ribbons of rain flowing down the glass window. *It's time to go!* But he just couldn't make himself leave without saying a word of farewell to Yongbaek. Taeil casually settled next to Yongbaek and thumped him on the shoulder. "What's with that sleepy face?" he said with a laugh. "Do you want a cigarette? It'll wake you up."

Taeil was ashamed that he couldn't do anything else for Yongbaek. It struck him that the white cigarette looked like a thin piece of bone. Yongbaek gave a hesitant wordless moan but then held out both hands for the cigarette. Most of his own cigarettes had been taken away from him by his so-called friends. Yongbaek made a gesture of lighting a match and then abruptly made his way to the monitor's desk. Taeil gave an involuntary shiver, but Yongbaek soon returned and offered the lit cigarette to Taeil first before finally taking a puff himself. Crooning his wordless moan, Yongbaek peered at Taeil's face with innocent eyes. He squeezed his own cheeks with his hands and pointed first to the acetylene lamp and then to Taeil's face. And then he shook his head and hands over and over, as if he were a stubborn toddler. He was saying that Taeil didn't look well. Looking terribly worried, Yongbaek gripped Taeil's wrist and rubbed it against Taeil's cheek. It was a scene, Taeil thought, that he'd most likely remember for the rest of his life: Yongbaek's eyes, the feel of his palm on his cheeks as if they were Yongbaek's own. Yongbaek's gaze was unfocused and weak, and yet somehow his wide, black, unmoving eyes contained in them a certain steadfastness and even an aloof, transcendent dignity. What kind of look could prevail against the eyes of a child? Taeil blinked rapidly, trying his best to suppress the tears that were threatening to brim over. Through the haze of his tears, Taeil thought he saw the masklike expression slip from Yongbaek's face for just a second. Taeil lowered his head and averted his gaze.

There was no time. Taeil surreptitiously took a deep breath. He made a gesture of fumbling with the buttons on his pants as he exited the room, his face fixed in a buffoonish expression. Although he had the sensation of blood rising to his cheeks, the blood deep within him had coagulated into stillness. The monitor at the desk was rifling through a magazine filled with illustrations. At one point Taeil had thought the monitor's face resembled that of an owl, but today it looked more like that of a donkey. In the hallway, he couldn't help but glance back at the room. The interior of the room was strangely bright. He walked down the chilly concrete hallway in his military-issued socks. Like asphalt, the floor was blackish and cold and hard and unmoving, and it seemed to stretch on and on with a vast subterranean emptiness. Taeil boldly soldiered on. The guards were standing at attention in their usual places, as if they were just part of the décor. The acetylene lamps were swaying. Their calm light turned the rooms into walls and the hallway into a fantastic, otherworldly space. The thought randomly came to Taeil that this hallway had a beautiful deep solitude to it.

He passed one person coming back from the

bathroom, and he knew there were two or three people behind him who were also on their way there. He mustn't let them pass him. Taeil walked through the entrance of the annex. The monitors were changing shifts. Although the monitors did nothing but casually glance at him, his heart gave a great thump and he felt the blood in his veins freeze. There didn't seem to be anyone in the stall he was aiming for. His body cast a long shadow over the door. His heartbeat sped up even more at seeing his own shadow, but he swiftly opened the door and then sat there on the toilet for some time, gathering his breath. And then, all at once, he forgot everything that had happened in the past. While keeping a sharp, fierce eye on the door, he inserted his fingernails under the first nail head and proceeded with his plan. His hands shook, his whole body shook. A handful of maggots were sluggishly crawling on the ground near the nail. *Stay calm, stay calm. The time, the time—Swiftly, calmly, calmly . . .* He tried to steady his racing heart. If the monitor were to approach, the shadow thrown by the acetylene lamp would probably reach Taeil first.

"Ah!" As he brushed the maggots away with his palm, he nearly cried out and stumbled. One nail had already been pulled out. It was impossible. He was sure he had pushed it in. A pitch-black fog of apprehension rose up before his eyes, blocking his vision. He involuntarily turned around. No enemy in sight. *Someone knows!* But then why had nothing happened? He carelessly plugged the nail back in and tried to stand. But nothing had happened, right? Every single one of his thoughts marshalled together into a single lightning strike that rent his brain in two. His thoughts had already separated from his body and were racing to meet the vast wilderness beyond the scoop opening. There was still time to bring his body back, but somewhere a voice was shouting that there would never be another chance. One of the laborers gave a cough in that moment and positioned himself at the end of the row of urinals. Taeil was overwhelmed. He wrenched the nails out, carefully pried up a board, and slid his body down the hole. The waste bubbled up over his feet. No one was using the urinals now. He stuck his head back up and moved the board back to its original position. He could see the walls of the urinals beyond the door, but there was no sign of people. *There's still time—* He sunk the nails back into place and stuck the crowbar into his waistband. And then he gently let his entire body plunge into the human waste. The stench pierced his nose like a drill through the skull. He thought he would throw up. He closed his eyes and violently shook his head. It was like being immersed in a low-pressure oil tank. The waste was cold and thick and heavy, and it ate away at his skin like a swarm of fish, oozed into every opening of his clothes, invaded his entire body. His body temperature plunged. The awful odor continued to wreak havoc on his stomach, which was still digesting its last meal. He nearly fainted from the smell. It was dark in the hole. If he delayed any longer, he would most likely be unable to locate the scoop opening. There—a faint light, peeping through the chinks of the wire mesh. Taeil aimed for that light that was both dim and dazzling at the same time. Using the beams below the toilets as a guide, he made his way forward. But he was only able to advance about two or three yards before he ran into a low ceiling. Above him came the faint dull thudding of feet along what was most likely the aisle between the toilets. He had no choice but to swim. He swam towards the light. He swam as hard as he could—but he did not get far. It felt like he wasn't swimming in water but in porridge: he was constantly forced to pause, his feet scrambling for purchase, as he used his hands to push away the obstacles that blocked his face. He was seized with an irrational fear that he would be dragged down into a bottomless abyss, into some unknown hell, the moment he ceased moving his hands and feet. He panicked. Struggling even just a little caused waste to pour into his mouth. He tried his best to spit it out. A sneeze was threatening to erupt. He hastily covered his mouth with his hand. Waste splattered into his eyes and nose. In this way, he finally reached the scoop opening. The light from the outside world was struggling to force itself in. He wiped his face with his filthy hands and used his head to push against the window, but the window rejected his efforts with a low banging sound. Taeil carefully applied sewage to the iron grill over the window, attempting to dampen the sound of its creaking.

As he struggled to wrench the grill off with the crowbar, he heard the sound of the monitor's footsteps grow more hurried. The sound rippled out, increasing from a single pair of feet to multiple ones. It was joined by the banging of the stall door. The noise echoed eerily within the dark cave. Taeil was desperate. With a dull low creak, a gap opened in the window. But because he had to use one hand to support his body, he wasn't able to put any more force behind the crowbar.

"Ah, over there! He's over there!" The shout rolled over him like a violent wave. The guard had stuck his head down the hole. "You idiot! Come out quickly!"

A shrill whistle was being blown. And then came a sudden gunshot that tore through the air. What in the world had happened? Taeil would likely have misinterpreted the sound as a signal alerting people to his escape, had he not seen the guard's surprise. It was, in fact, a complete coincidence. The whistle abruptly stopped. And then came a confused voice from above him: "It-it's another one! Another escape!" For Taeil, the problem wasn't who had escaped; it was that another escape was happening at the same time as his. The situation was developing at a bewildering speed. Taeil managed to break the glass window to the scoop opening. The crowbar caught in the wire mesh. With a click, the lock flew off and the window gave way. The rain hit his face like a shower. The rain was white and bright. Taeil crawled out on his elbows. The area was slippery, and he couldn't get a good foothold. He'd managed to get almost his entire body out when he heard the howl. A German shepherd had emerged from the shadow of the building and was charging at him from around twenty yards away. A Japanese person with a gun and several overseers followed behind, kicking up a spray of muddy rain as they ran.

The dog flew at him with a leap. Taeil slammed the window shut and scuttled back into the human waste like a turtle retreating into its shell. Following the wall, he desperately swam towards the corner. The dog was growling and worrying the wire mesh of the window with his teeth. Several stakes, the kind used for railroad ties, had been embedded into the walls like wainscotting. They had become slippery and slithery from their exposure to human waste, the same texture as rotten flayed skin. The walls offered him no handholds. After long effort, he was finally able to touch what felt like a beam that was supporting the ceiling in the corner. The top was blocked off and he wasn't able to put his hands around the beam, but he was lucky enough to find a hollow to grasp. The darkness began to completely dominate him. He despaired. Overcome with dizziness, he felt the energy leach from his body to the point where he considered lying down and giving up right there. He was frozen to his core, and his feet were numb and stiff. He thought he might become delirious with fever at any moment.

But in that instant, in that tiny break, his spirit grew terribly calm. Projected on the wall of his mind was a blurry, distant image of himself trying to flee to a foreign country. It was joined by the white-clothed figure of his mother, who could always be found standing off in a corner of his dreams. He was crying. His cool, clear tears were the merest drop in the bucket of the filth around him. He felt like his tears belonged to someone else. He felt like the axis of his soul was sinking into a calmness borne by the concentration of all of his different selves. At the same time, his body was going numb. He decided to die. Put another way, he wanted a feces-filled freedom.

The dog stopped barking at the same moment a human voice called out. "Nariyama!" The voice echoed through every inch of the vast darkness. "Hey, answer us—! You can still live if you come out now, Nariyama. You'll die in that shit tank. Nariyama, come out now!"

Taeil's energy returned when he heard the voice. A surge of hatred rose up in him. He fought against his stiffening body with all his might. Why would his body not listen to his spirit? The voice continued to call to him from beyond the scoop opening, roaming through the empty darkness. It was the same kind of voice one used to coax a child, cajolery and cordiality wrapped around a lie. Suddenly, a blindingly bright beam of light cut through the darkness.

"It's time to come out. Harimoto was caught, too . . . We're bringing him in."

The voice told him they would use Harimoto to catch Taeil. But Harimoto hadn't been captured yet. *Harimoto—Harimoto?* . . . That was a surprise. It was a surprise that the "loyal" Harimoto would flee.

"Don't wanna come out? We're gonna release the dog!"

"Release it!" Taeil screamed. The dog hurled itself into the light. It flew at him with its head held high. The wandering light hit Taeil, as if creating a path in the dark for the dog to follow. The dog silently advanced, a big black shadow limned by the light. The dog was at an advantage. But it, too, didn't seem to know how to deal with all the shit; it struggled hard to swim. Its speed slowed. Taeil clutched the crowbar and waited. He had confidence. Dogs were weak in the water and couldn't leap upon their prey. When the eyes gleaming yellow within the black shadow that was its body appeared before him, he swung the crowbar down, aiming for the head. Unlike when he'd struck Yi Myeongsik, Seong Taeil managed to break open the head of what was attacking him. The dog yelped and nearly toppled sideways like a capsizing boat, but then managed to right itself again. It sunk its teeth into him. As it did, Taeil's hand lost its grip on the beam. He frenziedly bashed at the four-legged creature that had attached itself to him. The crowbar made a dull thumping noise as it connected hard with the dog's body two or three times. The dog let go of him.

"It's all over." Someone was shouting, somewhere far beyond his consciousness. In that moment, something brighter than the light flashed in the dark. Gunshot shook the cave with a roar, and a bullet exploded against the wall. The flash came again. He tried frantically to dodge the bullet that was flying towards him like a spear. The crowbar fell from his hands. He groaned. With his last strength, Taeil put his tongue between his teeth and bit down. He toppled sideways. In that instant, both his body and his soul floated up. There was a golden light in front of Taeil. In it twinkled luminous crystals as clear as jewels. He couldn't hear the gunshots anymore. In the sprawling world deep within his muddy consciousness everything was shining—no, the light itself was disappearing, leaving behind only a flash. Taeil swam as hard as he could into the light. The world of human filth was gone. He swam through the light, screaming something desperately. He swam for a long time.

But when the pitch-black darkness finally closed over his eyes, Seong Taeil hadn't even swum a yard.

A Tale of a False Dream

One chilly morning in March, I stood in a corner of the Y. Station terminal, waiting for the bus. I was exhausted because of my dream from last night. Traces of the dream were still alive inside me, like ink that had spread underneath my skin and around my heart. I was also exhausted from having just emerged from a pedestrian tunnel that had been crammed with a swarming horde. Apparently around two million commuters passed through Y. Station on a daily basis. The department store attached to the station dominated the view, looming high over the passersby like an enormous castle wall. There were clouds above the building. I watched the clouds scud across the blue sky, feeling the weight of the entire building pressing down upon my shoulders. Last night's dream had been a peculiar one.

My body had been inside a mesh bag that seemed made of cobwebs. A nest of hermit crabs had taken up residence inside my stomach, which was covered in a kangaroo-like pelt. The hermit crabs used their claws to tear at my guts and feed upon them. My guts were as tender as the flesh of a fig. Strangely, there was no blood or any stabbing pain as the hermit crabs scavenged my body. It might have been due to the white-clothed dwarf priestess who sat crouched in my abdomen, ceaselessly intoning a mantra. She was old and wrinkled and impossibly hideous, and she'd cast a spell on me. She unspooled my intestines for the hermit crabs. As they feasted, they squirmed and wriggled like an infestation of maggots. Eventually the transparent mesh bag was scooped up into the air by some unknown thing and fastened to one of the white clouds racing across the sky. Below the massed clouds was the country of Japan. My hermit crabs and I were being flown at full speed towards the west, towards the country of Korea.

It had been over twenty years since I'd last visited. But the place where I alit was not my hometown but an unfamiliar part of the land. I walked leisurely along a dusty rural road, clothed in white Korean clothes. The road eventually led to Seoul, where it wound its way through the great gate of Namdaemun to Jongno and then to the eight-sided pavilion in Pagoda Park. It was there that I stopped. The pavilion had become a gathering spot for the unemployed. The crowds of people in the park soon engulfed me, and I found myself participating in a public debate on whether or not to entrust the funeral of President Q. to the suzerain state where he'd died. It was argued that the autonomy of the people relied upon purging the land of foreign powers and the ghost of Q. Underneath my ill-fitting Korean clothes, a cold sweat was trickling down my skin and pooling into the crevices of my body. As I gripped the hand of a student beside me and participated in the debate, a chilly, dismal wind blew through my agitated heart. I engaged in the debate while cradling my torso, which was as empty as a crab shell whose meat had all been devoured by a hungry human. I was afraid the student might detect my hollow stomach. Any words that burble out of a person with a hollow stomach are as empty as air bubbles. But wait a minute—something this ridiculous couldn't possibly be real. Even though we *were* in Korea, a country where it was said that ghosts and goblins went unchallenged even in broad daylight, something was off. I set out on a journey through the eight provinces of Korea, searching for something to replace the guts that had been gouged out of my now-empty abdominal cavity.

One day, I stood on a spot where you could see a hill that contained the cave of a certain gentleman thief, located at the very end of a wasteland. A straw scarecrow who looked just like one of the seven incarnations of Hong Gildong,* the leader of the League of Those Who Help the Impoverished, was walking towards me. Copying the dwarf priestess, I intoned a mantra that was meant to turn the scarecrow back into straw that I could then use to fill up my stomach. But the mantra wasn't very effective, and the scarecrow seemed to have

---

* A legendary figure, popularized by *The Biography of Hong Gildong*, written by the 17th century writer Heo Gyun. Born in Seoul as the illegitimate son of a nobleman, Hong Gildong left home as a youth, rebelling against the feudal order and taking part in peasant revolts. As the leader of a group of bandits called the League of Those Who Help the Impoverished, he stole from feudal rulers and distributed their ill-gotten riches to the poor. With his powers of magic and divination, he was able to seemingly appear and disappear at will throughout the land. He eventually left Korea and established a utopia called Yuldo on an island in the sea.

powers of his own—powers that were typical of Hong Gildong, who was a master of the astrological art of transformation. In any case, the scarecrow soon revived and moved to block my way.

"I see that you're a human with no guts. A pity—you can't serve your function as a human being like that."

"Who do you think you are, to say such rude things to me?"

"You're the Mr. R. who arrived from Japan, aren't you? I'm the spirit of Hong Gildong, who protects the eight provinces of Korea."

"You call yourself Hong Gildong, but you don't know a single thing about who I really am. You should be ashamed of yourself."

"It's my contention that you're not a true Korean. For one, how can you explain the fact that you don't have any guts?"

I was at a loss. I was unable to come up with a lie, even a cowardly one like that I'd left them behind for safekeeping in Japan. "That's funny, coming from you. You're a coward who abandoned Korea and ran off to your so-called utopia."

"You're wrong. I was expelled by Korea's parasitic

government officials. It was not I who abandoned Korea. That my spirit lives even now in the eight provinces of the peninsula is proof of that."

"If that's the case, then why did you try so hard to gain a cabinet post in the Ministry of War from those same parasitic officials?"

"You don't know anything. They had no choice but to give me that post, as I'm the embodiment of the will of the people."

I myself had no choice but to plead my case to the spirit of Hong Gildong and his full-fledged Korean guts. It was not that I was born without guts. I'd simply lost them on my way to Korea. Since there's supposedly a Hong Gildong in each of the eight provinces (including the real one), it wouldn't hurt for him to bequeath me just one set of intestines, would it? "That's a rather self-serving request. Still, I'd be rather inclined to grant it, if that didn't mean having to neglect one of the eight provinces. Guts are important to many people." Saying thus, Hong Gildong used his powers of astrology to disappear into thin air. I'd been forsaken. Alone in that endless wasteland devoid of even a single hill, I continued to call out his name, searching for guts I could make my own.

All of a sudden, a monstrous hermit crab about the size of a child appeared before my eyes. It was naked and shell-less—without a home, in other words. It lumbered towards me and tried to crawl through the hole in my stomach. "Haha, I'll be your guts!" it said.

"This is ridiculous!" Horrified, I began to run away. A disembodied voice roared at me from the sky above the wasteland. *What happened to your guts? You cannot call yourself Korean if you don't have guts.* Desperate to flee from the voice's assault, I clapped my hands over my ears and continued to wander through a wasteland that was now like a desert aflame with the glow of the setting sun. A huge wave of sadness crashed over me, threatening to carry me off somewhere unknown. Tears flowed down my face. *Ah, I see.* The feeling that I'd been betrayed by everything and everyone began to slowly rise up within me. My brain began to swell, and there came the sound of breaking glass. The left and right sides of my brain cleaved apart with a clunk, as if having fallen off hinges. I wrapped the moist halves of my brain in a towel and tried to force them back together, but the moment I did a terrible pain shot through my skull. I collapsed onto the sand. My eyes rolled back in their sockets, and my four limbs went stiff. I raised a voiceless cry. *Ahh, I've gone mad!* The wind snatched at my wild, brittle, vanishing voice. With my hands pressed to my head, I attempted to stand, having admitted to myself that I'd gone crazy. But my heart was failing by the minute, and I was seized with fear that I'd suffocate and die at any moment, die alone in this desert. Something was blocking my mouth, preventing me from calling out for help. A cry tore from my throat. My wife was holding my hand and shaking me awake. I awoke, limp and exhausted.

In the past, people all over Korea used woodblock-printed books for interpreting dreams. You may still be able to find them in the South Korean countryside. Just ask the village wise man. He'll be the one smoking a long pipe, a white moustache and beard obscuring his face. The villagers still consult books on dreams and astrology and divination for any number of matters in their lives. These books, their covers ragged and their pages worn and dirty from years of use, are stuffed full of the impoverished villagers' wishes and fears about their dreams. A sick person traveling on a boat or train, for example, indicates a journey of death. If you see a rising dragon, you will be visited by fortune and fame. If you see a school of fish in a clear stream, treasure will soon be yours. These are the kinds of things that are written in the books, which are meant for interpreting dreams and what they portend.

But so-called modern man no longer has an interest in such things, and his dreams have become nothing more than a mechanical manifestation of human physiology, like the wavelengths from an EKG. Their auras of mystery torn away by the power of science, dreams need not linger into the dawn. They no longer have any staying power. Even so, occasionally some dreams with the audacity and tenacity of old do manage to step into the full light of day. I don't believe in dream interpretation books, but whenever I encounter one of those oh-so-human dreams, I feel a desire to step into the dream world myself.

The bus I was on was full; it zipped along the road, ignoring the people who were waiting at the bus stops with their hands raised. I was hemmed in on all sides by the shoulders and chests of the passengers around me. My head was stuffed with the remnants of the unpleasant dream that still lived inside me. My body felt languid, as it did after a wet dream. The experience had left a deep, clear impression upon me. The entire dream had been in Korean. It was perfect in how it had woven the

Korean language into the very structure of my thoughts and feelings. That wasn't something that often happened in my daily life. What also left a lasting impression on me were the Korean clothes I'd worn. I've never worn those kind of clothes in my life. But in the dream, I'd participated in the public debate in Pagoda Park as the sleeves of my *durumagi* (overcoat) fluttered in the wind. I was moved by the sight of myself in those clothes. Come to think of it, back in my school days (over twenty years ago now) I once had a dream where I was clad in a *durumagi* over dazzling white Korean clothes. Not only that, I sported a hat on my head just like those worn by the nobles of old, straw sandals on my feet, and a long old-fashioned pipe in my mouth. It was the same kind of outfit that an old man from the countryside might have worn a generation ago, the kind of outfit worn by those wise men who interpret dreams in villages as I mentioned before. I wasn't a wise old man, however, but a callow youth through and through, and the clothes made me look ridiculous. Not only that, it wasn't Korea but the crowded shopping street of Shinsaibashi-suji in Osaka I found myself swaggering through. I composed my face into the stern, sober expression of an elderly man, blew smoke from my three-foot-long pipe, and looked contemptuously around me as I walked through Shinsaibashi-suji towards Dotonbori.

I have the feeling that this clownish dream figure of mine from twenty-some years ago reflected my feelings towards Korea at the time. But what about last night's dream? It was a dream that had violently slammed down upon me with all the force of a typhoon. And what about the unresponsive fleshy guts that had been crammed inside me?! Even if it was just a dream, the sight of the hermit crabs munching away at my guts was just too much.

Immediately after escaping the dream, I was hit with a hunger for intestines—hot, plump, hefty intestines soaked in a bubbling bath of blood. I hungered for live intestines so taut that they'd spring back like a snake if you twisted them, intestines that steamed with the smell of fresh blood, the kind of intestines you might feed to a lion or falcon. (I wasn't a talent like Lu Xun, but at times like these I couldn't help but indulge in such literary flourishes.)

My stomach felt hollow as I rode the bus. Not because my guts had been eaten in the dream, but because I'd been ordered not to drink or eat anything after dinner last night in preparation for an X-ray of my stomach they were going to do at the hospital I was headed to now. I wasn't looking forward to the barium I would have to drink in the cold, dark room, the transparent green liquid that looking like it was suspended in midair. The old, slim, white-haired doctor would force the mineral liquid into my stomach, which had been lopped to one-third its original size. I'd choke it down, imagining the liquid radiating light like a green jewel from my throat to my nasal cavity and then spreading luxuriously in the dark across my entire face with all the sticky texture of inorganic matter and the smell of an inanimate object. Reality would flip, turn into a world of photographic negatives, and from atop the radiographic stand I'd feel my life float up from my body. It may well be that the dream was the result of the abdominal surgery that had left a nine-inch scar from my solar plexus to my abdomen and my anticipation of the barium I'd have to drink. The dream had left both my body and soul fatigued. My feelings had sunk down into the depths of my languid body and now crouched there, waiting. Had last night's dream overtaken me? My heart felt strangely hollowed out, just like my stomach. Come to think of it, despite its fantastical nature the dream had been a rather dreary one, tinged in the gloomy tones of twilight. The feeling of heaviness still jumbled up inside me gave me the illusion that I'd left not my house but the Korea from my dreams this morning. I held on tight to the hanging strap that dangled above me inside the bus that was racing through the capital of Japan.

A buzzer sounded. Someone was getting off at last. The bus pulled up to the next stop. People began to alight as soon as the doors opened. Now that I'd gotten some freedom of movement back due to the newly expanded space, I put a hand in my inner pocket, checking to make sure the patient's registration card I'd stuck inside my notebook was still there. But my fingers brushed against something else instead. With a sense of relief, I recognized it immediately: Certificate of Alien Registration, No. 199,000—I rarely forgot the loathsome thing. If I left the house without it, I'd spend the whole day restless and uneasy. We were required to carry this particular form of ID with us at all times and to produce it to the authorities whenever they asked. The police used the Certificate of Alien Registration as a pretext to hassle you about all sorts of things; you never knew when and where you might become a target. The harassment was no small matter. There were cops who sometimes even tailed me to the public baths, pouncing on me the moment I was naked. A black fingerprint taken from my left index finger was splayed out in the middle of the thin card. It's true that there are many kinds of IDs in this world, but to require a fingerprint on one? It was unprecedented, surely. There's a reason why Koreans—who make up about ninety percent of foreign residents in Japan—call the cards "Korean dog tags." My "dog tag" was enclosed in a stiff case that could serve as a shoehorn in a pinch, which I knew because I usually used it in that way. Whenever I went in to renew the card, I'd get into trouble with the police over how ragged and shapeless the case had become. Reassured, my fingers mechanically put the certificate into the opposite inner pocket of my jacket.

I was pushed towards the front of the bus by the surge of boarding passengers. There, I was startled to hear the plaintive, maybe even distressed keen of what sounded like a small dog. The keen rang out strangely clear and crisp through the morning air. An image rose in my mind of a small dog's legs being crushed and dragged by the wheels of a bicycle. I shoved my way through the sea of shoulders and stuck my head out the window. There were no bicycles in sight. What I saw instead was something very different from what I'd been envisioning in my head. Not a small dog, and not in danger. Two adult dogs, both white with black spots, were in the midst of mating. The female dog was being supported by the roots of a plane tree that was illuminated by the light of the early spring sun. I couldn't believe I'd thought it the whine of a small dog. It was March, a little early for mating season. I smiled wryly. But then in the next instant my wry smile crumbled all at once. I couldn't believe it. A cowardly blush of shame was beginning to spread across my cheeks. I'd been the only one to push his way through and stick his head out—.

I shifted my grip on the strap and looked around me. My heart tensed in surprise at how swiftly my surroundings had changed. All around me were cold, unmoving faces as frozen and still as the morning air. There was no reaction at all to the scene outside the window. Either they hadn't seen it, or else something from the outside world had blocked their view. Of course, it was childish to be so perturbed by the sight of dogs mating. Still, what was with this oppressive indifference and silence? Not even a single eyebrow twitched. It was eerie. I realized that I was isolated from my fellow passengers as thoroughly as if clear glass had been wedged between me and their jostling, flesh-and-blood bodies. Any movement threatened to shatter the glass. It was within such an atmosphere that I raised my head and looked at the clock that hung above the driver's seat. The round clock face looked back at me brazenly, with all the confidence of something that had belonged here since before even the bus came into being.

My body stiffened. I'd unconsciously been trying to contain my body in its own narrow space so that it didn't touch any of the bodies that surrounded me. *This is quite the predicament.* I felt like I was being smothered by some invisible vacuous bag. And then I soon felt an insurmountable rupture arise between my body and the brazen faces of the people in the full bus.

Even just standing there, our bodies touching and swaying, these people were rejecting me.

Everyone around me is Japanese.

There were many napes near my face. They lacked the smell of the earth. The bus was instead full of the smell of concrete, concrete that had imprisoned the earth down deep. *This is quite the predicament.* I was on my way to a hospital that was permeated with the smell of plaster and rubbing alcohol. This was, without a doubt, Japan. I sometimes forgot I was in Japan. But here I was, going to a Japanese hospital, riding a Japanese bus, speaking Japanese, and even copyediting a Japanese-language manuscript as a part-time job. A voice speaking in Japanese abruptly rose over the sound of the vibrating bus and ricocheted against my earlobes. Two men who looked like work colleagues were having a conversation next to me. "I'll be liberated once the section chief comes back from overseas." The word "liberated" detached itself from the rest of the conversation and burrowed deep into my ears. Because they were talking in Japanese, their words entered my head not as if I were listening to a casual conversation but as if I were listening to a portable radio—one that was uncomfortably crackly and muffled. In other words, I was being met with abrupt resistance by the Japanese language that I regularly used. The bus was noisy with that Japanese.

"Ahh, *yeogiga Ilboniroguna* (this is Japan, I see)," I murmured in Korean. The heavy echo of the words on my lips revived the thick, oily atmosphere of last night's dream, which had been constructed out of Korean. Every shudder of the bus expanded the emptiness in my heart even more and made that feeling of rupture swell further.

"*Haebang* (liberation), huh." There was no logical connection to my mutterings. It was just that I couldn't let the word—which, for the Korean people, contained all the nuances of independence, fatherland, the ethnic nation, history, freedom, the police, imperialism, and more—pass by me without comment. It had the power to dredge up the August 15, 1945 within me, and to collapse the past twenty-some years into a single moment in the blink of an eye. The bright sense of rupture created by that August 15 liberation was now welling up like a dazzling, frothy spring. But it's strange how memory works by association. As August 15 opened up inside me, a certain woman's face manifested itself, caught in the rupture of that day.

It was the face of U., a proprietress of a certain bar in a neighborhood full of small casual places to eat and drink, a little removed from the livelier area around K. Station. It was a tiny bar, with a single plain wooden counter served by a single woman, but it was tidy and clean. A Japanese friend of mine, a journalist named F., had introduced the place to me about half a year ago, and I'd gotten in the habit of occasionally dropping by. Her face reminded me of someone's, but for the life of me I couldn't recall who. (I wouldn't realize until later that my irritation was due to the fact that her face resembled that of another woman from twenty-some years ago.) She was a widow who was approaching middle age, and she was beautiful. But her beauty was refracted by the original shape of the face that had lodged itself deep in me.

A woman who fought against a constant sense of shakiness, U. possessed a lopsided loveliness marked by tension and disequilibrium. She had a wide but languid brow and dark eyes full of passion. There were times when the fine contours of her face would fight to hide the intense emotions surging up from deep within her, and it was during such times that her face shone with an almost agonizing allure. It was an allure that came less from her looks than from her expression, and it stirred up memories that had been long buried in me. But it wasn't enough to fully uncover those memories, and I was always left with a feeling of frustration.

That's why I was so shocked when the image of her face rose up in my mind's eye like a balloon as I stood there in the bus, along with the memory of August 15. I even gasped. Within the sound of my own startled voice I was finally able to find what I'd been searching for in her face. The moment I found it, my chest tightened painfully. The blurry, uncertain image I'd been unable to grasp for so long was at last coming into focus. It soon revealed itself as the figure of a woman sitting in dimness. It was no longer U. but the young woman who'd slipped onto the streetcar in the midst of that devastating summer.

August 15, 1945. The large sunflowers clustered in the small hospital garden had been shaking wildly since noon. It was a muggy Tokyo day. That afternoon, the sun shone endlessly over the ruins as if intent on scorching the skin off the earth. I'd come from Osaka to Tokyo to take care of some business, after spending half a year in Keijo (Seoul). Nineteen years old at the time, I considered myself to be a very devoted and serious-minded nationalist. I'd been in a hospital for Koreans when the moment I'd been so anxiously awaiting finally arrived. Immediately after the broadcast from the "Emperor of Japan," I finished up my lunch with my compatriots and made my way to the Minowa depot train station. There, I stood among the charred rubble and waited for the Ueno-bound streetcar.

On a day in which both people and the rusty red iron frames of the burned ruins wavered in the heat like melting candy, it felt strangely unreal that the dirty yellow streetcar was the only thing that moved through the landscape like a living thing. The other passengers—one old woman and several men with luggage who had the air of the merchant about them—waited for the streetcar with their heads hung low. They were silent, and there was no telling whether they knew each other or whether they'd gathered like that by chance. I realized that I alone stood apart from the others, at the other end of the traffic island, as if I were the only one waiting for something different. The streetcar that pulled up had fragments of glass still stuck in its empty windows. The first thing that caught my eye inside the car was the sight of the war notices pasted on the window frames, spouting propaganda slogans like "A Successful Conclusion of This Holy War" and "One's Fate in Battle is Everlasting." Their torn ends flapped in the air like tattered wings.

A young woman hastily boarded the streetcar. It seemed like the conductor had been waiting for her;

the door immediately closed upon her arrival, and the streetcar set off. Struggling for breath, the young woman sat down directly across from me. I was seated to the right of the entrance, in other words next to the door in the seat that abutted the conductor's chair. The young woman had most likely chosen her seat because it was easily accessible from where she'd boarded. She kept her eyes downcast, looking embarrassed by the fact that she'd rushed onto the car. She held a square package wrapped in cloth on her knees. Her shapely body was enveloped in indigo-patterned working pants that she'd probably slept in. Bare feet peeped out from her geta. The toes on her handsomely shaped feet were aligned in a nice curve. She must have walked a long way through the bombed-out streets—her feet were covered in a light film of dust. There was such an air of immaculate cleanliness about her that it was hard to believe it was really dirt on her feet. I wasn't able to see her face, however, as she kept her gaze downcast for some time.

As others pressed handkerchiefs to their faces, this woman kept her head bowed and her body still. I got the sense that she wasn't actually doing so out of embarrassment for having rushed onto the streetcar. This vehicle, which was even now cutting across the ruins with a strange calmness that belied the events of the day, was weighed down with sadness. Why did these people have to be here at this time? Where in the world were they going? I'd boarded the streetcar with the desire to see with my own eyes the spectacle of Japanese soldiers committing group suicide at the square in front of the Imperial Palace. And yet these people were quietly going on with their normal lives, even in this historic moment. The streetcar that was immersed in sadness demanded that of me, too. It was using the palms of a gentle woman to call to me. I rejected that call with clenched fists. Amidst the calm, I was tense as a porcupine. Across towns, villages, and fields all throughout Korea, my compatriots were no doubt raising their fists high and embracing, sobbing, exulting, dancing, and dashing through the streets. I could imagine them erecting flags on the mountaintops and shouting *Manse! Joseon dongnip manse*! (Hurrah! Hurrah for Korean independence!), could see the joyful, tear-streaked faces of the friends I'd left behind in Keijo. I would shout and cry, too, if I were there. I would cry with all my heart. But I was not in Korea or in Keijo but in Japan. Where in this country could I possibly give such a shout? To me, it would be a sacred shout, not something that could be released just anywhere. On this day, I was too composed. I was too calm for my age, even calmer than the adults. I therefore looked emotionless. What would happen if the person looking at me was someone who'd been an ardent "imperial subject" until August 14? Even if one tried to gauge the day's emotions in others, they could only be understood in terms of one's own sentiment. I looked at the people around me and saw only dubious adults full of disgrace. I thought: I'll soon return to my homeland. In the meantime, I'll refuse to shout *Manse!* in Japan. If I find I can't endure it any longer, I'll climb some mountain by myself. Alone, surrounded only by the clear, clean air on the mountaintop, I'll suck the ozone into my lungs and scream *Joseon dongnip manse*! until I lose my voice, until my throat tears apart, until I collapse. I've clenched my hands into tight fists for so long for that purpose. I felt a fateful rupture between my fist and the gentle palm, one that couldn't be changed. Even so, there was no need to shout here and now that I'm Korean. All I could do was close my stiff eyelids, while the dazzling, revolving axis of history remained tightly held in our—in my—fists.

Eventually I opened my eyes again, and my gaze fell quite naturally in the direction of the woman in front of me, who was crying with her face down. The conductor came and clipped our tickets. My eyes caught hers when she raised her head at the conductor's presence. They were dark, deep eyes. They shone with a fierce wavering light that I could tell was holding back a rising sadness.

After the conductor passed, she immediately cast her eyes down again. I waited hopefully for another glimpse of her face. She was a beautiful woman, around two or three years older than me, with surprisingly taut cheekbones framed by a round face. Her sad, pale cheeks and dark eyes glittering with tears were balanced against a wide white forehead. I was attracted to the strange, disproportioned beauty of her handsome face.

The woman gently dabbed at her eyes with her handkerchief. As the streetcar rattled past an empty stop amidst the burnt-out ruins, she unexpectedly lifted her face, revealing an expression filled with an almost shamanistic resentment. She kept her eyes fixed on me. But then her bright, shining tears began to betray her. One fat tear after another fell onto her lap. The luminance of her bloodshot eyes radiated an almost gruesome beauty. I immediately shrank back into my seat. My heart was pounding, and I felt overwhelmed. The look had contained an insistent invitation to sink into a deep shared feeling as a fellow Japanese.

Even so, why was she able to look at me like that? Why didn't she try to wipe away the tears that were even now falling before the gazes of strangers? How could a woman who'd so earnestly hidden her face suddenly find the ability to boldly look someone in the eye? I'd already been feeling a certain awkwardness ever since getting on the streetcar, and so I soon realized that she was throwing a wordless accusation at me because I had no tears. I intuitively grasped that we, the only young people in this shaking streetcar, were strangely in touch with each other's inner states.

The light in her unblinking eyes softened, as if a switch had been flipped, and her tears continued to seep out. For some reason, something that had been wavering and building up at the corner of my eye finally overflowed in that moment, sliding smoothly down my cheek and wetting my lip. Resigned to the tear stains on my cheeks, I closed my eyes. Hot tears swelled behind my eyelids, the pressure growing and growing, until the tears finally forced their way past my eyelids and down my face. It was puzzling. I didn't understand what was happening. It was clear that the beautiful young woman was the catalyst. But why in the world should that be? Why was I so affected? I didn't understand. All that was clear was my own sense of guilt at having revealed what shouldn't have been revealed, what had pierced me through the heart. A violent power had stirred up something deep in my body that was now aiming for the gaping hole that had been opened up.

Something unexpected happened. As I looked helplessly at her, feeling cursed, feeling as if I might get sucked into her deep, dark eyes, her face suddenly tensed and twisted into the ugly expression of one who has been possessed. With that, she threw both her package and her upper body onto the unoccupied seat beside her, covered her face with her palms, and let out a wail. Her round shoulders shook violently, and an awful, ugly sob escaped her lips. It was both a pitiable and bizarre sight. Then it hit me: she assumed that I was Japanese, and that the tears I had accidentally shed came from the same source as hers. The realization unnerved me. Her unexpected behavior based on this misunderstanding sent me reeling in a completely opposite direction. It severed the thin thread between us.

I stood up in agitation. The thing that had been stretched taut within me began to crumble apart, and a great wave of emotion rushed into the gaps left behind. My body twitched and trembled, engulfed as it was by this whirlpool of emotion. I shook my head like an obstinate child, turned my back to the sobbing woman, and gripped the hanging strap. Beyond the empty windowpanes, the desolate, windy city stretched out towards the horizon. The sky that bordered the charred rubble was achingly blue. It made the ruins stand out even more than usual. My retinas still retained the faint image of the white collar that ringed the woman's round shoulders, framed by short black hair and swathed in indigo cloth. Although my eyes were momentarily fixed upon the deep brown expanse of the city, they could still see the prostrate body of the lamenting woman. What in the world did any of this have to do with me? I carried within me the enmity of my people, which was far too great to feel any sort of sympathy with her. Even though it was not in any way her fault, the enmity that came from being a member of an oppressed people, a

Korean who had done everything he could to survive within a constant state of humiliation—that enmity was just too great. At last, I felt myself standing on the same ground as them. And I could see a bright rupture. The Genkai Sea had been sundered, and the water was spouting up towards the heavens. Underneath the sun, in the midsummer sea, where the mountainous sprays transformed into a shining rainbow—the rupture was there.

I was annoyed and bewildered by this woman who wouldn't stop crying. The cowardly tears that wet her cheeks; the oddly lonely streetcar with its solitary soul; the exceedingly ceremonial silence, like the subdued atmosphere inside a hearse, untroubled even by the woman's lamentations; the scenery outside the window, with its endless line of blank billboards painted over in white: suddenly, it all looked ridiculous. Even the woman's broken sobs now sounded like the voice of a petulant child, and then like someone laughing. My bewilderment abruptly switched to an almost unbearable swell of amusement, as if a key had been turned in a lock deep inside my body. I continued to grip the hanging strap in my confusion. A laugh tickled the back of my throat. I could hear a giggle forming in my mouth. The swelling laughter trapped in my throat was threatening to burst out of me at any moment. I told the conductor that I wanted to get off at the next stop. In the tired old streetcar hurtling forward at full speed, the conductor gave me a cold look and informed me that the next stop was not Ueno. I knew that, I told him; I wanted to get off now.

"Something happen?" The conductor looked at me in the same way police officers do. "I'm telling you, the next stop isn't Ueno."

"I know that!" I shouted. "When a passenger tells you he wants to get off, you have to let him off!"

As soon as the streetcar screeched to a halt, I forcibly opened the doors and jumped out. Then I began making my way through the empty ruins that shimmered in the haze of the midsummer afternoon, watching all the while as the streetcar sped away into the distance, its wheels echoing against the rails. The image of the woman was still etched into my mind, and her sad, shaking voice still rang in my ears. I raised one arm to my face and swiped at my tears with a fist. As I gazed at my wet palm, the hot sunlight beating down upon me, more tears began to fall from my eyes. I recalled the noon broadcast in my memories. The moment we'd been waiting for had finally come! A new era was finally here! I gave a mighty kick to an empty can nearby and looked up. The sky was spinning round and round, aflame with a heat that was giving off a white light. The skeleton remains of the buildings swayed and shook. An intense emotion that was neither sadness nor amusement clawed its way up my throat and spouted up into the air.

I looked up at the dazzling blue sky and roared with the laughter of a madman. I laughed again. As I did, everything around me seemed to grind to a halt. My laughter rose up towards the sky that stretched over the burnt ruins, and my face collapsed into a mess of torrential tears and sweat. The sky that loomed over the desolate landscape was achingly clear and beautiful. Through the prism of my tears, the endless blue of it fractured into kaleidoscopic shards that no longer held within them the color of the ruins.

Back in the present, I spent almost an entire day at the hospital getting poked and prodded and X-rayed. There wasn't anything else I particularly needed to do, aside from stopping by the small Korean-run publishing company I worked at part-time to pick up a manuscript they wanted me to copyedit. I made a little side trip to S., a newly emerging subcenter in the city that wasn't too far from the hospital, and had a meal at one of the Korean restaurants there. For the first time in a long while, I had a desire to surround myself with the hustle and bustle of downtown. I entered a large bookstore in a building near S. Station. Unlike the uniform flow of pedestrians in the streets, the people inside the stuffy bookstore were jammed against each other in a disorderly jumble. A thought suddenly came to me, and I made my way to the dictionary corner. By the time I got there, I was so hot I had to shed my coat and wipe the sweat from my nape. I took down a one-volume encyclopedia from the shelf with both hands and began flipping through the pages. My own actions felt strange to me, and I found myself smiling wryly. Last night's dream was still alive inside me: I was looking for the entry on hermit crabs.

An animal somewhat like a cross between a shrimp and a crab, with a soft underbelly. They generally have one pair of claws and normally live in a univalve shell. As they grow, they move into increasingly larger shells. Aha, so they move into increasingly larger shells as they grow! I eventually found a seat at the café in the back of the bookstore and ordered some black tea. The thought had already occurred to me that the monstrous naked hermit crabs had been trying to move into my stomach. And then there was the matter of the mating dogs this morning. And wasn't it strange, I thought, how the face of the woman from August 15 had the same shape as the face of the bar proprietress U. . . .

Over twenty years had passed since that August 15. Whenever I greeted the anniversary of our liberation and recalled the events of that day, the memory of the woman in the indigo pants always appeared, even though we'd only been together for a very short time inside the streetcar. I no longer had any memory of what had happened after I leapt out of the car that day. It was obvious that I didn't go to the square in front of the Imperial Palace, no doubt because of the shock I'd received from my encounter with the crying woman. For some reason, what had happened in the streetcar was the only memory that remained clear in my mind. Even after the day itself had passed, the feelings from that day still had no outlet precisely because I, being Korean, had known that the woman didn't know I was Korean.

Although we had the misfortune of being unable to share in the same feeling, it was most likely for that reason that the woman still lived inside my August 15, even if the reverse were not true. It's for that reason that my chest tightened even now at the thought of the woman I'd met in passing, whose name I didn't even know.

I left the café and reentered the crowd outside. Walking through the boisterous streets underneath a cloudy afternoon sky, I found myself wanting to see a real live hermit crab. As I wandered around, trying to find a likely place where a peddler might be selling them on the street, I next found myself wanting to see the face of U. again. I sensed that there must be some critical difference between the face that had suddenly come to mind and the face I was trying to see now. It was that difference I wanted to see. I descended into the subway.

I settled into a seat at the end of the subway car. The doctor had given me a shot of alpha-lipoic acid and some other things when I'd told him I was tired. But it felt like the tiredness had pooled around my heart. The subway car was empty enough that I could see the faces of the people seated opposite me. Several passengers were also looking silently at the people around them, with eyes that were feckless and expressionless. The elderly man in a suit seated across from me looked at me with inscrutable eyes. Outside the window, the sound of the train's red-hot wheels scattered against the swiftly passing walls of the tunnel. When the train came to a halt in front of the platform, I became even more uncomfortably aware of the man's unfathomable eyes on me. Also the full-color advertisements inside the car. The subway map. The sound of each station being announced over the intercom. And the women in kimonos. Every single passenger. For a moment each and every one of these things made me feel uneasy. This was Japan. I could feel that I was in Japan. Not only that, I wasn't here as a passing tourist. This was a place I'd lived in longer than in my own fatherland, to the point of no return.—This was a Japan that had trapped us in its borders, a country where we might have gained citizenship and gotten naturalized, had it not been our former colonizer.

As I sat inside the subway car that was now headed towards K. Station, I thought about the journalist F., the man who had introduced me to U.'s bar. I recalled an evening when we'd been taken to a so-called Korean nightclub by a Korean businessman he knew and several of his Korean friends. Inside the club was a group of women in traditional Korean dresses of silk and velvet whose hems trailed to the floor. The red, yellow, purple, and white of their clothes made for a gorgeous spectacle underneath the lights that were like dull oxidized silver. They looked like a school of fish swimming together at the bottom of the sea. Someone was playing a tune on a large piano in gleaming black. Next to the pianist sat a man in a blue Korean *jokki* who was banging along on a *janggo* (Korean drum) on top of a dais. The man was elderly and balding and bespectacled, with a deceptively long face. An enigmatic smile hovered on his lips as he played. Soon he launched into a long solo performance of a Korean folk song. He closed his eyes. As the tempo grew faster and jauntier, the rhythm seemed to flow through his wildly moving hands up to his shoulders, which danced along to the beat. I could clearly see the sweat that glistened on his wide forehead. That enigmatic smile culminated in an ecstatic trace that shook my own flesh and shrunk the distance between us in a single swoop. I soon learned that he was, incredibly, Japanese. When I told F. that, his mouth dropped. *Is that really true?* F. had been born the son of a colonist and had spent his elementary and middle school years in Korea. That he was studying Korean now was proof of how he was still beholden to a certain sentimental feeling towards Korea. He'd recently traveled to South Korea as a special correspondent and while there had learned some new songs I didn't know. He sang them often, with rather imprecise pronunciation. Part of him was still immersed in the Seoul that had raised him. His sentiment was so thoroughly rooted inside him that if anyone tried to wrench it away against his will, it would most likely tear apart his very heart. Even so, I had no doubt he would still shout with joy.

The *janggo* performance ended, and there came a lull in the cheerful banter and solicitous interventions of the colorfully dressed women. F. leaned across the table and turned his gaze from the *janggo* over to me. No, it might be more accurate to say that he folded his gaze inwards, to his own heart. A faint smile appeared on the lower half of his face. "Mr. R.," he said in a voice like a groan, "I can't wrap my mind around the *janggo* we just heard. I'm in a bit of a shock. Those emotions—I wonder if we could call them the emotions of a person who's fallen under the spell of Korea . . . The old man was incredible. He could've been me in the future, in my old age."

I murmured a vague assent to F. and then fell into a silent reverie. It may have been because of the alcohol, but there was now no hint of a smile on F.'s swarthy, masculine face. Humor had never come easily to him.

"I've finally begun to feel a reaction to that old man. There wasn't any room for reaction during his performance, but now . . . "

"Reaction?"

"I'm talking about jealousy. Look at him sitting there. He's surpassed me! I guess this is what you'd call the sentimentality of a fraud who's finally realized that he's a fraud. Though even an amateur like me can tell there's something clumsy at times about the way he beats the *janggo* . . . Say, whaddya think of his blue *jokki*? Korean clothes suit him surprisingly well."

"I'm still thinking about what you meant when you said the old man could be you from the future."

F. gave me a quizzical look.

"What I'm trying to say is that you need to let Korea go. You're clinging to it too much."

"Yeah, I've still got a ways to go . . . Even I know that much, as sentimental as I may be. But letting go of Korea is out of the question right now. I want to do just the opposite."

"It may be because I'm Korean, but I can't help but wonder about that. You won't be able to really appreciate Korea until you let it go. Obsessing about it isn't good for you."

I felt a sudden distaste for my own admonishing attitude. I'd been trying to go easy on the alcohol for health reasons, but now I was struck with the desire to drain the glass that was in my hand. Chasing alcohol with alcohol, letting your intoxication lead to more intoxication—I missed that world. I used to drink myself into oblivion in that world. Come to think of it, it wasn't so different from the feeling one got from talking ponderously and earnestly with an old friend, intoxication flowing through every pore of one's body . . . I poured beer into the now-empty glass and encouraged F. to go on.

"You tell me I should let Korea go, but I can't just change my emotions like that. I've always been a Japanese person with nationalistic tendencies, so it may be that I have no business getting attached in the first place. But I do think it's possible for someone to get attached to Korea *because* they're Japanese. Look at me, for instance. You know I don't have a homeland, right? Japan's not my homeland, although it's my country of citizenship. The place that's been living inside me since I was a kid, the place I feel most at home—it isn't in Japan. It's in the hills and red clay roads of Seoul. If Seoul isn't my hometown, then what is? What am I supposed to do? If that's denied to me, Mr. R., then I'm no different from a person without a past."

But Korea doesn't exist for your sake, or for the sake of any colonist and their sons. I didn't say that aloud. F. was a person who never boasted about his journalist credentials. In that sense, he was quite an independent man. When it came to Korea, however, he had a tendency to become all too maudlin. Our booth was now empty except for us and a woman in a flattering purple velvet Korean dress who was sitting next to F. With nothing else to do, she kept topping off our beers. F. urged her to eat some of the hors d'oeuvres we'd ordered. She took some fruit from the thick glass plate on the table and ate it with a straightforward alacrity. The other members of our group were dancing with some women on the rather cramped dance floor. The air rang with the steady beat of the *janggo*. The woman began to get up. F. tried to stop her, but she had no interest in talking with us. The woman—a second-generation Korean in her early twenties who could speak no Korean—invited me to join her on the dance floor. I gently refused.

"You know that no one can deny you your hometown," I said to F. "As long as it's not a colonialist nostalgia for 'the good old days,' that is. But if that's the case, then what about a person like me? I'm the opposite of you, Mr. F. If you don't have a past, that means that Zainichi Koreans like me who were raised in Japan don't have a past, either. That is, you feel that your home is Korea, whereas I *cannot* feel that my home is Japan. I'm unable to feel any attachment at all to the Japan that's crammed inside me. You say that you love Korea, that it's part of your soul. I can't say the same thing about Japan. I don't know how to explain the twisted emotions that come from such a dilemma . . . In that sense, it could be argued that you're more blessed than I am."

"Blessed? I don't like that word at all. It has a stuck-up sound to it. It's a sinful word, at least for a Japanese person. That's a low blow, attacking me with that word while I'm drunk. I have no idea what to say in response . . . But if that really is the case, what does that mean about our ability to communicate with each other? Is there always going to be a sense of rupture there?"

"Communication is something that comes afterwards. I guess I'm trying to point out that we both need to be more aware of that rupture. We need *more* rupture—we need to cut ties completely. You need to let go of Korea. It may just be my selfishness speaking. But maybe that'll help keep you from turning into a pale imitation of that old *janggo* performer, at the very least."

I laughed, and for the first time F. did, too. "Is that the best I can hope for in life, to become a master *janggo* drummer? Perhaps that's not so bad. At the end of the day, though, I still find myself wanting to shout my love for Korea. Ahh, I appear to be drunk. There's this ache deep in my flesh that feels like homesickness. There's nothing I can do about it. Maybe it's a byproduct of the aging process, hahaha . . . "

The other people in our group came back to the booth then, having finished dancing, and our conversation ended there. As the memory played back in my mind, I marveled at how I'd emphasized the idea of rupture to F. then. In the bus this morning, surrounded as always by Japanese people, I had felt something shudder down my spine. Was it a feeling of rupture? If so, it meant that the dazzling luminance of August 15 had already vanished. Mixed in with that feeling may also have been a vague fear of the assimilating forces that crept closer by the day. Even amidst the noise of the subway I could hear F.'s groaning voice once again, crawling up from the subconscious depths of my mind. *I wonder if we should call his emotions the emotions of a man who was bewitched by Korea . . . The sight of the old man . . . It may very well have been F. in his old age.* There was a throbbing in my ears, and a murmuring that had all the weight of self-derision . . . Several days ago, I'd taken a walk around Y. Station with a friend of mine. With a forced smile on his face, my friend had told me the following: *Over twenty years have passed. What will happen to us Zainichi Koreans if the division of our homeland continues like this for another ten years? The so-called first generation will slowly die out, leaving behind a growing community of second- and third-generation Koreans. Don't you think that'll only accelerate the assimilation process? The situation is quite serious.* At that moment, a middle-aged man in a suit passed by me, his gaze averted. What was he thinking about me in that moment? I highly doubt it was about my identity as a Korean or what it meant to be

Korean.

My mother, who was now deceased, had walked around Japan in her Korean clothes. For all their lives, she and other such women had stood atop an austere rupture, though they didn't particularly sense it as such. I couldn't help but wonder if it was a problem that no one inside the subway car could tell I was Korean, and that my own heart remained completely untouched by such an environment. I needed to become the type of person who thought it only proper that I walk around in Korean clothes, just as I'd done in my dream—to be unafraid of getting onto the bus with the equivalent of a label on my forehead proclaiming I was Korean, to look as foreign as a Westerner.

I got off at K. Station and made my way to U.'s bar. The neon lights of the neighborhood shone prominently against the early evening gloom. U. was stretched out next to a red electric stove in front of the bar counter. She was reading a newspaper. As soon as she saw me, she hastily got up from her seat. Nodding to me in greeting, she moved behind the counter and prepared a wet hand towel for me. It was so fresh and hot that you could still see the steam rising from it.

“I came here today just to see your face,” I told U. in a joking tone, then immediately regretted it. What a clumsy line! But U. gave me a bright smile that deepened the laugh lines around her eyes.

“What makes you say that, Mr. R.?” she said, her gaze averted, as if confronted with something blinding. My own eyes remained firmly fixed on her face. Under my scrutiny, the face of the sad young woman from that distant summer afternoon finally began to show itself . . . Exposed to U.’s radiant beauty in this way, something deep inside me was struggling to respond in kind. She was wearing a kimono dyed with a fine navy blue pattern that made me think again of the young woman in the streetcar, whose working pants had sported a similar pattern. Similar enough, at least, to further link the two in my mind.

I poured some beer for U. and clinked my glass against hers. There was no way for her to understand how I was feeling, of course. I took a sip of beer and then placed the glass on the counter. As I did so, I was struck by how the meticulously scrubbed, plain wooden counter matched the immaculateness of U.’s skin.

My heart felt caught between U. and the counter

and immersed in an entirely different world. Had the young woman continued to weep after I leapt from the streetcar on that August 15, 1945? What had she thought of my abrupt actions? There was no way of knowing. On that day, I had been in one world and she'd been in another, sadder one. That wasn't her fault, but it wasn't my fault, either. We had coincidentally come face to face with each other before being expelled from each other's individual worlds, that was all. And through that twist of coincidence, she continued to live within the August 15 that was inside me.

Rather unusually for her, U. had put some white powder on her face. I searched her face for that different face from the past. U. moved about restlessly, affected perhaps by my contemplation. As I watched her chopping up ingredients on the narrow counter and opening and closing the refrigerator, her face slowly began to harmonize with the face of the woman from the ruins, and for a moment—a very brief moment—it looked like it was not U. but that other woman who was standing there. How strange it was. The only thing that connected the two women to each other was me. U. had no idea that another woman's face was at that very moment superimposed onto her own, like a magic-lantern picture projected onto a separate image. U. by no means enjoyed a charmed life, which was reflected in the volatility of her beauty. One could certainly see how the events of August 15 could have shaped it. Her weary expression had a kind of housewife quality to it, one that seemed more suited to a family kitchen than to a bar. You could still see the shapely lines of U.'s body underneath the kimono she wore. The smell of the raw fish on the counter was a sharp contrast to the feminine scent pooled around her nape and chest. As she threw me a glance, her lips half parted, I couldn't help but sense something sexual. A sour smell, the kind born from a darkness that has never seen the sun, seemed to emanate from her mouth. And I thought I saw in that moment something peel away from her face, leaving behind only a mask of makeup. It wasn't something she'd deliberately discarded. No, this strange thing had slipped off her face on its own.

I'd come here wanting to see U., all the while thinking about that woman from August 15 whose name I didn't know. I'd thought, too, to tell U. all about the riddle that only her face could solve. That had still been my intent when I first sat at the counter. But *something* had disappeared from U.'s face, and all that was left was a dull, painted prettiness. My desire to talk to her vanished the moment that *something* did. The only thing I felt now was a growing hollowness inside me. In the past, I'd always felt something like frustration whenever I looked upon U., as if her beauty was being illuminated by that original form hidden inside me (that much at least was finally clear). But it was dawning on me that today would be different. While it was nice to be spared the discomfort that always came with that frustration, now that the riddle was solved I was left with only a sense of unfulfillment and emptiness.

Was the beauty that had until now been lodged in U.'s face only a phantasm? If so, would the woman from August 15 disappear in the same way? It was strange how one's expectations could so easily go up in smoke. It may be that my expectations were nothing but phantasms. No, that wasn't true; my expectations had been met. U. had returned to being just another bartender. *I guess these things happen.* By tomorrow, U.'s beauty would no longer be an illusory, radiating force inside me but a real, material thing. It was probably better that way. If we're to understand the things that are reflected upon a person's face as phantasms, then what should we call all those countless dreams that wander amongst the evil spirits of the night world? It's said that dreams are falsehoods. But even falsehoods have the power to strike people down. The night world is not a place that simply exists to store the dregs of the day world. It has the ability to make people feel grief, pain, joy, anger. Or maybe not. Perhaps it's more accurate to say that dreams are lies after all, holding power only over people who are still enslaved to superstition. People like me.

This had been some day. A day without a single tranquil moment, although the only off-putting thing that had happened was the incident with the mating dogs this morning (and even that was fairly trivial). All I did was go to the hospital, walk around the shopping district, and spend some time at this bar. I'd spent the entire day in a dream—no, in a strange state where my physical body had been unable to completely separate itself from a dream. In that sense, it was a day with a fierce undercurrent to it. A day that stunk of falsehoods.

"Is there a place around here that sells hermit crabs?"

"What? Hermit . . . crabs?"

"Yes."

“What an unexpected question. Does one of your children need them for a school project?”

“Something like that. Do you happen to know what they eat? Fig seeds or food like that, maybe?”

“Hmm, I wonder. There’s a man who sometimes sells hermit crabs on the street corner. I’ve seen him feed them cucumbers and pickled radish.”

“Is that so?”

Even I thought my own interest in the topic odd. U. told me everything she knew about hermit crabs, thinking that it was for my children. She ended by mentioning that she thought peddlers usually went around selling them on the streets from late spring into the summer, though she couldn’t be sure. I too had seen the peddlers she was talking about. They would attach strings to the hermit crabs and let them crawl around on the ground on sunny street corners. I hadn’t thought it would be so difficult to find one today. After leaving the hospital, I’d made my way through the shopping areas of S. Neighborhood, searching for hermit crab sellers. I’d also kept an eye out for them on the busy streets around K. Station. Because of what had happened on the bus, I found myself wanting to see actual hermit crabs moving around. I had the uncanny feeling they were connected somewhere (maybe above my stomach . . .) to the sense of rupture I'd felt. I was determined to return home with one of those grotesque, funny-looking arthropods.

A few customers entered the bar, and I used that as an opportunity to leave. It was dark, and the unexpected arrival of snow had turned the air chilly. As I exited the alley into the main street where the buses ran, the snow began to fall in earnest, blanketing the night in white. The snowflakes tickled my face like a swarm of tiny insects. I stroked the part of my belly where the hermit crab monsters had resided and smiled to myself in the snow. I crossed the bus lane and made a beeline for the station. It was possible that a penniless hermit crab seller was somewhere out there on this cold and lonely night; you never knew. Abruptly a thought came to me: *How do you say "hermit crab" in Korean?* I couldn't remember. I was certain I'd been speaking Korean in my dream, so I should have known the Korean word for the animal. But it just wouldn't come to me. How could that be? My ears began to ring, and my heart suddenly felt heavy. Was it just a temporary lapse of memory, or had I in fact never known the word? If the latter, that meant that I'd been speaking gibberish in my dream. Ahh, how false dreams were, indeed. I smiled wryly as a bitterness filled my mouth. The traces of my dream still lingered in me like a hangover, refusing to die. Like alcohol, it had spread throughout my body, sinking deep underneath my skin. Was I really R.—or, to put it another way, was the R. inside the dream really me? What a bizarre and off-putting dream. With a bit of embellishment, one could easily turn it into the type of tale that was told of old. One could title it "A Tale of a False Dream." As soon as I got home, I decided, I'd look up the Korean word for "hermit crab." It had been a false dream—or so I kept telling myself, anxious to reject the dream that had gouged out my heart as well as my guts. Even so, part of me wanted to hold on to the fact that the dream had been composed of the Korean language. As I stood there, underneath the snowy night sky, I could see my own red-chapped face, contorted in a bitter smile, as clearly as if I were looking in a mirror.